In the
Last
of the
WILD
WEST

George Williams III (signature)

George Williams III

Tree By The River Publishing Inc.
Ann Arbor, Michigan

Published by:
Tree By The River Publishing, Inc.
Ann Arbor, Michigan

Non-fiction books by George Williams III:

Rosa May: The Search For A Mining Camp Legend (1980)
The Guide to Bodie and Eastern Sierra Historic Sites (1982)
The Redlight Ladies of Virginia City, Nevada (1984)
The Murders at Convict Lake (1984)
The Songwriter's Demo Manual and Success Guide (1984)
Mark Twain: His Life In Virginia City, Nevada (1986)
Mark Twain: His Adventures at Aurora and Mono Lake (1987)
Mark Twain: Jackass Hill and the Jumping Frog (1988)
Hot Springs of the Eastern Sierra (1988)
In the Last of the Wild West (1992)

Layout and cover design by Robert Pierce

Library of Congress Cataloging-in-Publication Data

Williams, George, III, 1949-
        In the last of the wild west: a true story/ George Williams III.
            p.   cm.
        ISBN 0-935174-28-1 : $27.95.--ISBN 0-935174-27-3 (pbk.) : $12.95
        1. Storey County (Nev.)--Politics and government. 2. Political corruption--Nevada--Storey County--History--20th century.
        3. Prostitution--Nevada--Storey County--History--20th century.
        4. Williams, George, 1949-   . I. Title.
        F847.S8W55   1992
        364.1'534'092--dc20   91-45656
                                                              CIP

{Reader Please Take Notice}

This is a true story although I have exaggerated some scenes for the sake of satire. But only slightly.

Information regarding the criminal activity of the pimp and Storey County officials was obtained from the following: confessions of those involved in criminal activities, numerous eyewitnesses, Federal investigators, the FBI, the IRS, Nevada journalists, former Nevada Prison inmates, Nevada Department of Investigation, Nevada Prison Records, Nevada Archives, the offices of the Nevada Attorney General, former U.S. Attorneys, Reno City Police, Reno City Attorney, former Washoe County District Attorneys, public records of Washoe County and Storey County, Nevada; numerous books and articles, unpublished manuscripts, prostitutes who worked in Storey County, and former and current law enforcement officials, county, state and Federal. Reports in the *Nevada Appeal, Reno Evening Gazette* and *Reno Gazette-Journal* were helpful. I am particularly grateful to the men and women in Nevada law enforcement who trusted me and shared useful information. You have my sincerest thanks.

Some names have been changed to protect the innocent. I have also changed the names of some Storey County officials; those boys would only glory in their increased notoriety. Sorry fellas, I won't give you that. Besides, a hundred years from now when we're all dead and the boys are likely stoking ovens, their names won't matter.

I have, however, published the names of all State of Nevada employees and politicians, some of whom either purposely or negligently frustrated research into corruption in Nevada politics. The Nevada Attorney General was informed by numerous people of crimes being committed by Storey County and Nevada officials and refused to investigate, indict or prosecute.

I am particularly grateful to the pimp whose threat upon my life and the lives of my family infuriated me to such a degree that I tripled my research efforts. Thanks for the fuel.

Except for portions of the *Virginia City Voice,* for reasons sufficient to the author, no part of this book was written nor published within the state of Nevada.

CONTENTS

Part Four: *Into the Wilderness*

Part Five: *And the trouble follows*

Part Six: *Endings and Beginnings*

For my wife and children who lived it.

"Then the King will say to those on his right, 'Come you who are blessed by my Father; take your inheritance, the kingdom prepared for you since the creation of the world. For I was hungry and you gave me something to eat, I was thirsty and you gave me something to drink, I was a stranger and you invited me in, I needed clothes and you clothed me, I was sick and you looked after me, I was in prison and you came to visit me.'

"Then the righteous will answer him, 'Lord, when did we see you hungry and feed you, or thirsty and give you something to drink? When did we see you a stranger and invite you in, or needing clothes and clothe you? When did we see you sick or in prison and go to visit you?'

"The King will reply, 'I tell you the truth, whatever you did for one of the least of these brothers of mine, you did for me.'"   Matthew 25: 34-40

Be good and you will be lonesome.   Mark Twain

Thus saith the author...

I had reached the ignorant conclusion that we needed to get away from the terrible city and find a small rural town where people were normal and everyone was happy and no one bothered you. I was only looking for Paradise. This urge to hit the trail for the wide open spaces slayed me around the first of spring each year. As the spring flowers bloomed I began to pant for the highway like a dog pants for the blood of the neighbor's cat. I fantasized about taking my family away from the city and would have done it long ago if I had had the money.

Then something awful happened. My writing became successful. Almost miraculously, one day we had the money to hit the trail. And this is the adventure that followed...

PART ONE

Leaving Southern California

CHAPTER ONE

God Is A Black Slave

The seed for this adventure was planted one hot smoggy afternoon as I was having a heart attack in Southern California, or thought I was. I sat in the back room of a grocery store amongst the fruits and vegetables feeling like I was about to meet God face to face. A young grocery clerk nursed me. He looked scared and helpless.

"You're gonna be all right," he said. "The paramedics are on the way. Take it easy."

God, I hope they get here fast. I feel like crap.

I was weak. My palms were sweaty; my eyes were dilated. I was shaky and having difficulty breathing. I felt like I was about to pass out. My heart was pounding like a jack-hammer. I thought it would burst through my chest and smack the grocery clerk in the face. Wouldn't that be horrible. I sat on a sack of potatoes and leaned against the freezer and felt the cold against my back. *Dear God, what a place to die.* I gave the clerk my phone number and he called my wife. She was racing to the store.

I was only in my early thirties but I was worried about my heart. Heart disease runs in my mother's family. My cholesterol level was extraordinarily high. I was worried I had inherited my mother's bad genes and bad luck.

There's one good thing about dying. All the nonsense we waste our lives worrying about goes out the window. What really matters becomes instantly clear: God, eternity, heaven and hell, sin, family.

I felt God's heavy presence amongst the fruits and vegetables. He had been waiting to hear from me since I hadn't talked to Him for a while. I thought I'd better settle with Him while there was time.

"I'm sorry, Lord for letting you down. I'm sorry for the wrong things I've done." The clerk looked embarassed. So what. I was the one about to leap into eternity. You don't care what people think when you're dying. Suddenly God's opinion is more important than man's.

"I've always believed in you Lord and I've tried to be good. I know I am a sorry excuse for a human being. I know you've made better people than me. But I've tried to be good. I've *always* tried to be good. I don't mean to be bad. I want to be good with all my heart, and I end up being bad again. I don't understand myself. It's like something inside me makes me do the bad stuff."

I tried to divert the Lord to some of his other troubled creatures. "Besides, you've made—and please forgive me Lord—but you've made some really terrible people. I mean, some of them are much worse than me—if you can believe that. Why, they do really awful things. They murder and rape and steal and some of them are just plain mean and they hurt people for no good reason and they start wars. Look at Hitler. What an awful human being! He murdered millions. He deserved to go to hell. But me Lord, I'm just a small time sinner. I'm nothing great. Please forgive me, Lord and let me into Heaven. I don't want to go to hell. Dear Jesus, save me."

It was a pretty lame prayer. But I was nervous about dying and there wasn't time to get real elaborate. The Lord knew what I was trying to say. He knows everything.

When you're healthy and everything is going fine, hell is a make-believe place fired-up preachers rant about. But when your heart is giving out, hell is just as real as Texas—blazing, deadly and final.

And then my brain shut down and it all went black and I heard Him.

"Hey, you! Boy, wake up. You ben goin' down de wrong road."

"Wha? Who is that?"

"Boy, wake up. You ben doin' de w-r-o-n-g *stuff!*"

"Who is that?"

"God Almighty, fool. Ain't you nevuh heard mah voice?"

"No, not exactly Lord. Why are you talking like a black slave?"

"I love de black slaves. I can talk like anybody I wanna talk like. You gotta problem with dat boy?"

"No, sir."

"Das right. You don' worry 'none bout wha' ah sound like. You jes shut up and listen."

"Yes sir."

"Boy, ah had my eyes on ya and ya ben blowin' it bad. Wha' ah give ya a brain for? I seen ya a hustlin' and a bustlin' and tryin' to be some hot shot writer and workin' yo' butt off tryin' for that immortality stuff. Boy, wha' ah give you a brain for?"

"I've been doing something wrong?"

"Wrong? Hey you, boy, wake up. Ya been missin' de point, bub. Ya ben a worryin' about makin' money off dem books ya write so ya can feed yo' missus and the chilin'. And ya ben doin' preedy good sellin' dem, too. But ya ben a worryin' so. Always a worryin'. And now ya a lyin' back here knocked out n' all messed up. Boy, don' ya know ahs God Almighty an' ah ben lookin' out for ya?"

"Well, Lord..."

"Shut up and listen, boy. Ya ben a workin' in yo' little room, in yo' little head and writin' by yo' self and not seein' hardly nuttin' aroun' ya. I wan ya tuh start seein' whas a goin' on with de people aroun' ya and start usin' that good brain ah gave ya n' put dat pen in yo' hands n' help em out."

"Me? How can I help them, Lord?"

"Ya gots to get out of yo' room and listen to 'em. Ya gots to hear 'em with ya heart, what deys sayin' and feelin' and thinkin,' and wha' deys hurtin' 'bout. And den ya be honest and do de right thing and help like ya can."

"But Lord, there's so much pain and evil in the world. It's frustrating and awful. It breaks a man's heart. There's so little I can do."

"Boy, listen to me and listen good: *Do wha' ya can. Do de little ya can.* Das all I ask. Dey's a bettuh place a comin'. Ya gots no idea. But dey's a bettuh place. And all dat ya bring to dis place is dem folks ya help where's ya at now. All ya take with ya is dem people. Ya see? No gold o' silver, no fame n' high and mighty's, jus' dem people ya help. Ya got dat?"

"Sort of."

"An ya 'member this. It ain' goin' be easy. It won't nevuh be easy. And some folks won't like ya none. Why, dey didn' even like mah boy much, but he was a good boy 'nyway. Breaks mah heart to think wha' dey done tuh dat boy. But he be ahright now. Doncha be a worryin' none no mo, son. Ahs be right dare wid ya all de while."

Maybe I had been hallucinating. Or maybe I had been reading too much Mark Twain. Or maybe it really was God. Anyway, I came to as the paramedics banged through the big swinging doors into the back of the grocery store. They were young, big and in dark blue uniforms. They had equipment with them. They knelt down beside me. One of them opened a black case and started pulling stuff out.

"Tell me how you're feeling," the one near me said.

"I was standing in the check out line and all of a sudden I felt real weak, like I was gonna pass out. My hands got sweaty and I felt tight in my chest. I told the checker I thought I was having a heart attack and she called you guys."

"Do you have pain in your chest?"

"No. But it feels tight."

"Do you feel like you're gonna pass out?"

"Maybe."

"Have you been ill?"

"No."

"Are you taking any medication?"

"No. But I'm on a diet and I haven't eaten all day."

"All right." The paramedic unbuttoned my shirt and stuck white patches on each side of my chest. He connected wires to the patches and to the machine. "We're gonna check your heart and see how it's doing. Just relax. We're gonna help you."

So they checked my heart with the EKG thing and examined my eyes. "His eyes are dilated," the one near me said. "Let's give him some oxygen." They put the black mask over my face. "Hold that and breathe deeply." So I did. After a few minutes my shaky legs began feeling heavy and normal.

My wife rushed in with our next door neighbor. She was pale and terribly frightened. And she was beautiful, blond, with her sweet, kind grey-blue eyes. She looked like she was about to lose everything that made her life meaningful and happy: Me. *Dying on the ones you love. What a lousy thing to do to them. I don't want to die now God. My wife and kids need me. Please, don't let me die now.* My wife knelt down and grabbed my left hand and held it tightly.

"I love you, " she said.

"I love you too," and it sounded muffled and strange through the black oxygen mask.

The paramedics went about their business with their equipment. The one near me checked my pulse and listened to my heart with the stethoscope and took my blood pressure. Everyone looked real concerned. It was great. For once in my life I was the center of the universe's attention. Ironic dying could do what I never could.

"Your heart is all right," the paramedic next to me said. "Your pulse is a little fast. That's probably because you're upset. Blood pressure's a little high. It's hot and smoggy. Your blood sugar may have dropped from not eating. The smog, heat and lowered blood sugar probably brought this on. You'll be all right. Do you want us to call an ambulance?"

"No." I turned to the scared grocery clerk. "Thanks for staying with me. You really helped."

"It's all right." I shook his hand hard.

My wife drove me to the emergency room and they laid me on a table and hooked me up to the EKG machine and did their tests. I was still feeling shaky and weird. And I was still repentant.

The tests came out all right. There was nothing wrong with my heart. I wasn't going to die. At least I wasn't going to die today. I was astronomically grateful that God had given me a reprieve. I wasn't going to hell.

After my first collapse, I had more. Each time I felt like I was genuinely going to die. And each time I tried to settle things with God. After an awful attack in Death Valley, I figured it was time I discovered what was causing them.

I wasn't having heart attacks, although they felt like heart attacks and scared the snot out of me. I had hypoglycemia—low blood sugar. I was having low-blood sugar anxiety attacks caused by eating too much sugar and triggered by stress. Whenever life got complicated and I got nervous about it, my blood sugar went through the floor and I felt like I was going to die. I had to cut down on sweets, eat more protein and watch my carbohydrates. Exercise would help.

"And what about the way you live," my doctor asked.

I was your typical thirties man obsessed with my writing career and book publishing business. I worked too hard, worried too much and I ate the wrong stuff.

"Hypoglycemia can be the body's way of telling us we're living wrong," my doctor said. "Stress makes it worse. If you don't reduce your stress, you'll keep getting these attacks. You must change the way you live. Besides, hypoglycemia often leads to diabetes. And you know what that eventually brings."

"What?"

"Death. How do you feel about that?"

"Personally, I'm against it."

My body was unhappy about the way we were living. I would have to change the way I lived or die. All right. I was ready for a change for a lot of reasons.

CHAPTER TWO

The Ghost People

You should know about my wife, too. You'll need someone you can sympathize with. My wife deserves your sympathy. She's married to me. And she's been through enough hell the last three years to earn your sympathy.

My wife's name is Edie, *Ee-dee*. She is the best and kindest human I know. Of course I'm prejudiced. I worship the cushions she sits on. In my ignorant opinion, God may have made an error when He made Eve the first woman instead of my wife. Eve was an awful creature. She kept bad company and she was easily influenced. If Eve would have let that apple be, you and I would be living in Paradise right now. We would be lying around all day, stark naked and feeling perfectly comfortable about it. We wouldn't have to suffer the inconvenience of working for a living. Instead we got Eve where the trouble started. Believe me, my wife could have been trusted with that apple and we'd be better off for it.

Edie has common sense. This is good for me because I don't have any. Edie was born with common sense. It oozes from her. This wounds my sensitive manly pride and puzzles me. My wife has a built-in, natural understanding of the world. She's an expert on human nature and she expresses her insight simply and directly. "He's a jerk and he can't be trusted," she'll say about someone I think is next in line to Jesus Christ. Unlike my wife, I have goofed-up radar. I often see in others the high morals and character traits God never installed in their natures. Edie instantly knows what people are like and what motivates them. So I've come to rely on her judgement. She isn't as trusting as me. And that's good for me. Even at my age, I find it hard to believe some of the stuff we do to one another.

Edie has a practicality it seems women are born with. While I wander around in my head with questions of right and wrong and books and ideas, my wife cleans house, makes dinner, irons my shirts, feeds and yells at the children and reorganizes the messes I make. She does all this willingly. She takes great pleasure in the day to day work that must be done, and since I won't do it, she does. She can comfort a child better than I can, and cook better than I can, and care about people better than

I can, and she's much more thoughtful of others than I will ever be. In short, Edie is a much better person. I thank God for inflicting me upon this good woman and entrusting her earthly welfare to someone like me. But it must be all right. God always knows what He's doing.

My wife puts up with me and she's very good at it. She's the first one to get up in the morning, and while she's getting the kids ready for school and making them breakfast and shoving them out the door, I'm asleep. When I awake, she's smiling and glad to see me, unless I was bad the night before, and then she's not glad to see me and she makes me aware of my errors. But on the good days when I have behaved myself, she smiles and let's me know she's happy I'm alive and makes me coffee and treats me like one of her children. And for her kindness and patience, I am very grateful.

While I begin my morning of writing, my wife leaves me alone and doesn't bother me about bills or whether we're going shopping or anything that should be discussed right then. She knows I need a clear mind when I write. So she leaves the discussion of our domestic problems until I've finished. My wife is a saint and without her I'd be a miserable lost soul. I depend on her.

It wasn't Edie's fault we left Southern California in search of paradise. It was my fault. Edie can live anywhere happily. She isn't like me. She accepts the world the way it is and doesn't try to change it. She believes it is pointless to wrestle with a world that won't be changed no matter how many good men and women are born into it. I envy her serenity and her acceptance.

For ten years we lived in a small city in Southern California. We owned a house in a decent neighborhood. By "decent" I mean people were fairly normal. They had regular jobs; they kept their yards neat. They didn't steal from each other or kill each other or eat each other. It was a middle-class neighborhood near the center of town. Our dead-end street was lined with large, old carob trees that gave wonderful shade in the summer. Their shiny, mahogany pods fell in the autumn and spotted the streets and smelled a familiar musky smell when the rains soaked them. I remember how the pods crunched when I stepped on them late at night as I tried to walk worries away or tried to find the solution to a writing problem.

Our neighborhood was typical, houses lined up next to one another along a paved street that ran for a half mile, with neat green lawns and shrubs and flowering plants in every yard. It was an older neighborhood we could afford when we were first married. The houses were wooden shiplap like the old Venetian blinds with large front porches where you could sit and watch the neighbors water their lawns or wash their cars or rake the carob into the gutters where the street sweeper roared past early in the morning, sucked it up and carried it away.

Everything we needed was nearby and convenient. A grocery store was over the hill; a hospital was a mile away; there were hundreds of stores within several miles where you could buy anything you wanted; there were schools, libraries, colleges, street lights, stop signs, traffic signals and everything that makes for a regular life in a city. We probably could have stayed there if two things hadn't happened: Southern California turned into Hell and everyone we loved or cared about left our lives.

One of the last straws were the "ghost people" who moved next door. They were about our age, in their early thirties. The wife was slender and pale; the husband was slender and pale. They had dark circles around their eyes as if they'd been kept awake a couple centuries. They looked like co-stars from *Night of the Living Dead*. I called them the ghost people because of their reclusive behavior. Though we tried to be friendly in a neighborly way, the ghost people were peculiarly stand-offish. I didn't take it personally. Usually you don't dislike someone unless you know them.

When we were in the front yard and they drove into their driveway, they never said hello and their eyes never met ours. They hastily slid to their front door, quickly opened and shut it without saying a word and entered the dark world they apparently considered home. The ghost people stayed in their house until they left for work, with every window shade tightly drawn except for the kitchen windows which faced our bedroom. Their lighted kitchen was nearly always without their presence. Rarely seeing them move around in their house gave you the impression the ghost people crawled in their coffins and hid until morning.

The preceding owner of their house was a tidy Dutch widow on whose kitchen floor you could have literally eaten. She painstakingly watered her yard and pampered her flowers and shrubs. She daily inspected her lawn and if the grass was a quarter inch too high, it was instantly cut. Each year her house was painted a sparkling white and if a shingle was crooked the whole roof was replaced. The Dutch widow made a virtual paradise out of her ordinary city lot. Her immaculate house and yard were an example to the rest of us.

Then the widow died and the ghost people showed up. The Dutch widow's yard decayed day by scorching summer day, without the least concern for watering her lawn and pampered plants. The lush green lawn became a dry brown wig. The shrub leaves curled into crisp brown corn flakes and fell in piles. The lovely flowers wept and perished. The yard the widow so lovingly and attentively cared for, became a brown wasteland that would have killed the widow a second time if she saw it.

There were several fruit trees in their back yard that bore hundreds of pounds of luscious plums and oranges. The ghost people never laid a hand on the fruit. It fell from the trees and rotted on the earth. The waste made us sick.

They did weird things to the widow's house and yard as if to punish her memory. The horrible chemicals in the smog drifted to earth in a brown dust that piled on the white siding. The smog did that to everyone's house. You had to hose your house down like you hose down a car. But the ghost people let the brown dust pile on their house until the former bright white home was dull and sad.

They tore the wooden siding from the house and made gaping holes in its abdomen and then left the siding to rot in the dirt. You couldn't figure out why they tore the siding off. That sorry, old house looked wounded.

They dug up the back yard and made strange trenches and left the trenches open. The back yard looked like it had a monster mole living in it. They never put anything *into* the trenches.

The ghost people did their weird landscaping and home repair when you weren't looking. I mean, you never saw them outside *ever* doing anything. And the next day part of their house was gone or another trench had grown in the back yard. I think they came out at night and did this stuff while we were sleeping. I think they did it just to mess with my head.

It was none of our business, really, what they did. It was their property to do with as they pleased. It just disturbed us to see such a fine house and grounds deteriorate so badly. It wasn't long before the widow's happy home was the saddest house and yard and we were sorry the widow had died and the ghost people were born.

I still find it hard to believe, but the couple had a living daughter. Well, she was sort of alive. They kept her inside and you never heard her laugh or cry, even in summer when the windows were left open. The ghost people probably kept the kid locked in a closet.

The ghost people were strange but they are a good example of Southern California social behavior, to an exaggerated degree perhaps, but true nonetheless. Though millions live in Southern California, it is a common custom to not communicate or to communicate poorly with persons one meets during the day, particularly one's neighbor. A conversation that gets past, "Hello, how are you," is miraculous. Perhaps television has made people inarticulate vegetables. Maybe the smog has eaten brain tissue. Maybe it's the transiency. Maybe people just don't care anymore. Undeniably, Southern Californians have a fetish for privacy. The first thing people do in California when they buy a house is put a six foot wall around it and turn it into a fort. Which means a normal sociable human being often feels he is living amongst the Ubangis of of the Congo, entirely frustrated because he cannot communicate with a single soul of the millions living around him. It's not unusual to live next to a neighbor for fifty years and never learn his name nor what he does for a living nor his hobby nor his children's names. And when he dies, you learn about it when the realtor puts a "For Sale" sign in the front yard. Most Southern Californians consider this normal human behavior. I thought it was strange. And the longer we lived there, the stranger I thought it was.

We lived in Riverside, once a nice, easy going town beside the Santa Ana River, about fifty miles southeast of Los Angeles. If you drive up Mount Rubidoux in the center of town you have a full circle view of the town. Looking around, you can appreciate what a nice place Riverside is. Looking east on a rare, smog-free day, for miles in the distance there are thriving green lawns, bountiful trees and the rooftops of hundreds of houses. Many streets are lined with palm trees that lift into the air like grey telephone poles with shaggy green umbrellas for heads. There are acres of orange groves and in the spring time there is the lovely fragrance of the orange blossoms along the tree lined avenues.

The old business district is in the northern end with the county courthouse. Several municipal high rises loom over their smaller neighbors. They light up like golden temples when the afternoon sun hits their reflective windows and seem to draw the city's energy toward them.

East in the distance is rocky and barren Box Springs Mountain and below it the high bell tower on the University of California campus.

The Santa Ana River is just west, the sorriest excuse for a river. Usually you can jump or skip across it. The quarter mile wide river bed is generally as thirsty as the desert around it except for a sad stream that slithers down the middle and supports a ribbon of brush and trees. It isn't much of a river until it rains for a couple days. Then the river bed fills up, the river overflows its banks and threatens bridges. The Santa Ana River heads in the San Bernardino Mountains and winds through the inland valleys to the Pacific. Its main purpose now is to transport all the filth and sludge from the inland cities and dump it into the Pacific Ocean. Once the Santa Ana River was a brave little river with pride. But now it feels like a sewer, ashamed of itself and angered by what men have made it. Beyond the Santa Ana River and the bordering of trees, hills and mountains roll in the distance.

From Mount Rubidoux you can see that Riverside and her sister city San Bernardino, are in a basin formed by the San Gabriel Mountains to the northwest that toe-nail into the San Bernardino Mountains to the south, a dark, high ridge, some fifteen miles north of the city. The two mountain ranges form a barrier between the coastal valleys in the west and the High Desert in the east. The mountains are blamed for the bad air. They catch the Los Angeles smog like a baseball glove and hold it until a big breeze blows it over the mountains into the High Desert where it bothers the gentle desert souls who are tormented by the filthy air they have moved there to escape.

Mount Baldy is at the southern end of the San Gabriel Mountains. At nearly twelve thousand feet, it is the highest mountain in the area. Between Mount Baldy and the beginning of the San Bernardino Mountains there is a steep wide canyon buffeted with sandstone cliffs known as the Cajon Pass—that's *Kuh-hone*. More than a century earlier Mormon emigrants first used the Cajon Pass to slip down from the high Mojave Desert into the San Bernardino Valley. Now an eight lane, concrete freeway—Interstate15, and miles of train track run up and down the Pass sealing the former Mormon trail. The Interstate is one of several escape routes out of the smog choked coastal valleys. Cars and trucks day and night speed up and down the Pass like bugs on a twig.

If you ever got a craving for blue sky and atmosphere fit to breathe—and you got it all the time, you escaped the smog chamber of the San Bernardino Valley by driving up the Cajon Pass to the High Desert. There is blue sky in the High Desert part of the day. A new generation of smog is born in Los Angeles each morning. It takes the new-born most of the day to figure out how to infect the inland valleys. And it isn't until late in the day that it figures out, to infect the High Desert, it needs the afternoon winds to shove it over the San Gabriel Mountains. So if you go up to the desert early, you can see blue sky before the Los Angeles smog buries it in the afternoon. And then you have the sad ride down the Cajon Pass into San Bernardino Valley, where the air pollution is second only to Los Angeles. The lower you go down the Pass, the thicker the smog gets. You feel like you're driving back into hell.

Looking down from Mount Rubidoux, Riverside is laid out in a green valley and rolling hills border the eastern edge and rise above the town. In recent years, developers have destroyed most of the hills with housing tracts. They have bulldozed the sagebrush and paved the hills. They have planted humans where hawks and coyotes lived and hunted. They have run off the meadowlarks.

They have even run off the lovers. The hills were once perfect for love on a warm spring or summer evening. Discrete places overlooked the city lights and it was quiet except for the crickets chattering. When you were young and in love the hills were your bedroom.

In the hills you felt safe from most of the damage humans can do to one another. They were a dying refuge. Surrounded by civilization, the hills were uncivilized and free. Wild things lived there—cottontails and jack rabbits, coyotes, ground squirrels, roadrunners—strange birds that prefer walking to flying and eat rattle snakes; hawks and owls, gopher snakes and glassy black stink bugs with their butts in the air. Yellow breasted meadowlarks sang soothingly in the brittle bushes amongst the buckwheat, sagebrush and wild oats. Flocks of grey doves swooped out of the brush when you surprised them. You could still touch real dirt and see the desert the way God made it and man should have left it. What was wild and free was being murdered. Human need and greed was seeing to that. Now the only wild thing left in the prim, little neighborhoods was the next door neighbor fighting his wife.

In January and early February, the winter rains gave birth to a delicate carpeting of rye grass, and thick green shoots of wild oats and the hills became wonderfully green. You learned to appreciate the wild grasses. This was desert country. The sun would burn the grasses by mid-June and the green hills would dry up and brown. Gardens of spring wild flowers sprang up with the rye grass. Whole hillsides were plastered with lovely yellow flowers and another hillside was a wonderful baby blue. Fields and hillsides of waist-high mustard blossomed with tiny yellow flowers. The hills became a perfume factory with the sweet intoxicating scents of the wild flowers. And all across the hillsides was the steady, low hum of bees who went about their business collecting nectar from the wild flowers. The bees worked hard and long for they knew the flowers would not last. The sun would have them very soon.

When the hills greened they beckoned you to walk in them. You were happy when they greened if you were in love because you had someone to share them with. And you were sorry if you were without someone when the hills came alive. And then you wanted to avoid them, but it was impossible for the hills were too wonderful.

We escaped the city by going into the hills. There we could touch something inside each other it seemed we could not touch in the city. We could see things more clearly in the hills. A favorite hill overlooked the city. We just called it *the Hill*. We went there to share secrets on spring or summer evenings. We sat on a still warm granite boulder and enjoyed the view and the easy evening breeze from the coast. We smiled over the town where we had made our home together.

Often after work, I met with my best friend Tom Cooper on the Hill. Each of us was deep in his career. We worked hard and worried about the future. We poured Scotch into plastic glasses and it put a warmth in us and the city and surrounding hills took on a glow they did not have before the Scotch soothed the difficulties in a day. We talked as brothers and shared our dreams. We loved the Hill. There we seemed to get above it all and looked down on the city where we were trying to make our dreams come true. We couldn't imagine the Hill not being there for us.

CHAPTER THREE

Losing Home

I drove through the freshly built housing tracts, up paved streets that only recently had been sagebrush covered hills. The Chevy pick-up chugged up the steep streets. Reaching the Hill I found Southern California's latest victim. A bulldozer's blade had shaved its head as flat as a parking lot. A huge concrete slab entombed its body. A high chain-linked fence imprisoned the Hill. The granite boulders we sat on had been shoved over the cliff. Someone had bought the Hill and they were building a house on its head. Inside the fence were stacks of golden lumber, sacks of concrete, black rolls of tar paper, piles of pipe, a back-hoe, five gallon buckets. A sign was wired to the fence in blood red letters: NO TRESPASSING. I stared at the sign and white-knuckled the steering wheel. I killed the engine and looked with sadness and unbelief at the future.

I don't know how many times we had visited the Hill and enjoyed its view and talked deeply and laughed. So many times over the years. We took the Hill for granted. We thought it would always be there like the sun or the moon. If change could come to the Hill, there was no stopping the changes.

The Hill had been a lovers' roost for generations. I felt some sadness for the teenagers who would have to find another Hill, if it was possible. The builder of this house had no idea of what he had done and likely didn't care. It was like a lot of changes lately. Pagan invaders had come out of nowhere, swept into our town by the thousands and took it from us.

There was a way around the fenced property to a neighboring hilltop. I started the engine, hit the pedal and sped down the street, turned right and drove up a hill. I parked the truck and walked up a worn path through the sagebrush and the brown, sun roasted heads of wild buckwheat. I smelled the sagebrush and the straw-dryness of the wild oats and it smelled good.

I felt the cool breeze from the coast when I reached the crest of the hill. It was dusk and the sun was about to sink into the Pacific. I found an old friend, a large flat, granite boulder near the pepper trees and sat down. I turned toward the dying sun, now a reddish-pink sliver. In the distance a brown smudge stretched across the horizon like a stage curtain and rose into the sky. And where it trailed off, the clear sky lifted into the heavens. It was the wall of smog blowing in from Los Angeles as it did nearly every day. It would intrude into our valley and pile against the San Bernardino Mountains. It would smell bad and burn our eyes and make us wish we were far from it. It wouldn't take long to blow in from the coast.

The sun slipped into the Pacific and night slid on the earth. A cold breeze blew up the mountain and swept my hair back. It woke me up. I looked out to the thousands of lights in our city, some red, green, silver and yellow, their light quivering gently in the night air. In the distance the straight lines of bright blue lights outlined the airport runway. A river of white headlights climbed the canyon at the foot of the Hill. A red trail ran in the opposite direction. I heard the steady swishing of the rushing cars.

Everything we had taken for granted for a decade was being rearranged by forces we could not control. Many old friends had left town, either for new jobs or to get away from Southern California. Both my wife and I had lost our best friends. Edie's dearest friend was carted off to Atlanta with her husband who was transferred by his corporation. Tom Cooper was seriously ill and moved to Cleveland to stay with family while he recovered. He was the best friend I had ever had and I missed him. As an only child, I made family of my friends. Gone was Tom's wise counseling, friendship and inspiration. And where he had been, now there was a hole in my life. My father, the only immediate family living nearby, had packed up and moved to Georgia. My mother lived in New England. My wife's family was scattered across the country.

Our neighborhood had stayed pretty much the same for the ten years we had lived there. But now there were changes. The old people had grown older and died or gone into retirement homes. The children of the young families had grown older and bigger. The young families wanted bigger and newer houses. "For Sale" signs went up like flags of surrender and families moved out. Our children sadly watched their playmates leave them. A lonesome quiet sat on the neighborhood. It felt new and eerie.

The Dutch widow died and the ghost people moved in. The couple across the street divorced and their lives disintegrated. The young couple next door moved into a bigger house across town. The neighbor a few doors away learned he had cancer and his future was uncertain. The single mother with four kids, whom our kids played with, moved to escape difficulties with her ex-husband. A neighborhood boy who cut our lawn was grown up and gone to college. His sister who baby sat our children had discovered boys. Our pastor, a talented, humble man who wrote dramatic plays that encouraged and inspired the people, learned he had liver cancer. In six months he was dead.

The recent housing boom and influx of newcomers increased our unsettled feelings. Riverside County was the fastest growing county in America. Families who couldn't afford houses on the coast, searched the inland valleys for affordable housing. The population doubled, then tripled. Within several years a hole-in-the-wall on the outskirts mushroomed into a city of a hundred and twenty thousand. New houses blanketed the former wheat fields, lined up row upon row like army barracks, squeezed so tightly together a neighbor's snoring rattled the windows. Major American franchises opened their doors. A few years ago those same businesses would have chuckled about doing business in that run-down area. Within several years the former hole-in-the-wall had incorporated and declared independence from the county.

The newcomers worked in Orange County or in the satellite cities around Los Angeles. The freeways bulged mornings and evenings as the rivers of automobiles dragged along bumper to bumper carrying the workers from the inland cities. An accident backed up traffic for hours. A horse and buggy could make it home faster than the high-tech machines up and down the canyons.

Old friends were replaced by strangers we couldn't help resenting. The influx had changed our easy going town into a crowded city. Angry drivers hugged your rear end and cursed as they passed you or flipped you off. The animosity had become so intense, drivers were shooting from their cars, killing and wounding each other. We avoided the main streets and took the back roads whenever possible.

The city was different. My wife and I weren't the only ones who were disturbed by the invasion of strangers. Everyone felt the change and it made people anxious. Crime and violence had multiplied with the increase in population. There were increased rapes, buglaries, murders, robberies. A young mother with two children was strangled for a couple hundred dollars a mile from our home. A seven year old girl was raped and murdered a few miles away. We worried about our children's safety. When I took my nightly walks, I kept an eye out for passing cars, afraid a drugged-out teenager would blow me away for his idea of fun.

The entire face of a familiar small town, was continuously being re-shaped by the new construction. It was all happening too fast. You felt disoriented by the changes. In a week or two a new franchise restaurant was erected, a new row of office buildings appeared, a tract of houses was laid out, a great high-rise went up on a vacant lot that no one had wanted. Old buildings were demolished and new ones took their places.

The romantic Mission Inn in the heart of Riverside, with its Spanish mission architecture, its fountains and brick walled gardens, was one of the few buildings that communicated the past to the present generation. The Mission Inn was Riverside's cultural center. It was a warm place for weddings, receptions, high school proms and dining. Musical plays were performed in the theater.

Then the Inn was purchased by a company half way across the country. What did they know about this wonderful place? They had big plans. Contractors, crews and machines ripped the Inn to pieces and demolished a century of memories. And then the company ran out of money and left the Inn looking like a half-developed fetus. The demolition of that dear, old hotel caused the soul enough pain to consider murder. Five years after the take-over, the Mission Inn is still shut down.

The increase in new people had its impact on services. You waited in long lines at the grocery store, at the bank, the gas station, the post office, restaurants. And when a new bank teller greeted you with, "Do you have an account here," or "May I see some identification," you felt insulted.

"We've had accounts here for years," you whined.

"Sorry. I don't know you."

The town that had been a friend and home to us for twenty years, nearly over-night had become an alien country. Now we felt as lonesome and isolated as if we were living on Alcatraz. We wanted the old times and the old friends. We wanted our town the way it was. But it was gone, and it was going more day by day.

Worse, we were no longer comfortable with Southern California culture and attitudes. Southern California had come to symbolize all that had gone bad in America: the worship of material wealth, and the over-emphasis on how we look rather than what we are. We had a President in the White House from California whose influence seemed to solidify these values. He made it seem right to be greedy and selfish. He told a nation what it wanted to hear: *Money is Right*. I remembered when he was Governor of California, how he closed the state mental hospitals and the mentally ill were forced into the streets. And that's where they stayed, wandering in their madness like pitiful animals, scrounging for food and shelter. The California President was friend of the rich while he pretended to be friend to the poor, all talk and perfect moves. The nation loved and worshipped him. He was compared to John Kennedy. Kennedy would have rolled over in his grave. The hope of Kennedy's idealism and his call to help country and neighbor, lay dead in a new generation while the old man in the White House made a nation feel it was all right *not* to be our brother's keeper. And the fundamentalist Christian church had embraced the California President as if he were Christ. We held deep Christian beliefs. But there was something very wrong about wrapping the Cross of Golgotha around a mad new nationalism. The two were incompatible to us.

The California President was the symbol of a nation gone hay-wire. And in the land of extremes, Southern Californians had accepted his message with a savage enthusiasm. Southern California had become the spawning ground for self-centered, empty headed robots whose purpose in life was to look, think, act and consume like other robots. Every human being was to be a duplicate of another human being. *Franchised thinking*, I called it. An original human being with an original idea was poison. We didn't accept it and we wanted to get away from it.

Southern California had been a good place once. But now it seemed to have more people per square foot than any place on Earth and more were moving there all the time. Their gasoline powered machines burned the blue skies into mud. Their toilets turned the creeks and rivers into sewers. When our plastic trash cans cracked and fell apart, I asked the trash collector, "What's happening to these things?"

"Smog tears them up," he said.

If smog tore up hard plastic, what was it doing to our lungs?

We owned our house and we loved it as we loved the lives we had lived in it. But the friends and family who had warmed it and made it a home were gone. Now it seemed cold and empty. Now we were strangers in our own town.We wanted our old friends back. But they were gone and they weren't coming back. We needed new friends and a new place to belong to.

We wanted to go away and find a small friendly town with fewer people. We wanted to find a place where the air was clean and the skies were blue. We wanted real people who had real, normal values. We wanted to get away from the strange culture that aggravated us. We wanted to see hawks soar and hear coyotes howl and smell the sagebrush and live near it. We wanted some place where life was simple.

Was there somewhere in America a place where people still looked you in the eyes as they talked with you, and listened when you spoke? Or was that America gone for good now? We didn't know. But we wanted to find out.

We asked ourselves, where do we belong now? Where is home?

CHAPTER FOUR

A New Home

I had first visited Virginia City, Nevada eleven years earlier while writing a book about a prostitute and madam. My subject had lived in Virginia City during the 1870's silver mining boom. Her name was Rosa May. I had discovered Rosa May's grave in the cemetery at Bodie, California in Mono County. She had died at Bodie while trying to save sick miners in an epidemic. I had traced her story from Bodie a hundred and twenty-five miles north to Virginia City where she had worked in brothels before Bodie.

I had been working on the book for a year before I met my wife. Then we were married and I dragged Edie to Virginia City and we searched the Storey County courthouse for fragments of Rosa May's life. We loved Virginia City, Carson City and the Lake Tahoe region. It was beautiful, clean and lightly populated. We wanted to live there but I had not been published.

Our income began to change when I published my first book, *Rosa May: The Search For A Mining Camp Legend*. It took five years to research and write. I established my own book publishing company when it was completed. I hired a typesetter who slaughtered the manuscript with misspellings. I let her go and learned to run a computerized typesetter and typeset *Rosa May* myself.

I wrote letters to several hundred people who wanted a copy of the book. I offered them a first edition, autographed copy if they sent ten dollars prior to publication. Many accepted my offer. *Rosa May* was shipped to the printer; I paid the big bill with the money from advance orders. I shipped my customers their books, sent out review copies and sold the rest to stores.

I sent a review copy to the *Los Angeles Times Book Review* . After several months, nothing happened. I sent another review copy and a letter. Nothing happened. I telephoned the editor, explained we were a small regional publisher. We would appreciate it if he would take a look at our new book. Then I sent another copy. The editor was kind and sent *Rosa May* to a reviewer.

When the *Times'* positive review of *Rosa May* appeared, we received orders from all over the world. Encouraging letters came in from readers; our income increased. I was a successful author and publisher.

For each of the next eleven summers, we made many five hundred mile trips back and forth to Northwestern Nevada. I continued researching and writing about the men and women who had lived in the mining camps. In six years I completed and published six books, five on Western American history and one on the music business in which I had worked. The major American library journals gave the music business book high marks. Orders poured in from libraries and chain book stores.

I wrote a second book about prostitution, *The Redlight Ladies of Virginia City, Nevada*. Then I began a series of books about Mark Twain's life in California and Nevada. One, *Mark Twain: His Life In Virginia City, Nevada*, had taken us back to Virginia City for the summer. There I gathered information about Twain's twenty-one months as reporter for the *Territorial Enterprise* where Clemens first used "Mark Twain" as his pseudonym. We rented the old Virginia City morgue for an office. And there in that cold and dusty basement, I began to organize the information and write about Twain's life in Virginia City.

When Southern California went bad, we were all set to move to Virginia City. We had made friends there; we had an office. And Buck, a new friend, had made a curious suggestion.

Storey County had serious problems. There was a local newspaper that could have reported what was going on but it had not. Buck encouraged me to look into the dark corners and start my own paper.

I wasn't sure. I did investigative historical writing. I wasn't a hard boiled journalist that cranked out yards of columns each day. But then, I was deep in the heart of a mid-life crisis and I wasn't thinking clearly. How can I explain how I felt?

It was like this:

When a mid-life man in all the busy-ness of his life, catches his breath and looks behind and ahead, and sees the friends of his youth gone, family gone, dreams life-worn and his values have lost some of their inspiration, a hole grows inside him. He doesn't want the hole to grow, but it grows anyway. He has ridden along his road pleasantly with an occasional bump. It has all gone well more or less. But now he comes to a wash-out, where the road has been cut away by a flood and left a chasm that seems impossible to cross. A man asks himself, what am I to do now? Is there a way around the wash-out? Is it worth the trouble to find it?

I had a hole inside me big as Utah and wanted to fill it but didn't know how. Amongst the believers I knew, I looked for the God that gives men peace and makes men whole, and I saw men my age like me, afraid, doubtful, overworked and concerned for themselves and their families. And why not? Life is hard. Living takes more than air and food and water. It takes money. Lots of money. Men wear themselves out trying to get more of it. Certainly there is more to life.

When a man assesses his life, he weighs what he has accomplished. It is a man's work that gives meaning to his life. And so I asked myself, what have I done that really matters? What have I done that has made the world better? And in my weary state of mind it seemed I had accomplished very little. Half my life was over. Now I found myself asking questions I hadn't asked in years: What is truly important? What is worth giving my life for? Certainly, my wife and children. But this had nothing to do with them. This was my problem. This had to do with me. What can I do with the rest of my life that will matter?

The hole inside me didn't know. It just wanted to be filled, now and without complication. I poured myself a Scotch and soda and drank it, and another Scotch and drank it and afterward I didn't think about the deep questions. In the morning I would get up, eat breakfast and start writing. And when work was done I would have a Scotch and be with my family, go to sleep and get up the next morning and do it again. I had become a working and drinking machine.

I had written six books in six years, built a publishing company out of nothing, taken care of my family, been a father and a husband and I was tired. More tired than I knew. I wanted a break. I wanted to have fun. And I had worked long and hard enough to have it.

One day as I sat alone in my office after work with a Scotch in one hand and a cigar in the other, it came to me that I was lonesome and my life wouldn't change unless I did something about it. I needed to get involved with people. I needed to write about things that affected their lives. Wasn't that what God wanted me to do? Yes. That's what I believed He wanted me to do.

And where were the people I cared about now? They were in Virginia City. Maybe that's where I could work out this mid-life crisis thing. Maybe starting a newspaper and getting involved was the answer. I didn't know; I was uncertain about a lot of stuff. I had lost my balance.

We stayed in Virginia City at the end of that summer and enrolled our children in school. We drove back to Southern California for Christmas. A day after we got back, the news reported the rape and murder of a seven year old girl whose naked body was found near our home. The victim was the same age as our daughter.

It was the last straw.

We painted and re-carpeted our house, made the necessary repairs, put an ad in the paper and rented it. We cleaned out the house and garage and separated everything: what would go into storage, what would go to the dump, what went to the Salvation Army, and what we would take to Nevada. I filled the pick-up with several loads of junk and carted them to the dump. Our furniture went into storage along with my piano. I would miss it.

We rented a U-Haul trailer and filled it with office supplies, desks and chairs, pots and pans, sheets and pillow cases and stuff I can't remember. And at the end of the sorting, packing and cleaning, our home was as empty as a tomb. We felt like newly made vagrants.

The hardest thing for us to do was to leave our home. We had moved into it a few months after we were married and lived in it for ten years—longer than I had lived in one place in my life. I wrote my first book in that house and our children were conceived there and we brought them home from the hospital to that house and it was their first and only home. Our house was full of our lives. Or maybe our lives were full of that house. But leaving it vacant while we lived in Nevada was stupid. Renting it would make money and help us buy a house in Nevada.

This was The Plan: We would move to Virginia City and see how we liked living in a small rural town. I would start my newspaper and continue writing the Mark Twain in the West series. Earning a living wouldn't be a problem. We would run our publishing business out of the old morgue. We could practically run it out of a shoe box. All we needed was a post office and a telephone. If Virginia City wasn't what we were looking for, we could try some place else. And I would begin working through this mid-life crisis thing.

We wanted to find a small town far from Southern California smog and make new friends and be happy. We were only looking for paradise. We knew we might have to try several places before we found what we were looking for. We were willing to give up our home and our security in order to find a new home and a new life.

If Edie had known it would be three years before we finally settled down, and if she had known the trouble that lay ahead, we might have stayed where we were and saved ourselves the torture. But this is one of the good things about being human: *The future is always a surprise.*

We pulled out of the San Bernardino Valley on eight lane Interstate 15 and climbed through the smog up the Cajon Pass toward the high Mojave Desert. The smelly, brown air cleared into blue skies as we neared the Cajon Summit. The truck worked its way over the Pass with the packed trailer behind it, picked up speed and raced down the grade toward Victorville. The horizon immediately opened to the wide, flat and clear Mojave Desert, broken up by mud-colored mountains that rose into the blue sky.

We caught U.S. Highway 395 this side of Victorville and turned north. The two lane blacktop cut across the brown desert valleys. We smelled the wild smell of the creosote bushes and waved good-byes to the Joshua trees, strange, dark stick figures with their arms held toward the sky like scarecrows. We climbed and rushed down the highway into bluer skies. Beyond Ridgecrest we hit the southern wall of the Sierra Nevada, turned northward and fought the strong southerly winds up the long grade into the Owens Valley. The dark, massive and beautiful Sierra Nevada Mountains made a wall to the west. Along the eastern side, the high, grey and brown Inyo Mountains rose hard and sharp into the sky. North of Bishop we climbed steep Sherwin Grade. The pick-up moaned as it worked up and out of the Owens Valley into the mountains.

We followed Highway 395 north along the Sierra and passed the mountain resort towns of Mammoth Lakes and June Lake. There was snow in the high country. We stopped and the children played in the snow and we took pictures. The skies grew bluer and cleaner the farthernorth we drove; we breathed freely.

We came out of the mountains to the sagebrush covered Mono Basin with the high grey volcanic Mono Craters on the east. We passed through little Lee Vining at the foot of the Tioga Pass that leads up to Yosemite, then edged the western shore of Mono Lake, the great saline lake where thousands of migratory birds rendezvous each summer. We climbed the last steep grade over Conway Summit at 8100 feet and sped down into the cold Bridgeport Valley. We stopped in Bridgeport, said hello to friends and went on. Just north of Coleville we reached Topaz Lake and knew we were almost there. A load lifted as we crossed the

Nevada state line at Topaz Lake. We stopped at the border casino and ordered Scotches to celebrate our release.

We rested, then drove through Gardnerville, made Carson City and turned east on Highway 50, "the loneliest road in America," says *Life* magazine. We headed out of Carson City toward Virginia City. We smiled when we reached the dirt road that led to Buck's and saw the great cottonwoods that marked his ranch and our new home.

PART TWO

Into the Wild West

CHAPTER FIVE

The Washoe Mountains

The Washoe Mountains are east of the Sierra Nevada. Today they are often called the Virginia Range. But since the early miners called them the Washoes, that name suits me. The Washoe Mountains rise just north of Carson City, run parallel to the Sierra and northward toward and around Reno. Washoe Valley and the Truckee Meadows lie between the two mountain ranges, well watered and once pastoral. But on the eastern side of the Washoes around Buck's ranch, the valleys are desert.

While the Sierra Nevada range splits Eastern California down the middle with some peaks over fourteen thousand feet, and granite walls high as skyscrapers, clothed by vast pine forests, whose awesome snow pack creates streams and rivers that feed meadows and cities, the Washoe Mountains are child-less orphans. They are as bald as a brown shaved head. They look as barren as if an army of lawn mowers were let loose and obliterated every inch of vegetation. Except for gutter-size spring run-offs or canyon rivers born by summer cloudbursts, American and Lousetown Creeks are the only Washoe streams with barely enough water to fill a bathtub. There are no verdant meadows. And while the Sierra peaks are white capped in winter, their lower Washoe brothers are often snow-less and sad.

Though the Washoes seem barren and forlorn from a distance, if you leave the valley floors and climb into them, you find they are not as lifeless as they seem. On their western slopes where winter storms dump their left-overs, the Washoes are strewn with *pine nut* and *juniper* trees, *ponderosa pine, mountain mahogany,* even some *willows* and *locusts* in wet canyons or around springs.

Here in this hard-bitten high desert, brave plants survive through hot dry summers and frozen winters. The most persistent vegetation is the *sagebrush*, with twisted, dry, gray limbs and tiny, gray-green leaves. You can't take two steps in Nevada without stepping on a sagebrush. It would grow in your bed if you let it. Sagebrush nearly covers Nevada and like other high desert plants helps to keep what little topsoil there is from packing into the wind. Its wood is as dry as the desert it thrives in and makes a pleasant campfire on a cold night. If you crush the leaves with your fingers, a lovely wild fragrance is released and there is nothing like it. Nevadans are enamored by the sagebrush and boast proudly of this sad specimen as if it were a blooming rose bush. Their affection is so profound that the sagebrush is the Nevada state flower. Sometimes Nevada is called the Sagebrush State. The sagebrush can grow as high as a man's head where there is water. But on the dry tips of hills where the wind blows hardest, the sagebrush is clipped lower than your knee. The average size is about waist-high.

The dull winter sagebrush leaves become a brighter green with the spring rains and winter snow melt. The greening of the sagebrush and the rebirth of wild grasses bring a green warmth to the Washoes. In late summer and early autumn, the sagebrush blooms with tiny yellow flowers and when the first frost hits, the flowers become a rust color and the dry seeds are easily scattered. The sagebrush leaves go gray. These autumn changes in the sagebrush make the Washoe Mountains dull and gray-brown.

Thousands of years of heavy winds off the Sierra Nevada have blown much of the topsoil from the Washoes. What is left is a tawny gravel. The gravel plays an important part in the life of desert plants. It acts as a protective barrier that allows the rain and snow to trickle through it and into the ground. At the same time the gravel barrier acts as a strange mulch that slows the evaporation. Parched Nevada has an astronomically fast evaporation rate. You could put the Red Sea in Nevada and ten minutes later it would be a dry, alkali sump.

A small flat, round fern-like vegetation of green and maroon, grows in wide patches all over the mountains. It is the high desert's version of a lawn.

Foot-high clumps of *bunch grass* and taut, waist-high stalks of *giant wild rye* are food for the bands of wild horses and deer that live in the high country in spring and summer.

Rabbitbrush is nearly as plentiful as the sagebrush, a waist-high bush that looks like an overgrown weed. When the rabbitbrush blooms in May and September with its bushy, golden-yellow flowers, those who have allergies are the first to know about it. The eyes itch terribly and water in a continual pity party. The allergies are worse if the spring has been very wet. Then the rabbitbrush thrives like watermelon. The bright flowers burn a straw color in the autumn and the tiny seeds are easily blown by the fall and winter winds.

Indian tea is the strangest Washoe plant and grows in wide, bright green bushes waist-high all over the mountains. Its limbs are as gray and twisted as the sagebrush wood. But its leaves, if you can call them leaves, are green, leaf-less twigs, six inches long and about an eighth inch wide with tiny brown knuckles every inch or so. The blades grow vertically, making the Indian tea look more like a broom than a plant. The Paiute Indians made a flavorous hot drink by boiling the strange green blades.

From the valley floor there are dark places in the Washoes. You can't tell from a distance that the dark places are *juniper* and *pine nut* trees. They look like bushes from the distance. But up close they rise about twenty-five feet high and as much wide. The two trees look alike and newcomers confuse them because they are similar in size and grow about the same height and girth. But if you examine their branches you discover that the pine nut tree has dark green, spiny needles that smell like a Christmas tree, while the juniper has a flat, branch-like foliage resembling green sea coral. In the spring, the juniper tree grows hundreds of pale-blue berry seeds, while the pine nut limbs sprout golden sacks that burst with a bright yellow pollen. Though the juniper's fragrance is pine-like, it does not have the bite of the neighboring pine nut tree.

It is remarkable how these two neighbors survive months without water and long, severe winters. They thrive in this high desert wasteland as if it were the most wonderful place on earth. You would think they would make their homes in canyons where water collects. Instead, they prefer rocky slopes where there is drainage. Give the juniper and pine nut trees a good steep, solid wall of rock, and their astonishing seeds will dig in and build a home and live off that rock as if it were the Garden of Eden.

The above ground climate has no effect on the pine nut and juniper trees. Their life depends upon the underground water buried deep beneath the surface gravel and kept there by the earth and rock that prevents its evaporation. The pine nut tree is typical of high desert plants. It drills its tap root through rock and sand deep down to moisture and water. And if it doesn't rain for a couple years, it doesn't trouble the pine nut tree the least. For its source of nutriment is as true as the sun and if the water table drops, the pine nut just sends its steel roots looking for it. Because the pine nut's life is hard, its wood is dense, stubborn and as solid as stone. Trying to fell a pine nut tree with a pitiful hand-axe would be like trying to split a boulder with a butter knife. Chain saws are required to cut the wood for winter fires. The pine nut wood is a wonderful fuel, marvelously rich in oil, and burns long and hot, releasing a sweet, warm fragrance.

The pine nut tree, more than the juniper, has been a friend to men. By autumn, the trees have grown slender, palm size cones. The pine nuts, about the size of a shelled peanut, are tucked under the cone petals. The Paiutes gathered and shelled the nuts in autumn and retrieved a sweet white kernel from which they made a nutritious meal. The pine nuts were valuable protein during the long winters.

Early settlers and miners used the pine nut wood to build log cabins. Planks could be sawn from the trees, but the often short, twisted limbs did not make for very fine boards.

The Washoe Mountains are chameleon-like and change with the seasons. In winter, they are gray-brown and friendless, unless it snows and then they look salt and peppered. In April and May, the snow melt and spring rains awaken the Washoes to a lively green and they catch your attention and you get the urge to climb them. The normally drab desert plants burst forth with surprising color as if they'd just heard Vincent Van Gogh was coming by and wants to see them at their best. The *desert peach*, generally just a mean, high bush with briars that will puncture your tires, now bursts into the most beautiful rage of pink flowers. For several weeks the desert peach looks like the sweetest and friendliest thing on earth. Then the tiny flowers dry and a peanut-sized red and yellow fruit emerges which gives the desert peach its name. The fruit falls from the bushes, is blown by the wind or rolls down the hillsides. And then the desert peach becomes its old, mean self and you want to avoid it.

The dry stems of the rabbitbrush begin to green. The normally dull green *bitterbrush* sports tiny yellow flowers. Star-like blazing blue and pale blue *bachelor buttons* thrive on the hillsides and along roadways. *Mule ears*, a pea-green plant with long fuzzy leaves, break out with yellow sun flowers. The *Indian paintbrush's* red-orange bells dangle in the wind. Baby-blue and violet *lupine, sun flowers,* and the *ground sell*—often called *butter weed*, yellow *checker mallows, hawk bears, prickly poppies*—with five big white petals, a big yellow center and a spine that will tear your hands apart, and the beautiful five pointed, yellow, *giant blazing star*, the purple *California thistle* and the red-pink *Bull thistle*, a variety of *wild buckwheat* and *monkey flowers* and more flowers than I know the names of, all awaken in late May and June and clothe the sorry Washoes with splendor.

The spring greening grows in the nibble-size wild grasses, in the waist-high *mustard* and *giant wild rye* and the *tumble weed*. Ah, the tumble weed. Here's a real vagrant. The tumble weed is actually *Russian thistle* some fool imported to America. It spread like a plague across the Western states. The tumble weed starts out in the spring innocently enough as do evil things. It begins small and flat on the sand like a hand-sized, green spider, sucking up every molecule of water it can get its greedy tongue on through its single tap root drilled into the earth. At this stage, it doesn't even look like a tumble weed. If you squeeze the legs of this succulent spider-like thing, its vessels burst with water. It becomes self-confident and proud as spring warms the desert earth and begins to grow wider and raises its flat, spider body into a basketball-sized bush with mean little stickers along its stems, still green mind you, and fastened to the earth. Then as the summer sun blasts the desert, the surface water perishes and the green tumbleweed is torched yellow as wheat. The tumbleweed hangs around until the autumn winds whip the mountains. Then it lets loose from its tap root and is off wherever the persistent Nevada wind wants to push it, propagating its sticker seeds all the way.

There are secret springs in the Washoes where the hills tuck together or at the bottoms of mountainsides. Only the worst draught dries them up. Beside the springs are tall stands of *tules* and green patches of *water cress* with tiny, white flowers and barriers of *green nettles* and *willows*. Wild horses know where the springs are, as the Paiutes did, as do the foxes, deer, ground squirrels, quail, sage hens, chukar, pack rats, mice, coyotes and rattle snakes.

In late May and June, the cottonwoods along the creeks and beside the springs sprout millions of round white fibrous balls that are blown by the wind and look like a winter snow storm. In the center of these white packages is a tiny white seed. The strong spring winds blow the cottonwood seeds miles away from the creeks and rivers.

As the June and July sun roars, it burns the grasses into straw whisps and the wild flowers shrivel and die. The moist spring earth becomes parched. The Washoes lose their brief bright colors. Now the desert heat cools any desire to go climbing into the mountains.

With the first frosts in September and October, the cottonwoods along the creeks and springs turn as golden as butter; then the leaves turn brown and they dry and fall from the limbs. Then the cottonwoods become gray skeletons along the waterways. The Washoe Mountains wither to a dead-leaf brown and the dried-up tumble weeds are blown down from the mountains and pile against doors and fences. Then you feel less friendly toward the Washoes. Early winter withers the Washoe's sagebrush covering to a lonesome gray.

In January and February as winter takes hold, *pogonip* forms in the valleys and high into the mountains. Pogonip is the Paiute Indian word for "white death." The Paiutes knew what they were talking about. The pogonip is a dense, damp fog full of tiny ice crystals. The white ice crystals grow on every living thing, grass or twig, like salt. You go to sleep with the landscape gray and dull and wake up in the morning with the trees and mountains covered in white, though no snow has fallen. The Paiutes had the misfortune of living in this fog, breathing it, getting pneumonia and dying from it. For several days or weeks the pogonip hovers over valleys blinding roadways and depressing the human spirit. The only way to escape it is to climb high into the Washoes to about 5500 feet. Then, suddenly, you break through the fog into sunlight, blue sky and warmth. And looking down from this height, the pogonip lays under you like a pearly feather pillow.

CHAPTER SIX

Buck's Ranch

Buck's ranch was in the Washoe foothills on several hundred acres of steep, rocky land. It was a calm, silent isolated ranch. Few knew where it was; few knew Buck lived there. Buck liked it that way. The ranch was hidden, something we would learn to appreciate. Buck had invited us to camp there until we got settled in Nevada.

Locals nicknamed the valley around Buck's the "Banana Belt." Though only two thousand feet in elevation separate Virginia City from the Banana Belt, in winter the difference is killing. While Virginia City at 6200 feet is as frozen as the arctic, the Banana Belt is as sunny and cheerful as Bermuda.

Buck's home was a single-wide mobile strapped down to a level site where the original shepherd's cabin burned down. Part of the stone walls of the former cabin still stood behind Buck's mobile. In front, a waist-high stone wall made a fence.

Where Buck's trailer sat was the only truly level place. The rest of the ranch sloped like a child's slide. Shoulder-high sagebrush and rabbitbrush covered the hills and wild grasses and weeds grew in between scattered pine nut and juniper trees. Someone comforted by plush, verdant forests would likely consider the rocky, nearly treeless land, worthless. But we loved it. It was rugged and wide open. It was Nevada.

In every direction there were hills and mountains. To the south were the Pine Nut Mountains, dark, distant and brooding, with Rawe and Lyon Peaks at nearly nine thousand feet. Ten miles west was the great wall of the Sierra Nevada; over the ridge was Lake Tahoe Basin. To the northwest was McClellan Peak with several tall antennas. Red lights on their tips blinked through the night and warned airplanes to steer clear of the mountains.

Three big cottonwoods grew beside Buck's artesian spring. Years ago, shepherds built a six foot square concrete cistern, twenty feet deep, to collect the precious spring water. The spring was Buck's only water. Buck liked the idea that his water came naturally out of the ground. A dilapidated shed covered the cistern. Inside the well house an electric pump and pressure tank pumped water to Buck's house. A long hose went from the well house to Buck's strawberry garden. A chicken wire fence enclosed the garden to keep rabbits and ground squirrels from devouring the treasured strawberries.

The well house door was a sheet of plywood propped up by a two-by-four. You had to move the two-by-four to get inside the well house. Once you removed the door, you discovered a wonderful, dark world where a host of small frogs lived in the darkness and damp earth where the water pipes leaked. The frogs sprang to attention when the door opened and the daylight burst in. Some jumped into the cistern, and some squirmed into dark corners and hid from the light. The frogs had curious feet, like tiny hands with suction pods on the tips of their fingers that enabled them to climb up the concrete walls to the water pipes where they sat day and night, talking with each other, mostly about this new guy and his kids who kept opening the well house door and bothering them. Buck and I joked about the "protein" the frogs gave the well water. The water was not treated but it tasted all right anyway. In late autumn, the frogs disappeared from the well house and the children asked where they went. The frogs burrowed into the mud where they hibernated until spring.

In normal years, the spring water overflowed the cistern and made two small ponds below the cottonwoods. Skinny cottonwood saplings circled the ponds. Buck tried to plant trout in the ponds but the water was too warm and the fish died. The ponds were an oasis in the high desert and attracted an assortment of wild life—cottontails, jack rabbits, quail, ground squirrels, coyotes, frogs, wild dogs, wild horses, lizards, black birds and other birds. Some mornings we watched families of quail scurry to the ponds with their tiny flags on the tips of their heads, like brown question marks, fluttering as the quail sped across the dirt. Buck kept a five gallon can of bird seed and threw it out behind his trailer where the quail had breakfast each morning. We watched the quail peck at the bird seed. Nearby a family of ground squirrels played in a rock pile above their earthen homes.

In the spring, the black birds made grass nests in the branches of the shoulder-high sagebrush near the ponds. The mother birds flew away when you approached the nests and perched in a nearby cottonwood branch and squawked at you until you removed yourself from their territories.

Behind Buck's mobile was a low, primitive dugout built by shepherds long ago. The walls of the dugout were constructed of slender basalt slabs carefully piled up and covered by a sagging wooden roof. You kneeled to get inside the dugout. Inside there was an old conical-shaped oven made of red bricks that were cemented together with brown mud. The oven looked like a bee hive. Here the shepherds baked their simple bread in the floor of the oven that was flat, light colored stone. A hole in the top of the oven let out the smoke that puffed out a circle in the shed roof. Part of the oven had collapsed and the bricks lay where they had fallen. The dugout had probably housed many a shepherd but they had left nothing behind to know them by.

A weathered lean-to with a rusted metal roof, once used to protect equipment and store winter fire wood, leaned in the direction the wind most often blew. Rusted, ancient horseshoes were nailed to the outside walls. Beyond the lean-to, there was a toppled outhouse—a double seated outhouse. Cardboard had been tacked around the toilet holes to provide a slender insulation for the cold, winter nights. A crescent moon was cut into the door; remnants of wooden shingles partially clothed the worn roof. A fenced-in area where the shepherds corralled sheep was overgrown with weed and brush. A small lean-to in the corral was being shoved aside by sagebrush. There were a couple unused barns and a lean-to garage with a storage shed attached, the bare wood burned a deep brown by a century of hot summers.

You could tell by the unattended buildings and overgrowth, the place was no longer a working sheep ranch. Now it was just Buck's place. Spooky was the only animal that made its home there, Buck's strange, black mongrel dog. Spooky looked like the lonesomest creature on earth. Buck inherited her with the ranch. The previous tenant was an evil man who had a litter of pups he didn't want. He began to kill them but somehow Spooky escaped into the sagebrush, fled into the hills and survived. The dog killer moved out.

When Buck showed up, Spooky sensed he was a good man. She came down from the hills and gingerly made friends with him. Buck was the only person Spooky trusted.

You hardly ever saw Spooky during the day. She lived in the hills. She darted into the sagebrush to hide if she saw you. Late at night she barked outside Buck's door and Buck let her inside. Spooky curled up in Buck's bed and Buck talked to her as he scratched the tender place behind her ear and reassured Spooky it was all right. Then, just before dawn, she slipped out an open window and was gone for the day.

Wild horses snuck into Buck's ranch when he wasn't looking. The wild horses left their calling cards—mounds of fresh manure. Buck despised the wild horses—called them "damn nags" because they competed for food with range cattle. Many rural Nevadans, mostly ranchers, cursed the wild horses. Only newcomers admired the strays. And even they cursed the wild horses when they strolled onto a highway in front of speeding cars and were struck and killed.

Our new home was our travel trailer parked on a gentle slope under Buck's cottonwood trees. The wheels were blocked with boulders to keep the trailer from sliding down the slope. An extension cord ran to an electric outlet. A carpet made the entrance to the trailer. We would live cheaply and simply until we knew we wanted to stay in Nevada. At least we would try.

The children tied a rope to a cottonwood limb and made a swing with a small board. They fought over the swing and often went to the ponds and collected frogs and caged them in glass jars. They played with the frogs for hours. It was surprising to see how much pleasure children who had lived among the tinseled treasures could receive from Nature's simplest things. There were lots of lizards on the ranch that the kids called "blue-bellies." Although the lizards were black, they had metallic blue undersides. My son captured the blue-bellies with a nylon fishing line attached to a long stick with a simple noose at the end of the line. He carefully slipped the noose around the unsuspecting lizard's neck and yanked the line. The captured lizards became pets and the children played with them for hours. Then they let them loose and recaptured the lizards the next day.

In the wet years, there was plenty of water from Buck's well but in the dry years the spring nearly dried up. The ponds became dry, sun caked pits and we did not use the well water because Buck needed it. During the dry times we hauled in water.

We sat on the tailgate of our pick-up in warm weather and watched the sun as it set behind the Sierra, and marveled at the "Sierra wave," high, thin, pink and violet clouds, flattened against the sky as if God had smeared paint across a great plate of glass. The high, evening winds across the Sierra will do that to the clouds and it is wonderful to see.

In the twilight, brown cottontails with their white bottoms and gray jack rabbits with black stub tails hopped from the sagebrush into the dirt road and sat hunched, then leapfrogged away. The families of quail scurried nervously single file toward the ponds and if the children ran after them, the quail erupted into the air for a dozen yards and fell into the sagebrush covering.

Evening came and the stars were very bright in the cloudless black sky far from city lights that could dim their glory, and our noisy pals, the coyotes, came down from the mountains for food and love making and cried for one another. Their crying made the children raise their heads and widen their eyes and my wife drew closer. Sometimes the coyotes made a terrible racket and I chased them off, pitching rocks into the sagebrush. The air was alive and clean with the wild smell of the sagebrush. Often in the late afternoon and evening a light breeze rustled the cottonwood leaves and the rustling calmed dark thoughts.

There wasn't much room in our travel trailer but we had what was necessary and comfortable. It was a simple shelter with a stove for cooking and heat, a refrigerator, radio and television, toilet and running water, sofas that made into beds and storage space. Our children were young and small. Life in the trailer grew intimate and we felt closer to one another than we had in the big house in the city and we felt better for it. Somehow a simple meal in that cozy place smelled better and tasted better. Perhaps knowing we did not have to live in a trailer helped us to accept our little home more easily. If we ever felt we did not have what others had, we knew there were some who had less. Like the black African mother who cuddled her infant on her milk-less breasts and cursed herself because she did not have enough food to keep her emaciated child alive, or cursed her world or her God for letting her baby die a terrible death. There were people out there with real troubles. What other Americans had compared to us was unimportant. Our trailer would be home until we were ready to settle somewhere permanently.

Life was simple at Buck's. We had shelter and space. We had water and electricity. We had clean air and blue skies. No one bothered us. We were safe for the time. Buck's ranch would be our refuge longer than we imagined.

CHAPTER SEVEN

Virginia City

Two thousand feet above Buck's ranch, is Virginia City, slapped against the eastern slopes of Mt. Davidson high in the Washoe Mountains. The narrow wooden cottages and mansions hug the side of the mountain for dear life as if they are afraid they might roller coaster down the steep grade into Six Mile Canyon. Paved streets crisscross the mountain with century old buildings lined up in rows like spectators on bleachers. Their windows like open eyes stare from the mountain crow's nest out to the Carson Plains below and dark mountain ranges far in the distance.

What God made here, men have reconstructed in a hundred and thirty years of inhabitation. Left to itself, it was a mountainous high desert of sagebrush and rabbitbrush, a dry land, except when the snow melted into skinny creeks that twisted down the canyons where great cottonwoods and locust trees sucked up the precious water. The brown rocky mountainsides were darkened by pine nut and juniper trees that seemed to live on nothing but dry dirt and rock. The fierce Washoe Zephyrs bulldozed the mountains in autumn and shook the pine nuts from their cones and the Paiutes and the ground squirrels gathered them for winter grub.

In the late 1850's, white men hiked up canyons from the Carson River to Mt. Davidson in search of gold. In 1859 two Irishmen found incredibly rich deposits of gold and silver at what is now Virginia City. Naturally, the Irishmen didn't get rich. What they found was pounced on by other men and stolen from the discoverers. The two Irishmen died from the greed of men and from the bad luck that often comes to the discoverers of mineral wealth. The earth seems to punish those responsible for the theft of her riches.

News of the discovery hit the petered-out California mining camps. When the snow-buried Sierra passes cleared in spring, the fevered California miners swept over them like locusts for new strikes in *Washoe*— Nevada Territory. Thousands of California miners crawled all over the Washoe Mountains like bugs, digging into hillsides, blowing up rock ledges, clawing at the mountains in search of gold and silver. They hammered posts into the ground to mark their claims and their dreams of wealth. They dug caves into the mountain sides for primitive shelters, and lived in canvas tents or slept under the stars and sagebrush. They mowed down the pine nut trees for firewood and timber for cabins. They carved roads into the feet of Mt. Davidson, ran them in a grid north and south, east and west and gave them names. They built roads up the steep mountains so horse and mule drawn wagons could bring up lumber, food, equipment, dynamite, whisky and whatever men needed to live. Flimsy shacks went up like summer wheat. But when the vastness of the riches below the town was known for certain, they built sturdier buildings, many of brick, some six stories high.

They paved the dirt roads with crushed rock from the mine mills. They built stables and corrals and planted blackberries and apple trees and fed them with water pumped up the Washoes from a Sierra lake twenty-one miles away. In a couple years, the former barren mountainside was a small, dense city with people from around the world. You could buy anything you wanted in the many shops. Gas lines under the streets and into the buildings fueled thousands of lights. Then they built a railroad to Carson City and connected the isolated mining town to San Francisco. Men made a home where God never intended men to live. And that meant trouble.

Hell lets loose when you put men in an isolated, unfamiliar place. Virginia City was crammed with a hundred whisky mills and whores were imported to satisfy man's need for sex which is always multiplied in the wilderness. Boredom led miners to saloons and whorehouses; rotten whisky enraged them. They fought over women and mining claims, horses and cards, boots and shirts and anything that was worth having. Killings were as frequent as running noses in winter. From its conception, Virginia City was a contentious, troubled place that could kill the peace of the Apostles. It didn't seem to matter. Men and women flocked by the thousands to this isolated town on the top of a mountain in the empty Nevada desert. And most believed they would get rich for their troubles.

The truth is, only a few truly prospered. And for each that did, hundreds lost their fortunes or their hopes, their dreams or their lives. The popular histories like to boast about the once rich Virginia City mines. But they seldom tell you about the miners in the bread and soup lines during the boom years when drops in mining stocks put them out of work. Suicides were notoriously common; the latest victim hardly made a dent in the hardened consciousness. Some killed themselves by throwing themselves in front of trains, or hanged themselves or overdosed on opium or they drowned themselves in a bowl of water or drank themselves to death. Men craved gold and silver and when they couldn't get them—or couldn't get enough, they did the most sensible thing: they killed themselves.

Something evil happens to a piece of earth when men do bad things on it. The scores of murders, the greed, the contentiousness, the self-inflicted deaths, the whores and the perverted sex, caused something dark to grow at the foot of Mt. Davidson. And it grew despite the bright and clear sunlight and the clean mountain air.

The first boom in the early 1860's created a town about a mile square filled with narrow two and three story wooden and brick buildings. Early earnings from the mines yielded about 20 million dollars. The second boom in the mid-1870's produced profits of over 300 million dollars. The wobbling infant became a serious industrial city of twenty-five thousand, with huge, pounding mills pulsating twenty-four hours a day, pumping the clear sky full of white smoke. Half the people burrowed like animals in the scorching heat and hell in the mines below the town; and the other half weaseled around above it.

The deep mines and huge mills created monstrous piles of gold, grey and rust colored tailings as if the earth had vomited the mounds out of itself. The huge piles of tailings produced by the great mills that crushed and melted millions of tons of ore from the bowels below the town are still there today. The largest piles mark the richest mines and mills.

For twenty years Virginia City's silver mines were known throughout America. Their tremendous wealth helped the Union win the Civil War and financed the building of San Francisco. For fifteen years they affected the lives of Americans everywhere, sometimes directly, sometimes indirectly with the rise and fall of mining stocks.

Every mining town is dependent on a never ending source of minerals which always has an end. When the end of Virginia City's riches was reached at the tail of the 1870's, mining companies folded; miners lost their jobs and businesses moved on. By the turn of the century Virginia City had fallen to what Silver King John Mackay called, "poor man's pudding." The town was nearly deserted but the stubborn or faithful stayed. Some continued as miners and worked the left-overs of the great mines. A grocery store, a few saloons, a few empty hotels, Virginia City sighed into the twentieth century.

In the 1920's Italian immigrants moved in and bought great, worn buildings for very little. A handful of mills reworked the old tailings and employed a hundred or more men.

In the 1930's, the mining and milling dried up with the Great Depression and the town nearly emptied. A tiny population held on and catered to a few tourists who came up from Reno and Carson City to see the once great and famous mining town.

In the 1940's, with the increased number of soldiers at various military installations, several houses of prostitution reopened on D Street, the traditional redlight district. A half-dozen saloons on C Street benefited from the overflow that went bar hopping after a visit to the D Street houses. The houses of prostitution prospered until 1947 when the murder of a prostitute caused their closure. Still, a few stubborn souls stayed and held on.

In the 1950's Virginia City grew in popularity as a tourist attraction when Lucius Beebe and Charles Clegg resurrected the *Territorial Enterprise* and began touting the town as a great place to have fun. Saloon keepers installed slot machines. Tourists reveled in the wild, fast life of hard liquor, sin and gambling in the once famous silver mining town.

When the "Bonanza" television show became an international hit in the early 1960's, it created much interest in Virginia City, the alleged home town of the Cartwrights. The Cartwrights existed only in the imagination of a writer. Yet their creation, and the popularity of the television show caused a sudden boom in Virginia City. Speculators and business people purchased the dilapidated buildings, sprayed them with bright paints, rebuilt their interiors and opened casinos, saloons, gift shops, museums, antique stores, hotels. Tourism boomed; Virginia City came alive.

The town sold and resold its history and legends: the sudden wealth of two poor Irish miners, John Mackay and James Fair, whose discovery of massive amounts of silver and gold in the Consolidated Virginia Mine made them millionaires overnight; the story of how Sam Clemens, then a struggling newspaper reporter, adopted his famous byline "Mark Twain," and sky rocketed to fame; the tale of Julia Bulette, a caring prostitute, who nursed miners and firemen, shunned by the self-righteous and brutally murdered by an out of work baker, her skull crushed by repeated blows of a stick of her own firewood; the tales of poor men made rich by lucky mineral discoveries. These and other stories fascinated visitors as Virginia City grew in popularity.

By the mid-1980's Virginia City had acquired an annual tourist season that began in April and ended in October. Once again it was an active rural town with a full time population of 800-900. The great silver mines and mills were shut down; now the town's sole source of commerce was mined from its history.

CHAPTER EIGHT

The Morgue and the Neighborhood

Virginia City has always attracted writers. Samuel Clemens, perhaps the most well known, cut his journalist teeth in Virginia City 1863-64 while reporting for the *Daily Territorial Enterprise*. In Twain's second book, *Roughing It*, published in 1872, he gives an accurate, entertaining portrait of Virginia City's first mining boom.

Dan De Quille [William Wright] Twain's Virginia City roommate and fellow reporter, spent thirty years on the *Enterprise*. In March 1875, Twain wrote De Quille and invited him to Hartford to write a book covering the history of Virginia City. Virginia City at that time was the talk of the nation. In the summer of 1875 De Quille took a leave from the *Enterprise* and stayed with Twain at his home in Hartford where De Quille wrote *The History of the Big Bonanza*, today known as *The Big Bonanza*, the best history of Virginia City's rise written by a man who was on the ground at the camp's inception.

Walter Van Tilburg Clark, perhaps Nevada's most well known novelist, author of *The City of Trembling Leaves* and *The Ox-Bow Incident*, later made into a movie, taught school in Virginia City in his mid-years. Following his retirement, Clark lived in Virginia City where he edited the *Journals of Alfred Doten*, an important resource for historians. Doten was a Comstock journalist whose diaries provide an interesting and informative peek at Virginia City's boom and decline.

James Cain, author of *Past All Dishonor*, a novel cast in Virginia City, visited and wrote about the town and his portrait depicts the town's troubled effects on men and women.

Robert Laxalt, today's most popular Nevada novelist, Bob Caples, a well known Nevada artist and Walt Clark, frequented Gordon Lane's Union Brewery Saloon in the 1950's, then a popular hangout for writers, artists, photographers and musicians.

Lucius Beebe and Charles Clegg, homosexual companions, moved to Virginia City in 1950, resurrected the *Territorial Enterprise* and wrote a number of books on Nevada and the West.

Louis Lamour, popular author of numerous Western novels, visited and wrote about the town in *The Comstock Lode*. And there have been many others, drawn to the romantic mining town to escape the world "down below" looking for a quiet friendly place to write. I wasn't the first and I won't be the last.

The old Virginia City morgue became our office because we couldn't find anything better at the time. It was a basement in the Giandoni Building, the last two story on the east side of North C Street. It was the county morgue at one time and built in 1876 at the peak of the mining boom. Nothing from the morgue remained and the spirits of the dead who had lain around there never bothered us. The basement was dusty and dirty and filled with junk we had to clean out before we could use it. But the price was right.

A five foot trap door in the wooden boardwalk was the entrance to the morgue. We had to lift it to reach the steep wooden stairs that led down to the basement office. Once opened, we tied the trap door to the brick wall to stop the frequent mountain gusts from blowing it shut. A steel fence circled the trap door and prevented tourists from taking a spill down the stairs and breaking their necks.

At the bottom of the stairs there was a pair of doors that led into the basement. The morgue's office was twenty feet square with a bare concrete floor. Dust and dirt from the boardwalk blew down the stairs and under the doors and dirtied the floor. Each morning we dust mopped the floor but no matter how well we cleaned, the dust dryness stayed in our noses as we worked through the day.

The twelve foot high walls were made of red-clay brick. The mortar was disintegrating and fell to the floor in small piles of white powder. The ceiling was open rough beams. In one corner there was a hot water heater for the apartments on the second floor. Once in a while the water heater went haywire and hot water spewed out. We were usually there when it erupted and able to stop it.

Our ceiling was the floor of Dave Heffner's gift shop and we heard the footsteps of Dave's customers and their muffled voices as they walked through his store. The old wooden floor creaked where the customers walked.

The morgue was a good cool place in summer. But in winter, our large kerosene heater could not keep the high-ceilinged office warm. Each winter morning we lit the kerosene heater and the acrid kerosene smell filled the room briefly until the heater got going good. On cold winter mornings we huddled around the heater. As long as we sat close to it, we were warm but only a few feet away it was so cold we shivered.

We dragged everything down the steep stairs into the morgue that I needed to write, and everything we needed to run our publishing business: desks, chairs, book cases, computers, filing cabinets, books and shipping supplies. We applied for a business license, had a telephone installed and we were in business.

Early in the mornings of school days, we left Buck's ranch in the Banana Belt and drove across the sagebrush flats on Highway 341 into the Washoe foothills to the pine nut and juniper trees and saw the first mining holes in the mountain sides and the piles of rust colored rock beside the old diggings. We wound through Spring Valley and saw the dirt roads that went up the mountainsides to the upper diggings. The double yellow-line two lane went up a hill and then down into the gully that intersects Gold Canyon where the gold was first discovered. We came to the first *trees of heaven* along American Creek and the four big wooden cyanide tanks and the one large steel tank at the old mill on the creek and then up to tiny, run-down Silver City—locals called it "Sliver City"—past the cottonwoods and man made rock walls and the shed that is the post office through Devil's Gate where the lime green lichen covered rock walls nearly kiss. Whether the men who named this opening "Devil's Gate" were divinely inspired is not known. But they had it right as far as trouble is concerned for some of those entering here.

We climbed the narrow road up the canyon as it passes the first open pit mine on the left and the black holes of the old tunnels stood out in the wasted mountainside like caves, past the hillsides full of holes and tailings. The New York Mine's dark, high head frame on a hill above the road seemed like the gate keeper as we drove through Gold Hill, Virginia City's sister mining camp, passed the gray, yellow and rust colored piles of tailings and the gray corrugated steel buildings of the Crown Point Mill and the old brick Gold Hill Hotel. The canyon grew steeper and narrower and the canyon walls went higher and straight ahead, way up high was the famous, gray stoned Mt. Davidson. Our pick-up barely made the grade at the hair pin curve at Griener's Bend, I shifted into first and the truck heaved over the always windy Divide where Mark Twain was robbed and there, stretched out before us like a great surprise, Virginia City, fastened to the eastern slope of Mt. Davidson.

We drove down the hill on South C Street past the great hole in the ground known as the Loring Pit and the four story wooden, red and white Fourth Ward School that is now a museum. We reached the small cottages on South C Street and finally came to the two high rows of buildings on each side of the street that is the central business district. The wooden boardwalks were empty and only a few cars moved on the street and there were still places to park. The Mexican trash collectors were emptying the oak barrels into the big dump truck.

We stopped at Markham's Virginia City Market for orange juice and pastries and drove down C Street to our office. I unlocked the padlock, pulled the trap door open and we piled down the steep steps to the darkened office. We turned the lights on, and if it was winter, the kerosene stove was lighted and then there was the sharp smell of the kerosene in the room. We put a pot of water on top of the heater for hot chocolate and to moisten the dry air in the office.

Shortly before school, the kids left the office and walked together four blocks up C Street and then down Union Street's steep hill where the local kids used their sleds, to the elementary school on D Street.

My wife or I went across the street to the Longbranch Saloon or up to Julia Bulette's Restaurant and ordered a couple fresh coffees to-go. With the fresh morning smell of coffee filling the office we went to work, me at my cluttered desk writing about twenty-seven year old Mark Twain's struggles as a silver miner at Aurora, Nevada before he became a reporter in Virginia City; my wife at her desk taking care of book orders, mailing lists and a myriad of details involved with the publishing business.

C Street was our new neighborhood in this retired mining camp turned tourist town. Our office was in the heart of the business district and we felt a part of the hopes and trials of our neighbors who each year struggled to make a living in an isolated town entirely dependent on visitors. This was not easy. Half the year businesses prospered; half the year they nearly starved. It took a good dose of courage, business sense and luck to turn a profit each year. Each spring a new flock leased or rented empty buildings along C Street. With great hope, these naive entrepreneurs opened their doors, made it through the summer, saw their profits slide in autumn and when winter killed business, they loaded their trucks and high-tailed it down the "hill" to Reno or Carson City. The businesses we sold our books to, who in turn sold them to tourists, were survivors, people who had learned to take what they earned in the summer, hide it in their mattresses or stash it in the bank to live on during the long, often profitless winters. These business people were not only customers, but friends of ours. We had done business with some for six years.

Up the stairs from the morgue was the boardwalk, busy with people from ten in the morning until six in the evening. Boardwalks lined each side of C Street for three quarters of a mile. Slanted lean-to's covered the boardwalks, supported by wooden posts at the edges of the street. The over-hangs shaded visitors from the bright, high mountain sun. The narrow buildings that had survived several fires, were pressed tightly together along the boardwalk on both sides of the street, some wooden, brick or stone, some three and four stories high. Brightly painted, elaborate Victorian moldings decorated their faces. High narrow doors led visitors into the various shops and saloons.

Dave Heffner's gift shop was above us; beside him was Muldoon's Restaurant and bar where we sometimes ordered lunch that was delivered to us in the morgue. Next door was the Union Brewery Saloon, then the Brass Rail Restaurant where Glenda Heffner baked her tempting fruit cobblers and the sweet smell of baking pastries drifted down to the morgue and made us hungry.

Across the street from us was the Longbranch Saloon, then the Wild West Museum and then the Stope Restaurant and bar where Merle Koch's Dixieland band played Sunday evenings. Farther up was the Silver Queen Casino and across the street the Bonanza Saloon and Casino, then the Silver Dollar Hotel and Julia Bulette's bar and casino was on the corner.

The Bucket of Blood's white, two story began the next block where Dave and Gary played ragtime on banjo and piano. Next door was the Delta parking lot in the center of town where the tour buses dropped the tourists and the trolley car tour started. The Delta Saloon was across the street, the busiest place in town; Eleanor Ryan's Delta Gift Shop was next door.

Farther south there was the Red Garter Saloon where loud Dixieland music blared all day; then the post office, the grocery store, the Turquoise Shop and across the street, the Wagon Wheel Restaurant. In between these were loads of gift shops that sold anything from snake skins and gold nuggets, to T-shirts and jewelry.

Around ten each morning in spring and summer, the town began to fill. C Street was jammed with cars, campers and RV's, and all the parking spaces were filled. The overflow searched for parking in the big dirt lots down on E Street. Visitors hiked two blocks up the steep hills from the parking lots and when they reached C Street they were out of breath and looking for a place to recuperate.

Throngs of visitors wandered up and down the wooden boardwalks on both sides of C Street seven days a week poking their curious heads into the many stores, saloons, candy shops and casinos. As they passed the saloon doorways there was the clinking of slot machines, the whirring sounds of the one-armed bandits, the cacophony of numerous ringing bells which meant slot winners, and Dixieland music from several saloons. In the morning there were the sweet breakfast smells of toast, fried eggs and bacon, fresh coffee and maple syrup. And in the afternoon the sweet, seductive fragrances of hot candy, roasting giant hot dogs, fruit cobblers and candied apples poured from doorways. The boardwalks were always crowded and if you walked up C Street to the post office, you dodged visitors like you would dodge cattle. It was easier to walk in the street.

Every hour on the hour the bells of St. Mary's In The Mountains tolled, the beautiful red bricked Cathedral with the giant white spire and the gold Cross of Christ at its pinnacle—the most striking sight in town. There were the frequent blasts of the steam whistle from the Virginia and Truckee train, Bob Gray's miraculous twenty-five year restoration down on F Street, and the fire whistle bellowed every day at noontime.

A trolley wound through town several times an hour carrying visitors in two shaded cars. The driver blasted the history of the town with a microphone and speaker and smiling visitors with cameras and video cameras, recorded the sights to show family and friends back home. Each day during the tourist season, Virginia City was like a county fair that lasted until six in the evening. Then the tourists left, the boardwalks cleared, the saloons and shops emptied and a lovely quiet set upon C Street. Locals took over the town and filled the saloons and had their "after shifters" or tried to beat video poker and slot machines.

We took a break at mid-morning and walked up the boardwalk to one of the many restaurants and had breakfast. We always ran into friends and talked, talked, talked and someone was always eager to share a new joke or friendly town gossip. You could not help meeting friends and having a conversation if you went up C Street. Virginia City could be the friendliest place in the world. Often the talk was stimulating, always funny and something new was always going on.

We waited on the boardwalk when the children were expected back from school and looked for their small dark figures as they dodged the tourists and rushed to meet us. The kids did their homework as we finished our work or sometimes they played with local kids on the boardwalk or went to the park and played on the swings. In winter when the sun slid earlier behind Mt. Davidson and its shadow blanketed and darkened the town, it was bitterly cold and the icy mountain winds whipped along C Street and the paper in the gutters lifted into the air. Then the kids stayed inside, read or colored, and drank cups of hot chocolate made from the water in the pot atop the kerosene heater.

We believed we had found what we were looking for. We were part of a town and a community. Our friends were nearby. Our business and a portion of our living were made in Virginia City. There was little to no crime, except those crimes committed by politicians in the courthouse.The children could walk to school. A grocery store was down the street. There were lots of small town activities, community plays, baseball games, town picnics, benefits.

After work we met with friends next door at the Union Brewery Saloon until five or six, then drove down the "hill" to Buck's for dinner and bed. And for a long while life in Virginia City was a lot of fun.

CHAPTER NINE

The Town

The town was absolutely stuffed with an assortment of rough characters from known felons and hard-luck prospectors to burned-out and crazed Vietnam veterans. In that high, sweet mountain atmosphere, an ordinary city crazy was transformed into something near mystical. Dan Heath, an artist friend who illustrates books and paints many of the local business signs, once said to me, "Virginia City is a town of misfits who don't fit anywhere but here," and he was entirely correct. Many were a bit left of center. But if nothing else, they were all interesting.

The stable portion were people who had been born and raised in Virginia City or who had moved there long ago. They lived quiet lives in cottages and mansions above and below C Street. Some worked for the county or the state. Many were older and retired and met for lunch at the Senior Citizen's Center next to the Virginia City Park. Those who attended this place called it the *Senile Center*. Some even visited the Catholic or Presbyterian churches on Sunday.

C Street was where all the trouble and action was. Here floated in and out every six months an assortment of troubled souls who were trying to find peace, or trying to find someone to love or be loved by or a reason to live. Buck called them "six month wonders." They were without real estate or a stable career. Many were divorced, separated, or widowed and trying to re-connect with people and life. They had had bad times in other places and they were looking for a new start. Many were in various stages of alcoholism.

Virginia City grows alcoholics the way Idaho grows potatoes. It was a whisky drinking town in the beginning, and it hasn't changed a hair since. Anyone who wouldn't take a drink was suspicious. The town is a safe and good place for alcoholics. There's a saloon every fifty feet along C Street. You can choose a favorite haunt from twenty-five saloons in a half mile stretch. Drinks are cheap. A local drinker doesn't have to worry about driving drunk because home is walking distance away. If not walk, then crawl. One of the running jokes was that you could tell who the town drunks were by the splinters in their hands, referring to the way they got home down the wooden boardwalks.

These endearing souls took up part-time jobs and handed out change in the casinos, swept and washed floors, bartended, waitressed, or worked as clerks in the local businesses. They met after work and drank and chucked quarters into slots and video poker machines. They were a free-wheeling group that didn't take much seriously. They were taking a break from life; they were on vacation. Some called them losers. But this seemed unkind. Most had had tragic lives or had come to where they were by having made the same mistakes we can all make.

For some, Virginia City was an isolated hideout where they went to escape past errors, both personal and legal. Those inclined toward the lawless side felt they were in familiar territory and stayed. The town had a reputation for lawlessness which some mistook for independence.

Here was a nearly isolated town hanging on the face of a high mountain at 6200 feet, fifteen miles from Carson City and eighteen miles from Reno with maybe eight hundred full-time residents and tourism its only industry. It didn't have a full-fledged grocery store, a pharmacy, a hospital, no dentist, no doctor, no airport, the dump was about to be closed, no welfare department, an off and on gas station, no car repair shop, and if you didn't work for a local business, the state or the county, you didn't work. It was not a place where people came to begin a career or hoped to find one. It was a place where people who had done something somewhere else came for various reasons, nearly all of them foolish and unwise.

Virginia City had managed to retain the rebellious, devil may care, shoot from the hip, live-and-let-live spirit the young rowdies brought to the mountains a century and a quarter earlier. The last of the Wild Wild West was alive and well in Storey County. Gambling and prostitution were wide open and legal. Saloons could stay open twenty-for hours. You could gamble and buy a girl if that was what you wanted. Tourists fell for the fun, sin and adventure.

Simple geography helped Virginia City hold on to its past. It was in the middle of rugged mountains, fifteen miles from the nearest city and culturally and economically light years from the real world. And that's why people moved there. And those who lived there thought this was good. The town had a five channel cable television system that carried the networks, but most people would rather leave the TV off and go down to a saloon for fun and conversation.

The townspeople were absolutely, overabundantly in love with the West. Most regretted having been born a hundred years too late and having missed a wondrous, exciting era. They loved Virginia City and its mining history, praised those who came before them and proudly repeated their legends and stories. *Love* is not the word. They nearly *worshiped* Virginia City. They were proud to live in a famous silver mining town whose fantastically rich silver mines had made a tremendous impact on American history. They were a friendly, independent bunch and enjoyed celebrations, parties and parades and they were always erecting benefits for a local who was ill or dying or who had hit hard times and needed money.

The parties never ended. Autumn and winter were worst because the town was slow. You'd take a walk down C Street to the post office on a winter day with all the best intentions God had put in your head that morning, when a friend invited you into a saloon for a toddy, and the talk and the fun were warm and good, and when by-God you turned around, the sun was about to set and it was time for dinner! There were Halloween parties, Christmas parties, St. Patrick's Day parties, and parties after basketball games, and Joe Blow's birthday party, and so and so's anniversary party. You could have killed yourself on parties. And everyone who had a party, to your detriment, had meant well.

Every man wore Levi's and nearly every man's feet were clothed in some kind of boot. Some locals strutted around with cowboy boots and cowboy hats. If not a cowboy hat, then you wore an imprinted baseball hat whose brim kept the bright Nevada sun from your eyes and whose logo told others where your brains or your allegiances were. Members of the Jeep Posse wore baseball caps with the Jeep Posse logo. Firemen wore the fireman's logo. Marines wore caps with the Corps insignia and below it *Semper Fi*—"always faithful." Tobacco chewing was more popular than gum or cigarettes.

Like other rural parts of America, men expressed their masculinity with weapons. Pick-up trucks with rifle racks and rifles were common. Some carried serious knives strapped to their belts. Deer and antelope hunting and fishing were popular sports. Men enjoyed getting out in the hills in their 4X4's and camping.

It was a town of jeeps and 4x4's and pick-up trucks and dinosaur automobiles the size of yachts with monstrous, gas guzzling engines. We called them Nevada Mobiles or Highway Mobiles, big, ugly air conditioned Cadillacs and Oldsmobiles from the 1960's and 70's that could tear down the heart of a Nevada two-lane and make a soul feel invin-

cible to the desert, the heat, the wind and the sagebrush. Nearly everyone had one, or wanted one. Most of the backyards of Nevada have at
least one broken-down Nevada Mobile gathering dust and waiting for
the money to have it repaired.

The mistake newcomers made was this: they believed Virginia
City's romance, cozy charm, the high mountains and wide blue skies
would give them a permanent reprieve from the world they had left behind. Of course, it couldn't. Unless you were retired or independently
wealthy or had a business that was not dependent on the local tourist
economy, you had to work at a local shop or casino. None of these businesses made much, so none of them paid much.

So the innocent who had left the terrible city for the small town
found him or herself working a job for minimum wage. It would seem
disastrous. But to these city escapees, it was perfectly fine. Rural rent
was cheaper. You didn't need money for gas because you didn't need a
car; nearly everything you needed was available in town. So you elimi-
nated car payments, insurance, registration fees and drunk driving tickets. If you needed something in Carson City, you could get a ride or give
your grocery list to a friend. Locals were often paid in cash and avoided
federal income taxes. There was no state income tax.

Basic necessities were simple: a little money, cheap shelter, food,
heat in winter and of course, alcohol. Used clothing could be picked up
inexpensively at one of the thrift stores in Carson City. Thrift store shopping was a popular pastime; such shoppers were called "thrift store
junkies." I know about them personally. My wife is one. I couldn't keep
her out of thrift stores if I handcuffed her.

CHAPTER TEN

Storey County

Virginia City is the seat of tiny Storey County. Of Nevada's seventeen counties, Storey County with only 262 square miles is the second smallest county. Only Carson City is smaller. Storey County is sixty-nine times smaller than Nye County, Nevada's largest county at 18,064 square miles.

The Washoe Mountains run smack through Storey County like a herd of buffalo. The Washoes make it hard to get around the county. There isn't a single road that starts at one end and runs all the way through it. If you're in the southern part and want to get to the north end, you must leave the county, drive through Reno and pick up the northern part outside Sparks, Nevada. You're better off being a bird.

Virginia City is the only town in the entire county. Eight to nine hundred people live there. The rest of the 2500 residents are scattered around the county, most in three settlements.

The Virginia City Highlands, about nine miles north of Virginia City, is the newest development. Many who live here moved from California. After reaping a windfall from selling their California homes, they could afford to build large houses on several acre parcels. Many are retired or are well paid professionals. They tend to have more money and more education than the average county resident. And they are more politically aware and against the county being run by prostitution.

"Mark Twain," is a settlement of mobile homes in Dayton Valley at the foot of the Washoes about seven miles east of Virginia City. Here live retired people and families with school age children. Mark Twain can be reached from Virginia City by taking Six Mile Canyon road.

Lockwood is a working man's neighborhood in the far northern end of the county outside Sparks. It is also known as the River District because the Truckee River flows through it. The brothel district is located here.

Because only 2500 people live in Storey County, it is poor. Though the federal government pays a slender maintenance fee on its public lands, it does not pay county taxes. There is a small real property tax base; sales taxes are slim and a minor bed tax on motels and brothels provides little revenue. Consequently, the county suffers in public services. Until recently it was without a staffed county library. The county does not have a hospital, a health department, medical clinic, welfare department or college. The two most important public services are the sheriff's department and the volunteer fire department. Paramedics from the fire departments stabilize victims and rush them by ambulance or helicopter to Carson City or Reno hospitals. Local fire departments are staffed with a few paid employees and volunteers take up the slack.

The county is without a radio or television station. Newspapers, usually based in Virginia City, come and go. Consequently citizens are given little information about the doings of their public servants which pleases the public servants. I shouldn't call them public servants. They are public employees and elected politicians. The employees are all right; the politicians are the ones you must watch. The worst run for office after they fail at business or crime and have a marked similarity to the inmates at the local prison.

The county economy was based on two things: tourism and whorehouses. Virginia City, being a once very famous silver mining town, attracts thousands of visitors who gamble in the casinos and purchase various items in the many gift shops and museums.

In the second line of business, the county had the distinction of having the largest legal brothel in the United States. The man and woman who ran this place were infamous. They made the national news when they spilled the beans on their former attorney who became a federal judge and did bad things. I'll tell you more about them later.

In the past, silver and gold mining were the source of revenue for locals and outside investors. The big mining days are long over. Mining companies sporadically work the old mines and tailings but it is nothing steady and provides little employment.

Because of the county's shady reputation, large corporations are not breaking down doors to get in. Subsequently, there are few good paying jobs. High school graduates either must accept work at one of the gift shops or find work in Carson City or Reno. Many young people eventually move away because of the lack of suitable jobs. County and state jobs are highly coveted because they are steady and provide benefits. The local prostitutes are probably the highest paid individuals in the county.

Virginia City, being the Storey County seat and the population center, is where all the political action is. The courthouse is on B Street, a street above the business district. The courthouse was built in 1876 beside a big old barn known as Piper's Opera House. The courthouse is the home of the politicians, and like all politically infested buildings, lies are planted and thrive there as if it's a bean field. The courthouse is a two story brick building with an elaborate Victorian facade and a big flag pole planted on top. The front is painted yellow with white trim. A statue of Justice is inset in the cornice. Usually blindfolded, in this instance Justice has her eyes wide open which is sort of comical. Scantily clad in something that resembles a sheet, Justice holds a pair of copper colored scales in her left hand and a big sword in her right. The sword is for hacking off the head of anyone who tells the truth and the scales are for weighing bribes. For a time the weight of the bribery was so great, one of the scales had fallen and Justice held one lopsided scale in her left hand. God stole Justice's missing scale. He knew about Storey County justice. He giggled about swiping it. The scale has since been replaced but I don't know if justice has improved with the repair.

From the courthouse you can look straight up Mt. Davidson and see a big white "V" painted on the mountainside. The V is lighted at night and can be seen all the way from Dayton Valley. The V stands for Victory, Virginia City or Vice, we didn't know which.

On the bottom floors, stone steps lead up to the two tall dark doors. The District Attorney's office is on the left side of the stairs. *District Attorney's Office* is painted in gold letters on the big window facing the street. And on the right side of the stairs there is a big window with *Sheriff's Office* in the same gold lettering.

Joe Pastrami was Storey County District Attorney. Joe's life was good and happy before he became District Attorney. He had a wife and a family and he was in his right mind. Joe didn't mean to go bad the way none of us mean to go bad. Once he was an idealistic attorney eager to correct injustice. Then Joe saw how haphazard our judicial system works and Joe got cynical. American attorneys are the most cynical people in the world; you can't blame them, really. Anyway, after Joe got cynical he started drinking more. And then he cut a deal with a Storey county brothel owner—he was known as the "pimp." After that mistake, Joe started carrying around Guilt and Remorse. He drank to get rid of them. But when Joe woke the next morning with a throbbing hangover, Guilt and Remorse were smiling and waiting for him at the foot of his bed.

Joe was a funny likable character and supported the local saloon economy with the passion of Michelangelo. Joe liked parties. Nearly every night was a party to Joe and when he hit the saloons along C Street it became a festival for all Joe's friends. Joe bought everyone drinks and after they were all good and drunk, Joe got the urge to pull his pants down and hang his underwear on the nearest crystal chandelier. This stunt was sort of a tradition when Joe got drunk, and he was more drunk than he was sober. It was sort of strange seeing the Storey County District Attorney buck naked at the bar, but then that was Virginia City for you.

Joe was supposed to be the chief county law enforcement officer. But it was a lot of trouble prosecuting people you had to face on the street the next day. Especially when you had a hangover. So Joe became the town clown; life was easier that way. Joe got drunk and made people laugh. Everybody liked Joe and they laughed when they thought of him. He wasn't District Attorney for a while, and then he wanted his old job back. This was Joe's reelection slogan:

Bring back old time corruption.
Vote for Joe Pastrami.

The people laughed and voted Joe back into office. They thought Joe was joking about the corruption.

Being drunk a lot of the time sort of slowed down Joe's work as District Attorney. Often after his all night parties, Joe layed down on a bench in front of the Delta Saloon and fell asleep. Ole Dick Knight, the janitor who swept out the Delta, would find Joe the next morning snoring on the bench. Joe sounded like a motor boat. Dick went over and rattled Joe's shoulders.

"Joe, you dumb son-of-a bitch, wake up. You fell asleep on the street again. Get your drunken butt up." But Joe just laid there, as still as a corpse, sounding like a motor boat. Dick really shook Joe.

"Joe, wake up. Do you want everybody to see you sleeping here? Wake up."

"Wah, wahs that. What the hell...Get your damn hands off of me," Joe said.

Dick kept shaking Joe. "Come on Joe. I'm only tryin' to help ya. Wake up and get off the bench."

After shaking Joe five or ten minutes, Dick got him up and nursed Joe into the Delta Saloon where Harvey, the grey bearded bartender who looks like Gabby Hays, fed Joe coffee and Joe came around.

On other mornings after his all night parties with his pals, just before dawn when Joe's constituents were about to wake up and start their day, Joe Pastrami left the saloons, and after literally falling on his face several times, staggered home to bed or wherever he found rest. You could always tell when Joe had been on a serious toot because his face got all beat up like someone had tenderized it with a crowbar.

You could never find Joe to talk about legal business until about four in the afternoon. Joe's secretary covered for him. She'd say, "Joe is in a meeting," or "Joe's down in Carson City on county business," but you knew Joe was probably passed out or drunk. And if Joe came into the office drunk, she took him in hand like a mother. "For Chris-sake Joe, whatever you do in court today, *don't breathe on anyone.*" And she fanned her hands to get the sour odor of whisky away from her and back on Joe.

Joe had to appear with the sheriff two times a month at the public Board of Commissioners meetings in the courthouse. The Storey County boys sat up front at long tables pushed together. Joe was the most entertaining thing to watch if he'd been out drinking the night before because he was still drunk. He sat at the table with a silly grin fastened to his face like a cat that's swallowed a bird. He was a marvel of incompetence and brilliant at doing as little as possible to earn his salary. Whenever one of the Commissioners asked Joe about a legal matter, ole Joe just cupped his head in his hands real thoughtful like and said, "Well, hmm, that's an interesting question. And it certainly deserves looking into. I'll research that." Joe never gave the Commissioners a straight answer about anything. It was always, "I'll research that."

It was really something when Joe was drunk and started in on ole Pat Dixon, one of the county officers. Pat kept her hair clipped like a Marine and marched around the courthouse in knee-high, black leather boots like a lieutenant in the Gestapo. I think Pat thought she was a man.

Anyway, Joe Pastrami would get looking at Pat, and he'd get this screwy look in his eyes as if there was a bonfire in his brain, and it didn't matter that the Commissioners were discussing some serious issue, Joe would bear down on Ole Pat with his beady drunken eyes and blurt right out loud to Pat so everyone could hear him, "You ole lesbo," and everyone stopped talking and looked at Joe and tried to act like they hadn't heard what Joe said. So just to make certain everyone heard him right, Joe said it again, "You ole lesbo. Had a good woman lately, Pat?" And then you heard snickers and quiet laughs in the Board room because people knew about Pat and Joe went on, "I like the boots, Pat. Can ya get me a pair?" And if the audience got to laughing, Joe got inspired and entirely forgot where he was and really got on Pat's case, "So how do you do it, Pat? I mean, who gets to be on top," and stuff like that until Sheriff Dick felt compelled to do something.

"Joe," Sheriff Dick said, "if you don't shut up and leave Pat alone, I'll throw you out." Joe Pastrami just looked at Dick and said, "Oh, all right Dick," and then looked back at Pat and gave her one more shot, "You ole lesbo." Joe Pastrami was really something when he was drunk at the Commissioners' meetings.

On the opposite side of the courthouse stairs was Sheriff Dick's office. Although Sheriff Dick picked up a pay check from the county, he earned his real money like Joe Pastrami, taking bribes from the pimp, the brothel owner who controlled Storey County. You wouldn't know to look at Sheriff Dick that he was a crook because he always acted self-righteous as if he carried a Bible in his hip pocket. He hammered citizens about minor infractions as if they were rapists or murderers. All the while Sheriff Dick took bribes. Some knew about Sheriff Dick and it made them angry.

Sheriff Dick was going to cause me a lot of trouble. He thought I was crazy because I tried to tell the truth. Sheriff Dick thought only crazy people told the truth.

Sheriff Dick had a bunch of deputies under him. Most of them were good guys trying to make a living and support their families on terrible salaries. But he had two guys, Mad Dog and Heartless, who ticked-off a lot of people. The town gave them those nicknames. Or rather Mad Dog and Heartless earned them. Like all bad cops, Mad Dog and Heartless used their puny power to bully ordinary citizens. Consequently no one hardly had respect for them. You couldn't blame people, really. But I still felt sort of sorry for Mad Dog and Heartless.

The county School Board was beautiful, Ole Pat the lesbian with no children and four fools presided over by the husband of the county clerk. The President worked hand and hand with Al Ricardo, whom the President had hired as Superintendent of Schools. Al was a psycho case. For all the trouble Al caused, he was paid a monstrous salary. In fact, Al was the highest paid public servant in the county. The President thought anyone who hurt people as badly as Al, deserved it. No one knew about Al when they hired him. But they sure found out about him afterward.

I thought Al should have been hanged or murdered. I was going to make Al's life hell on earth with my newspaper.

The town didn't have a Mayor or a Town Council and that was a genuine problem for the people. There was just a three member county Board of Commissioners. One Commissioner was honest and disliked for his honesty; the other two were crooks who took bribes from the pimp and consequently were well liked.

The Chamber of Commerce was the governing town body, if any. It had an elected President, Vice-President, Secretary, Treasurer, etc. and an elected Board of about sixteen. The President at that time, Harry Hipowski, was a convicted child molester who was believed to have robbed the Chamber's treasury of a small fortune. Led by Harry's moral example, the Chamber got together every couple weeks and argued and disagreed about nearly everything but one: they all wanted more people to visit Virginia City so they could all make more money. They claimed to have great concern for the town's history but did little to preserve or promote it. The only reason they seemed to care about the history was because it made them money.

The Secretary of the Chamber was the real work horse who did nearly everything and worked like a black slave and was expected to do it all for nothing. The Secretary was always taken advantage of and consequently the Secretaries were always quitting, and afterward the former Secretaries were the most embittered people you'd ever meet. All of them tried hard to do a good job, and all of them did a good job. And all they got for their troubles were complaints and insults from the rest of the Chamber. The Chamber Board did a lot of talking, but little else.

The Chamber was able to organize itself to pull off one major event a year, Camel Races. In the old days, the Army used camels in the Nevada desert. Someone got the idea that they ought to have camel races to bring tourists to town. After arguing about it a long while, the Chamber erected the first Camel Race. Camel Races became very popular. First they attracted the whole town; then they attracted people from Carson and Reno; and then they drew people from everywhere. They finally became a three day drunk and the camels were the excuse for it. Camel Races attracted a rough crowd and any local with sense, got out of town that weekend.

The worst thing a newcomer could do was get involved in the local politics. Any person who was honest and was committed to doing something good for the community was slandered and despised. And the crooks and liars were usually elected to the highest offices and accepted as proper representatives for the community. It was the strangest thing.

CHAPTER ELEVEN

Bronco Lazzeri
and Gordon Lane

In the cow towns and mining towns of the American West during the 19th century, the saloon was a haven in the new hard country. Often there was a saloon before there was a town, usually run out of a canvas tent with two upright barrels and a plank for a bar. The infant settlements were without the town halls, community centers, churches and hotels where people had gathered in the East. The saloon became the central focus of human activity. In the isolated nervous boom towns of the far West, men found warmth and companionship in the saloon and more relevant news than was usually printed in the paper.

Not only could you buy whisky, wine and beer, but often free plates of meat, cheese and bread were laid out on the bar. This was wise on the saloon keeper's part. Food in the stomach made it take longer for the alcohol to have its effect. A drinker had to buy more drinks to get drunk. The food had another effect: a man with food in his stomach tended to cause less trouble.

The number of saloons increased as the Western towns grew. Each saloon catered to a particular class of men. A good saloon ran by an entertaining and respected saloon keeper attracted good men and became the heart of the community. Business was completed at the bar; news was shared; parties and celebrations erupted on birthdays, weddings, deaths and anniversaries.

There were always bad saloons, dives ran by the scum of the earth where rotten liquor was sold for dog prices. The people who ran these places were not bright nor charming. Often they dispensed women in back rooms as easily as they poured whisky. The hostile combination of whisky, loose women and men invariably led to trouble and to a blackened reputation.

But the Western saloon operated by a professional saloon keeper was a good place, warm and safe. They were run by strong minded men who knew how to handle trouble. A shot gun or a six-shooter kept beneath the bar and raised above the bar and pointed at the offending customer, usually caught the offender's attention. The trouble was completed before it started. If a man insisted on being a nuisance, he was escorted by the gun out the front door and told not to come back until he had sobered up. An apology and a plea for forgiveness was appropriate if the man wanted to be welcomed back.

A professional saloon keeper who ran a tight ship was as equally respected as the banker or the town judge. He held an exalted position and his establishment was generally more an estimation of the community than the local church if there was a church.

Such a place in Virginia City was the Union Brewery Saloon. It had a long and hospitable history.

One morning in the summer of 1949, Frank "Bronco" Lazzeri, dropped dead of a heart attack smack in the doorway of his Union Brewery Saloon. It was a surprise to Bronco but it wasn't a surprise to anyone else. Bronco had diabetes and he should have been taking better care of himself. Instead, he drank too much wine with his customers. Bronco was in his early fifties and fairly well-off for Virginia City standards at the time. He owned houses that he rented to poor families who sometimes didn't have the rent. Didn't matter. Bronco let it go. And if some months the renters didn't have money for food, Bronco bought the food. People were what mattered to Bronco, not money and profits. Bronco was a square dealer. Consequently he was beloved by those who knew him.

Bronco spoke English with a thick Italian accent you could have sawed in half. He loved America. When there was a shortage of water in winter, he poured wine on the saloon's grey wooden floor to mop up the dust and dirt, and the bitter smell of the wine hung in the air. Bronco was a character, full of humor and good sense. He and his saloon attracted the local miners and laborers who howled at Bronco's jokes. Bronco belonged in Virginia City. Said he came to town in the 1920's to escape the mob back in Chicago. Property was cheap. He bought a lot of it.

Bronco had been running the Union Brewery for about twenty years, off and on, at the time of his death. The saloon wasn't a brewery anymore but it had been one in the 1860's and 70's when Virginia City was a booming silver mining town. Everyone called the Union Brewery *Bronco's*.

Around the time Bronco died, Gordon Lane had the Wonder Lode Bar up on South C Street where the post office stands today. Just before Bronco died, the Wonder Lode burned down. The bar was open at the time of the fire and Gordon's customers helped him haul out his bar equipment and liquor inventory. Naturally, they deserved something for their labors. Gordon's customers drank up his liquor while they sat and watched the two-story Wonder Lode go up in flames.

Gordon Lane was thirty, a good looking young man fresh out of World War II. He had served on the submarines during the War. When he returned home to Burlingame, California south of San Francisco, he took a weekend trip to Virginia City and didn't go back but planted himself in the nearly deserted, old mining town.

What Gordon liked best about Virginia City then was that you could do what you wanted and nobody bothered you. The town was lightly populated, maybe three hundred people. Everyone knew everyone. It was the old Nevada. There were a handful of saloons, a restaurant, a market, the post office and a few whorehouses down on D Street. The water was piped in from a lake twenty-one miles away and fed into an open flume on the mountainside above the town. When the flume froze in winter, which it always did, the water supply was cut off. There wasn't water for several months until the ice in the flume melted. Then the population went down to Carson Hot Springs in Carson City or over to Steamboat Hot Springs on the other side of the mountains in Washoe Valley to bathe. The shortage of winter water didn't bother Gordon or the rest of the town's independent residents. No water kept out the "foreigners," the tourists.

Some of the town's residents were elderly and retired; some were hard-luck miners with claims out in the hills that barely paid enough to live and drink on and they were always hitting-up somebody for a grubstake. Some ran little souvenir shops along C Street and made meager livings from visitors. A lot of single men and "fly boys," from Stead Air Base came up on weekends and paid visits to the girls on D Street. Afterwards, they hit the C Street saloons.

There were a few mining companies working the old tailings that employed about a hundred and fifty men. These laborers were the blood and profit of the several saloons in town.

Virginia City had shriveled to a strange, quiet place with paint-less, wooden buildings and ghostly mansions whose grand years were decades past. Many of the brick buildings in the heart of the once thriving business district were vacant. Virginia City seemed to have nothing to look forward to. Certainly, anyone who moved there wouldn't get rich; they'd be lucky to survive. Like many Nevada mining towns that had brought prosperity and attention to the state in the latter half of the 19th century, Virginia City had become a dreary, unappealing place to most.

But there were people who liked the quiet pace of towns like this. Gordon Lane was one.

After the Wonder Lode Bar burned down, Gordon Lane had nothing better to do so he stuck around and bartended at a couple saloons. When Bronco died, the Brewery sat by itself all lonesome and needing a keeper. Gordon mulled it over. He loved the Union Brewery and he had had many good times with Bronco. He approached Bronco's daughters and made an offer on the saloon. The daughters agreed to rent the entire three story brick building for $85 a month. Gordon acquired a saloon that fronted on C Street, a huge basement to store all the junk he would collect the next thirty-five years and an upstairs apartment through which passed a few wives and an assortment of women until Anne lassoed Gordon permanently.

And so began Gordon Lane's thirty-five year reign at what became the legendary Union Brewery Saloon.

It was 1950.

Almost immediately Gordon ran into bad luck. The Korean War broke out and all local mining was shut down. The men working at the mines and mills whom Gordon depended on for business were let go and moved on.

And there was more bad luck. It came in the shape of a woman. She was a D Street prostitute who had the misfortune of getting herself murdered. The story goes that a jealous lover killed her, buried her in his basement, then hanged himself from a rafter. Bronco had somehow gotten hold of the noose the guy hanged himself with. The noose was framed alongside a newspaper article that told all about the woman's bad luck. That noose and the article still hang on a wall in the saloon.

The prostitute's bad luck became Gordon's. The county outlawed prostitution in Virginia City. This immediately killed an important attraction for male visitors. The weekend bar trade Gordon and others depended on, died.

Gordon and the Union Brewery Saloon hit hard times. Gordon was tempted to give up the Brewery, but as he said, "I was too damned stubborn." So he stayed and struggled through it.

Gordon learned something from the hard times: he couldn't depend on the tourist trade. Local customers were his bread and butter. Gordon decided to keep the Brewery a local bar. He would cater to the hard-luck miners and others who made Virginia City their home and be damned with the tourists. There would be no fancy painted doorways. Just a bare wood floor, wooden stools, a solid pine wood bar and a strong drink for a fair price.

With this in mind, Gordon started the long tradition of placing a wooden stool in the opened doorway of the Union Brewery Saloon during spring and summer when the tourists invaded. The tourists had previously sauntered into the Brewery and looked around the place as if it were a museum. And they had rudely stared at Gordon's local customers as if they were wax figures on display. The tourists made Gordon's customers feel uncomfortable. For their sake, Gordon put the wooden stool in the doorway. And kept it there. The stool told tourists, "This place is closed." But always, there were tourists who looked inside the bar and seeing people, were curious and slinked in. Gordon being a businessman did not turn away the lawbreaker. He was friendly, served a strong drink for a good price, and as long as the visitor didn't behave like an idiot, he offered the stranger a slice of Nevada unknown to most outside the state.

From the beginning of Gordon's tenure at the Union Brewery Saloon, he ran it as Bronco had, with a loose Western independence that befitted it. He hardly ever swept the floor and the dust grew on the shelves like moss. The grey, bare wooden floor, stayed grey and bare and was never varnished. The Union Brewery had the feel of an old, Western mining town saloon. You could almost smell the sweat of the miners who once drank at the same bar you drank at.

Over the four decades Gordon Lane tended bar in Virginia City, many visitors went home and told their friends about this wonderful saloon in Virginia City and the charming man who ran it. They came back year after year to visit Gordon and to feel the comfortable friendliness of Gordon Lane's Union Brewery. Gordon remembered them and greeted them with "Hello Joe," or whomever. These visitors brought their friends who in turn, brought their friends.

Year by year, Gordon Lane acquired a long list of faithful customers from everywhere and from all classes, from construction workers to governors. And every one of them considered Gordon and his saloon a warm oasis in an often difficult world.

CHAPTER TWELVE

The Union Brewery Saloon

The Human Beings met regularly in Gordon Lane's Union Brewery Saloon sometime after three in the afternoon. That's when Gordon Lane opened up the bar after climbing telephone poles all day repairing the cable television system he had built and was in charge of.

The Human Beings were unpretentious people who didn't care squat if you drove an expensive car, if you wore designer jeans, if there were strands of gray in your hair or a pimple in the middle of your forehead. They weren't concerned with the latest fashions. They either liked or disliked you for what you were, how you behaved and treated others. They were as human as the human animal gets, funny and sad, angry and forgiving, noble and sloven, pathetic and praise worthy, the meanest and the kindest, trustworthy and irresponsible and sometimes they drank too much or ate too much and passed gas and what went in their mouths generally came out the other end. The Human Beings were real—isolated islands of humanity in a culture that would like to package our personalities as conveniently as it packages cereal.

The Human Beings made the Union Brewery Saloon the friendliest place on earth when we first knew it. You could make more friends in the Union Brewery in ten minutes than you could make in the city in a century. It was a shrine to friendliness, good will, humor and honest to goodness conversation with anyone from a truck driver to a judge.

The Union Brewery was next door to our office in the morgue. Two doors away was more temptation than I needed and more laughter and conversation than I have found anywhere in my life. Anyone who spent an evening there and gave that sorry-looking place a chance would swear there was magic there.

Listen: A few years before we moved to Virginia City, Tom Cooper and I sped into town one spring evening. We found a single saloon open on North C Street. A warm, honey glow poured from the doorway, across the wooden boardwalk and into the street. Through the doorway we saw a bar and a crowd around it. We heard laughter and voices and a piano. Should we or shouldn't we?

We stepped across a wooden plank that was worn down as if a beaver had chewed it, and passed through the two high, opened doors.

The saloon was not large, maybe fifteen wide by thirty feet deep with a sixteen foot ceiling. The old bar was on the left and ran for about fifteen feet. The bartender's side of the bar was lined with a mess of liquor bottles and empty glasses all the way down the plank. The place was packed. The bartender was in his sixties, with a tanned desert face, a thick head of grey hair combed back, and keen blue eyes. He was short, slender, wearing an ordinary white T-shirt and khaki pants. He was obviously blasted. He weaved up and down the bar, grabbing customers' glasses, filling the glass with more ice, and freely pouring liquor back into the glasses and talking and laughing while doing it.

Unlike many modern bars, the bartender did not use a mechanical drink dispenser where a machine pumps out half a shot that is sold for full price. This happy inebriated bartender, tipped the bottle up without a pouring spout, and poured the liquor into the glasses as if it were water. He poured about two and a half shots and charged a dollar a drink. He was fabulously happy, took the customer's dollar and threw it behind him in the direction of the cash register. The drawer was half open; bills were strewn across the drawer; some had fallen between bottles left and right of the register and some had fallen on the floor; the bartender walked on them as he made his way up and down the bar.

Occasionally the bartender leaned across the bar to tell someone something funny; you knew it was funny because after he said it, he threw his hands up, his head back and his mouth opened in a perfect oval out of which came this high pitched howl. This incredible noise was followed by, "Hoo-hoo-hoo," like an owl. You had never heard anyone laugh like this anywhere. So at first you thought the bartender was simply manufacturing the laugh. But after he howled and went, "Hoo, hoo, hoo," a few more times, you knew this was the way the guy really laughed. It was interesting.

The back bar was piled with an army of liquor bottles, many with unrecognizable names that hadn't been manufactured in decades, some powdered with a fuzzy coating of dust. Above the back bar was a large mirror that hadn't been cleaned in years; you could sort of see yourself and the other customers in the mirror. Hanging from the high ceiling above the bar there was a crystal chandelier with four lighted globes, the crystals and the globes stained brown from years of cigarette and cigar smoke.

The floor was gray, bare wood planks that hadn't been swept lately or varnished in years. The bar was on the left. Against the right wall was a bench where those who couldn't find room at the bar sat. On the wall above the bench was Harold Parrish's collection of black and white photographs of the bartender and his customers. Harold's collection was almost a history of the saloon since the early days. Written below each photograph were the names of the photographed and the date the photograph was taken; many were of the bartender. The photographs always caught the attention of first time visitors who studied the collection.

Beyond the bench and across from the bar was an old, upright piano and someone was playing songs from the 1930's and 40's that seemed to fit this place. Forest Catlett was at the piano, a dear leprechaun in his sixties, his dark, oily hair slicked back, wearing a thin, neatly trimmed mustache like those worn by actors in the movies of the 1940's. Forest's chubby fingers effortlessly floated across the black and white keys. His playing was beautiful and everyone, young and old enjoyed the music.

The walls of the saloon were once yellow or beige but the paint had faded and now the color was something indescribable. The walls were plastered with all sorts of strange stuff: a map of the Virginia City mines, advertisements for beers and liqueurs that hadn't been made in years, old posters of local boxing matches and political candidates, cartoons cut out from various magazines and pasted on the walls. Beyond the bar on the left was a tall, old cooler that hadn't worked in years with two glass doors. The cooler was stuffed with all sorts of junk, the once white paint now yellow from years of cigarette smoke and customers rubbing against it. Humorous cartoons were taped to the cooler door.

Beyond the cooler was the old black, coal burning stove. The black smokestack went up and headed into the side wall. In the left rear corner there was a poker table with green felt and several wooden chairs; several people were sitting around it, talking, their drinks and brown beer bottles on the green felt. Someone was passed out in the old, padded easy chair in the opposite corner.

The saloon at first looked like a dive, the offspring of something between a college fraternity hangout and an old West miner's saloon shoved into the twentieth century. There was not a hint of pretentiousness. The bartender, who turned out to be the owner, obviously cared less what anyone thought of his bar. A sign above the back bar said it all:

THIS is MY HOUSE. IDO AS IDAM please. And another sign: THIS IS NOT A CHAIN STORE.

Two places opened at the bar. Tom and I slipped in and sat down on old oak stools.

"Whataya have, " the bartender asked.

"Scotch and sodas." The bartender somewhat clumsily from the liquor, made a few steps down the bar, grabbed the Scotch by the bottle neck, put two glasses on the bar, bent his head down as if to observe the glasses more carefully and filled them half-full of Scotch and the rest with club soda. He brought the drinks, banged them down in front of us and said, "Two bucks."

"Two bucks each?"

"Just two bucks." Tom and I looked at the deep, golden color of the Scotch, nodded to one another and laid two dollars on the old bar. The bartender picked up the bills and threw them in the direction of the cash register, missed his mark and the bills floated to the floor.

This was Gordon Lane or "Gordy" as he was known to locals. Some considered him a legend. This seemed accurate. For he had been serving whisky in Virginia City for forty years and hadn't gone insane, or died, but was still walking and talking. Articles about Gordon and his saloon had appeared in National *Geographic*.

After a few drinks, Forest took a break at the piano; I took his place and pounded out a few tunes. Tom went to the back of the saloon and studied the portrait of a beautiful young woman dressed in a blue Victorian gown. Half-lit, he began to fall in love with the portrait. Tom approached Gordon at the bar, "Will you sell me the portrait in the back?"

Gordon looked confused. "What? That," and pointed to the lady in blue.

"Yes. How much do you want for it," Tom asked.

Gordon raised his right hand and threw it out as if he were shooing away a fly. "Whataya, nuts? It's not for sale."

"I'll give you three hundred dollars for it," and Tom meant it.

Gordon made the same shoo-fly gesture, turned and walked to the opposite end of the bar. Money didn't mean much here.

We hung around the Brewery the rest of the evening, talking with the locals. They were simple, fun loving people who enjoyed conversation and understood the give and take of conversation. Coming from California, they were gold. We called them the Human Beings for they seemed so entirely human.

As the evening drew on and Gordon grew more tipsy, the drinks were poured stronger and more bills piled on the cash register and in between the bottles beside it. More bills covered the floor as Gordon weaved up and down the bar serving his customers. More bottles piled on the bar, all with their caps off and ready to be poured.

Sometime that first evening we felt it for the first time, almost imperceptibly, then stronger and warmer. The Union Brewery's magic: a strange mixture of the warmth from the liquor and conversation, an intimate, friendly, golden glow the saloon took on late in the evening from the cigar smoke and torch songs from World War II; the good will and friendliness of the people, the exchange of the latest jokes, a strange loss of time, the dice game called "horses" that excited and charged the players. There was a bizarre time warp. You had walked in for a drink and when you looked at your watch it was eight hours later and you didn't know how the time had gone so fast. You had just had a few drinks and talked and listened to these curious people tell the most outrageously funny stories, most of them based on their personal experiences, and the piano music had been wonderful and Gordon howling and "Hoo-hooing," weaving up and down the bar and throwing his money around as if it were confetti. I had never seen anything like it.

Gordon Lane's Union Brewery Saloon was a no-frills bar that sold a strong drink for a fair price. Gordon didn't whip up strawberry daquiris or Mai-tais or other tourist drinks. Gordon said he was in the "whisky business." Inserted in his match box covers it simply read: *We Serve Whisky.* The Brewery was by and large a man's bar but women were welcomed and more or less tolerated.

Which leads me to this: Although the Union Brewery first appeared to be a wild, no-holds-barred place, for all its apparent looseness there were rules. Gordon laid them out, sometimes subtly, sometimes not so subtly. Congenial drunks were tolerated and allowed to stay until they passed out. Then they were told to get something to eat or sleep it off in the easy chair in the back corner. Sometimes the over-served person slept in the chair all night after Gordon closed.

Tourists who asked Gordon dumb questions were tolerated unless the visitor's question was particularly irritating. Then Gordon simply answered politely and moved to the other end of the bar and left the visitor unaware he had been put off.

Women were not allowed to swear; women who did were asked to leave.

Anyone could play the piano providing they could play well enough and Gordon felt like listening to it. If Gordon didn't or if you played badly you were asked to stop.

Around seven in the evening was Gordon's dinner time. Locals were aware of this and checked their watches around quarter of seven and got ready to leave. At seven P.M. Gordon closed the bar and went upstairs to his apartment, had dinner, watched the world news and napped. Sometimes if it wasn't busy he kept the saloon open and quietly ate dinner at the bar. Either way, you got the message you were to leave Gordon alone at dinner time.

If Gordon closed the saloon at seven, he opened back up promptly at nine. The locals piled in and the piano players, who earned their livings playing in the casinos up the street, all came in and played for nothing. Sometimes two of them sat on the piano bench and played together and others gathered around and sang songs. It was all clean and honest fun and that made it more special for it was happening in a bar.

Another rule was that Gordon's wooden stool was to stay in the doorway to keep out the tourists who would only interrupt the proceedings. Usually, Major, Gordon's big German shepherd was sprawled asleep on the boardwalk in front of the doorway. It seemed that only daring persons with character or guts ignored the stool and stepped around it and went inside the Brewery. That was the way Gordon wanted it. Tourists stopped and cautiously peeked inside the saloon but only the most daring stepped over Major and slipped past the wooden sentry.

In the thirty-five years that Gordon Lane ran the Union Brewery Saloon it was perhaps as vital to the community as the sheriff or the fire department. Like a good Western saloon in the last century, it was a local club house and served as a meeting place for various town functions. People of all ages gathered there; the young and old talked and laughed with one another and understood one another and liked each other. This was something that made the Brewery unique. That and the fact that people of all classes found something comfortable about Gordon and found something in him they understood and felt close to. Gordon had this wonderful ability to make you feel as if he had invited you to his private party and you were a part of a special fraternity; you felt a sense of family and belonging in Gordon's place and you were always welcome. For every two or three drinks a customer bought, Gordon bought one. Sometimes as the evening grew late, money became less and less of an issue, though Gordon never forgot he was a saloon keeper. Gordon would simply come over and say, "Let me freshen that up," and pour a shot or two into your half-empty glass. Often during an evening he raised his glass to his customers, "Happy days," he said. The people lifted their glasses and gave back, "Happy days, Gordon." Other times, Gordon self-mockingly said to the crew, "One of the distinct pleasures of being in the whisky business is having a good drink with such fine people as you are an *example of.*" They had heard it hundreds of times but it was a tradition that always brought laughter.

The mixture of Gordon's customers was fascinating: lawyers, truck drivers, writers, photographers, artists, tourists, cooks, bartenders, local business people, politicians, judges, musicians of all ages who played all types of music, carpenters, brick layers, house painters, all interesting, most of them funny, all characters in their own right. Yet all these varied people were able to talk with one another and get along with one another. I never heard of or saw a fight in the Union Brewery while Gordon ran it. Violence was unthinkable and entirely out of character.

Some of Gordon's customers were from out of state and they returned each year to visit and bask in the genial camaraderie of this special place. They spoke of Gordon with respect and humor and told stories of special moments they had had in his saloon. Gordon and the Union Brewery were woven into their memories and into their lives. Gordon didn't realize how greatly people appreciated his humor, his good will and honesty. He was very modest.

When Gordon got tipsy—which was the usual case, for he drank behind the bar right along with his customers, he sometimes reached for a little busted-up plastic guitar with broken strings and strummed it as he sang to his customers. He had a voice that reminded you of Rudy Valee. If Gordon had a theme song, it was probably this one and he sang it with a smile in his clear blue eyes:

> *Fairy tales can come true,*
> *It can happen to you,*
> *If your young at heart.*

I believe Gordon believed that. For he still seemed uncommonly youthful although he was in his sixties. His body may have grown slightly stiff at times, and the creases in his tanned face slightly deeper, but the youth was always there in his eyes and in his talk and humor.

There was always someone playing Gordon's piano. The music and good times flowed. Many evenings a number of very good musicians showed up and played along with the piano players. They all played for the fun of it. Gordon supplied them with a steady stream of drinks.

Gordon had a tremendous capacity for alcohol and he drank any mixture of it all night long. He could drink whisky, followed by beer, by a rum and coke, followed by wine, followed by a gin and tonic followed by vodka and orange juice. He called this method of imbibing, "drinking scientifically."

"You wouldn't eat the same thing for breakfast everyday, would you," Gordon asked, "Then it makes no sense to drink the same thing day after day." What would have made most humans sick as a dog, didn't trouble Gordon the least. And the booze seemed to have had no lasting effect on his personality or health. Forty years later, Gordon was as slender and healthy as a race horse, and his good looks were still attractive to young women. Getting lots of exercise climbing up and down Virginia City's telephone poles fixing the cable television system was partly responsible. In the early years, it was not uncommon for Gordon to keep the Brewery open to four or five in the morning. Then he closed up, and went to work repairing the three channel cable television system.

Gordon Lane had a remarkable ability to accept a wide range of extraordinary characters and personalities. Behind the bar he was fair with nearly everyone, from common thief to judge. He took a person as he was. Trying to change life and people was a waste of time. It was this unusual acceptance of others that made him marvelously likable, and drew people into his saloon. Gordon's place became a common ground for all types who ordinarily wouldn't mix. And this was very good.

There was always an excuse for a party in Virginia City, someone's anniversary or birthday, a reunion, Halloween, Christmas, St. Patrick's Day, someone's death or retirement, or maybe it was Monday or Thursday evening, any excuse, when word lit up and down C Street that something was going on at the Union Brewery tonight. The eyes widened; a smile split the face; the heart kicked up. Someone usually prepared a batch of food and laid it out on the poker table in the back of the saloon and the people came in and ate and drank and the party began. Several musicians showed up. Gordon's piano fired up and the music started and continued and people danced or tapped their toes on the floor or their hands on the old bar, and people were happy and kind to each other and the troubled world outside was shut away where you hoped it would stay forever. The Brewery was a wonder; it was magical and human and honest and warm; it was a home to many who had no true home. I loved the place.

CHAPTER THIRTEEN

The Human Beings and the Bad Crew

The Human Beings adopted us and began teaching us the ways of the wild West. I was trainable and perfectly ripe for a new life amongst the nuts in Virginia City. I felt helplessly at home in this lopsided town of misfits who didn't fit anywhere, but here, in a once great mining town in the wilds of Nevada.

After writing alone most of the day, climbing up the wooden stairs from our office to the daylight and happy hearth of the Union Brewery Saloon, was like letting me out of prison after a million years. I took my place on the old oak stool at the far end of the bar near the wood burning stove. Years before it had been Highway Harry's place but Harry didn't come in anymore since his tractor rolled off steep Geiger Grade and took Harry with it and injured him badly.

Into the Brewery came people whose lives were very different from ours. Most were people who worked in town: carpenters, brick layers, lawyers, bartenders, waitresses, cooks, local politicians and shop clerks. Most couldn't have cared less about writing or literature. This was good. We needed a place to get away from work. People were themselves and left their public facades outside the door. The Brewery was our common ground and here we had common interests: a drink after work, the latest jokes, town news, laughter and just a little peace of mind in a world that was mad, madder than us. A spirited conversation was as greatly enjoyed as if it were a prime rib dinner. People treated each other fairly for the most part, and when they sinned, it was usually against themselves and not others.

The Human Beings were a treasure chest of unusual characters. Many had nicknames bestowed upon them by those who loved and accepted them for all their quirks. Mexican Richard differed from Big Richard who was an Anglo. No Ears Harry really didn't have ears. Said a dog chewed them off. You couldn't keep Talking Helen quiet but she was a spirited lady of seventy and a wonderful human being. Little Bit was Laurie who was more than little. Gordon Lane was G-1; Gordon

Churchward was G-2 and Gordon Oliver, was G-3. PSA Jim worked for PSA Airlines at the Reno airport. Chief was Harold Frankhauser who had bartended in Virginia City for about thirty years. Chief had a terrific dry sense of humor, and if he liked you he complimented you by greeting you with, "You asshole," or "Go to hell." Don't know how Frank got the name Chief.

Wally White Shoes, really wore white shoes. But some called Wally, Mr. Christmas, because each year Wally decorated many of the local businesses and Victorian homes with his own Christmas lights and did it for free on his own time. Did such a great job that the Reno television news did a story about him.

Feets was the manager of a local casino who walked in quick small steps. Alex the Russian was a young man in his twenties of Russian blood who became too happy when he drank vodka. Doc was the local veterinarian. Balderdash always said "balderdash" when he disapproved of something. Bill *Wrong* was Bill Wright the district attorney.

Forest Catlett spent his evenings in the Union Brewery Saloon seducing Gordon Lane's old piano into heavenly music. He was a little man in his sixties with dark, oily hair combed back with a thin Clark Gable mustache. His costume was consistent and practical: green work pants, a faded shirt, a warm overcoat and he always carried a paper bag full of his life's treasures: cassette tapes, sheet music and assorted artifacts from his past. And powdered garlic. Forest always poured the garlic into his beer. Thought it kept him healthy. Forest carefully and tenderly laid his bag of treasures on Gordon's bar as if that paper bag were a part of him. Every thing in that bag had a story behind it.

Forest had been a professional musician since the nineteen-forties and played in the big bands in those wonderful nightclubs that have been dead for decades. Their deaths left Forest afloat in a musical world that many fondly remembered but now was only populated by past good times and memories. Now Forest lived by the skin of his teeth. He showed up in Virginia City from the Bay area during the warm months and played piano for tips. His home was his car. That is, his home was a succession of cars. If anyone was ever a testimony to the existence of invisible beings who watch over drunks and children, Forest was it. Forest's guardian angel was on duty whether Forest was awake or unconscious. A car had never been built that Forest Catlett could not kill. He went through used cars like Kleenex. The reason they didn't last long was because Forest's guardian angel kept breaking them. He broke them because he didn't want Forest driving drunk, which Forest always did.

Forest had a list of drunk driving tickets as long as your arm and a score of warrants for his arrest for failure to appear on them. Every day of Forest's life outside of a jail was a miracle. I think Forest Catlett had more miracles to his credit than Christendom has acquired in the last two thousand years. Forest's guardian angel killed Forest's cars by breaking water pumps and fuel pumps and transmissions and flattening tires and making them run out of gas. Every time you met Forest he had a new used car and a story to tell about the death of the last one. Forest would buy a car for a hundred dollars and wonder why it smoked like an Eastern factory or why the transmission slipped or the clutch didn't work. One time he bought a car in Carson City, one of his usual hundred dollar specials. He headed out of Carson on Highway 50 toward Virginia City. About the time he reached the Virginia City turnoff, a total of six miles, the rear transmission ground to a halt. Forest hoofed it to Virginia City and told us about his latest automobile tragedy. Forest Catlett was one of the most endearing men and he could produce wondrous music out of the most crippled piano but he was his own worst enemy.

Crazy Bob really was crazy. Crazy Bob leafed through the trash barrels along C Street looking for food. If Crazy Bob didn't like the menu, he strolled down Six Mile Canyon to the dump for the delicacies it held. The dump was Bob's super market. Americans are such wasteful creatures. But this was good for Bob. He always found enough food at the dump, more than enough. What he couldn't eat at the dump he stuffed into a sack and hauled up to his shack in the hills.

Crazy Bob was tall and strong as a bear. His mouth was full of bad teeth, his hair unkempt and dirty, his whiskered face gray with grime, his pants black and his coat greasy and dirty. Bob's home was a shack on a mountain top outside town on public land. Crazy Bob was an enigma to a small town like Virginia City and no one knew quite what to do with him. He wasn't the sort of crazy where he harmed himself or others so you couldn't lock him up. You couldn't give him a room in town because Bob had a habit of burning them down by accident or negligence. Finally someone suggested they build a shack for Bob outside of town on federal land. This was done by a group of caring souls. The shack was without windows or a front door to keep out the vicious winter. That was Bob's arrangement. The boys had put in windows and a door but Bob thought he would improve their architecture and smashed the windows and tore off the door. It looked better to Bob that way. I don't know how Bob survived winters in that shed. At 6200 feet, even summer nights can be cold. Bob probably got so juiced-up with antibodies from his treks to the dump that it would have taken an epidemic to kill him. A small wood burning stove sat in the corner of Bob's shed and probably helped keep Bob warm. I'm surprised the boys let Bob have the stove. Bob had burned down a couple former sheds.

At one time Bob was as intelligent and sane as the rest of us. Some knew Bob before he went crazy. They said Bob was very intelligent. He had gone to college and served in Vietnam. They said the war and bad drugs made Bob crazy. And yet sometimes Bob leveled out and was as normal as the President. We said prayers for Crazy Bob; God could do for Bob what no one else could. But Bob being crazy, he was probably luckier than the rest of us.

And there was Planet Janet, a hippie from the 1960's who refused to let go of that decade and lived as if it had never ended. Drunk or her brain fried on something she had grown in her back yard, she floated down C Street making friends of anyone who would listen to her endless monologues about the universe and everything and everyone in it.

Tin Cup got his name sensibly. He carried his own tin cup into the bars, handed the cup to the bartender who poured his drink and handed it back to him. Tin Cup was the only patron in any bar that ever drank out of a tin cup.

Roller Skatin' Murray was one of the many Virginia City pianists. Roller Skatin' Murray participated in nearly every Virginia City parade, and there were many. Murray twisted and swirled down C Street on his roller skates as happy as a leprechaun. He was one of the characters who gathered at Gordon Lane's bar and entertained the crew at the piano.

George the Meatman came over from California several times a month. If you needed a ham or a roast or a prime rib or a pig, George could get it for you cheaper than you could get it in town. George took your order and two weeks later drove into town in his beat up car and delivered your meat and collected his money. Then he went down to Gordon Lane's bar and talked to Gordon for a couple days and got drunk and happy. George was in his sixties and had been coming into Gordon's for about thirty years. He was stout, fat bellied, grey haired, a couple days stubble and wore ancient eyeglasses. A white T-shirt stretched tightly over his tummy. George was the talkingest man you'd ever meet. He could solo for hours as long as you listened and sometimes that didn't matter. George was retired from the railroad. His trips to Virginia City and Gordon Lane's bar were less for business and more for the pleasure of seeing and talking to Gordon. George loved Gordon and considered his bar a happy oasis in a world that had grown colder with the years.

There were many others who floated in and out of Virginia City as if it were a circus. I have never found more vulnerable and endearing human beings in one place, whose troubles they each turned into self-deprecating laughter and whose individual tragedies could break the heart of the most cynical. These dear souls always had a kind word for you or a joke. If a day was gloomy a word from them would let in the light and make you feel less lonesome. You sent up many a prayer on their behalf. And I would not be surprised if they sent up many a prayer for you.

The nicknaming of these characters was a sign of familiarity bestowed on the one nicknamed and denoted that the person nicknamed had character, or at least was well known in the community for something be it ever so small or strange. Some of these characters made up our new family. But my uncles and advisers were a group of senior men, most double my age known as The Bad Crew.

The Bad Crew was comprised of some of the best men in Virginia City, all old-timers. Gordon Lane was the Pack Leader and his bar was the meeting hall. Doug Kick, an Englishman who recited bawdy limericks he had acquired in the English pubs and imported to America, was Entertainment Director. "Jack" John Curran, Philosopher in Residence, was a former drinking partner of Doug's and Gordon's who had reformed himself and resembled Mark Twain when he was old and white haired. Jack made profound statements on situations, whose comments I understand, were more profound in his drinking days. Jack was a retired surveyor and a terrific banjo player. Tiny Carlson, a man whose bulk could literally darken a doorway, and who continually advised local businessmen how to run their businesses, was Business Adviser. Balderdash, the manager of a saloon and casino, was Sergeant at Arms. He told jokes that were so bad, so unbelievably bad—and took such perverse pleasure in telling them, that you had to laugh. Louie Beaupre, Court Jester, was a black bearded Canadian woodsman who wore a buffalo cape in winter with a Canadian Frenchman's cap on his head. Louie could tell more jokes in an hour than most of us will tell in a lifetime. He drove a gray primered 1963 Chevy pick-up that roared happily without its muffler. A real alligator head was strapped across the top of the cab and the monster's opened white-toothed jaws clutched a female mannequin's leg. Louie's snow shoes were attached to the sides of the truck.

The Bad Crew was given its name by Doug Kick, who upon seeing the above gathered at Gordon Lane's bar always said, "It's a bad crew." But Doug meant it was a very good crew.

They were—and are still, entertaining sociable men. Most of them went through the Great Depression and World War II and that seemed to make all the difference. They liked small towns and they did not like cities because people were unfriendly and rushed around and didn't take time for others.

The Bad Crew took me in and shared values: You treated others as you would like to be treated. You kept your word. You told the truth. You put others first and took time to talk to people. There was nothing wrong with a drink as long as you didn't allow it to ruin your life. Real men could drink whiskey and not make a fool of themselves. But then, sometimes that was all right too. Sharing the latest joke was as important as earning a living. Money was something you needed to buy things. But money was nothing you hurt others to get or wasted a life chasing after. People are what matter.

The Bad Crew were ordinary working men with an extraordinary appreciation for life and people and they were extraordinarily tolerant. I probably learned more about tolerance from these guys than I did attending the last ten churches.

The Bad Crew spontaneously appeared on late afternoons at Gordon Lane's bar. And during this time the Crew would put on a show that could wake up the dead moldy Saints and make the Angels in Heaven roar with laughter. I lacked the experience and wit of these men so I was their audience. Each took turns relating the latest joke or comic story about one of the town's characters or a past incident that had taken place at the Union Brewery. These gentlemen provided the laughter the soul was sorry to have missed thus far in life; an hour with these guys could permanently erase the day's worst disasters.

The humor, for the most part, was clean and often corny. This is a typical joke Gordon Lane told:

There were two friends, now old men, who had played baseball in their youth and loved baseball. Each promised the other, that if one died, he would come back to tell the other whether or not there was baseball in Heaven.

One of the two died, and went to Heaven. One day he appeared to his friend.

"Well," *the living friend asked,* "Is there baseball in Heaven?"

"Well, I've got good news and bad news," his friend answered.
"What's the good news?"
"Yes, there's baseball in Heaven."
"And the bad news?"
"You're pitching Saturday."

And another:

A duck hunter shot a duck that landed on a nearby farm. The farmer came out and picked up the duck and told the hunter, "This is my duck because it fell on my property."
"No way," the hunter said. " I shot that duck and I'll keep it"
"The heck it is. The duck landed on my property and it's mine."
"That's not fair," the hunter said.
"Tell you what," the farmer said, "we'll settle this the way we farmers settle quarrels. Here's how we do it. First, I kick you as hard as I can in the groin. Then you do the same to me. We do this until one of us is left standing. The winner gets the duck. How's that?"
"Sounds fair," the hunter said.
The farmer began the competition and kicked the hunter fiercely in the groin. The hunter let out a howl, dropped to the ground with his hands between his legs. He screamed and groaned and moaned and kept on for about fifteen minutes. Finally, the pain subsided somewhat and the hunter weakly crawled to his feet ready to take his turn on the farmer. But just as the hunter brought his foot back and was ready to let go the farmer stopped him.
"Never mind," the farmer said. "Keep the duck."

One of the games these men played to amuse themselves was a dice game called "horses." In the early years it was called "razzle dazzle." I don't know how it got the name "horses" because it doesn't have anything to do with horses. Horses was played at the bar with any number of players but about six players seemed to make a good game. The loser bought the players a round.

The game was played with five dice and a rubber cup. The dice were put into the cup by a player, shook up and rattled to the player's satisfaction, and then the dice were slammed down on the bar where they rolled out of the cup. In the first rounds, each player shook the dice and tossed them on the bar. The player who had the best throw, meaning the greatest number of high dice, say, three "fives" or four "sixes," was considered "out" of the running. The players each took turns until only two players were left.

Then the two players played each other. But now the rules were different. Each of the finalists was given three rolls of the dice. The goal was to try to get the highest number of high dice. Say you made the first roll and got two "sixes." You laid the two "sixes" aside, put the remaining three dice in the cup and rolled again. If in the next roll you got a "six" you laid that aside with the first two "sixes" you got in the first throw. If in the third and final roll you got two more "sixes" then you had five "sixes" which was impossible to beat. "Ones" were aces, which meant if you needed an extra "five" or "six," you could designate the ace as such. Each of the two players got three tries of three rolls each. The player who got the best two out of three rolls was the winner. In some bars, players played for money. But at Gordon Lane's, horses was always played for drinks.

CHAPTER FOURTEEN

Talking Helen and the Pig

"Talking" Helen was one of Gordon Lane's local customers. She is a stout woman of seventy-three whom God made to teach humility and patience to everyone who knows her. Helen wears thick lensed eyeglasses that look like goggles. She suffers from glaucoma. She is known as Talking Helen because her monologues usually contain a significant amount of insults to the one being talked to. Helen has a high pitched, agitated voice like a banshee. She uses a collection of words that make her speech a chain saw that can cut out the heart of her victim. Helen is tough, opinionated, honest and you know exactly what she thinks of you the moment she opens her mouth. She can carve up the meanest and toughest man with her tongue and her victim will keep his mouth shut while Helen destroys him.

Talking Helen is absolutely notorious in Virginia City. She knows everyone and everyone knows her. I think everyone in the state of Nevada knows Helen. You can take Helen a hundred miles out into the middle of the Nevada desert, find a bar, and half the people would know Helen and the other half would have heard of her.

Unlike some retirees, Helen likes to keep busy and working. So she works part-time at a local business. She is highly sociable. All of Helen's family have died and she has adopted half the town and they have adopted her. To us younger folks, she is a feisty older woman we take to heart and look out after. Helen is family.

Besides letting you know what Helen doesn't like about you, the second most important thing in Helen's life is cooking. She is an excellent cook and she will tell you so. And if you forget it she will remind you. Before retiring she cooked in the big Vegas casinos. She is a member of the Culinary Union, and she will remind you of that too, that she is in the Union. Helen considers her membership in the Union a badge of her professional cooking skill which she takes dead seriously. Talking Helen is considered by many the best cook in the community. Helen's reputation gives her great pride.

Behind Helen's tough talk is a kind hearted elderly woman who wants to be needed and at heart cares deeply about others. She gives a party every year on her birthday, usually at the Union Brewery Saloon. She prepares all the food herself with the delicacy and precision of a surgeon. She spends a small fortune on these parties. On the very day someone should be thinking of Helen, she gives of herself, of her food and money to others.

Each of Helen's parties is to be an exhibition of Helen's culinary skill. Therefore she demands perfection of herself and everyone who works with her. And if you don't do things the way Helen orders, she'll climb all over you with that wailing voice that could wake up a mummy and make him sorry he's alive again. During the preparation for these parties, Helen becomes even more agitated than she usually is. She reminds you of a keg of nitroglycerin that is rattling around, ready to blow herself and everyone around her to hell.

On her seventy-second birthday, I made the mistake of offering to help Helen with her party. About a week before the party, Helen called and laid out the preparation details like a general readying for battle. Helen pointedly informed me that I was the private in her army. And if I ever forgot my rank, she set me straight. In Helen's army I had no opinions but hers, and I didn't know anything about anything, but particularly I didn't know anything about preparing food.

For her seventy-second birthday, Helen had decided to roast a pig outdoors over a grill of coals. I was to escort her to the place where the pig had formerly lived and where he had met his Maker by a butcher's knife outside Fallon, Nevada, about an hour and a half drive from Virginia City. The pig was hanging in a walk-in cooler. I was to drive Helen to the pig and we were to invite the pig to her party. Then we were to go to Fallon where Helen would shop for the rest of the party stuff. I was ordered to be at her door at nine AM sharp.

My wife and I met Helen on time and drove her to Fallon in the pick-up. During the course of the trip, Helen informed me I was a miserable creature and if I had better ideas about myself, I had better change them. Which I did. By the end of the day I was convinced I was a pretty sorry mess.

We picked up Helen's pig and escorted him—it was a her, to the basement of the Union Brewery Saloon where the pig spent the night in a walk-in cooler. The next morning I promptly picked the pig up at nine-thirty and hauled it to her next to final resting place, a barbecue under a wooden gazebo in the Virginia City park. There we placed coals in four corners of the barbecue and lit them and when the coals went grey, we placed the pig on the grate, spread-eagled, wrapped in aluminum foil.

We were to roast the pig for ten hours. Helen told us the coals would last *the whole ten hours* and we were not to disturb the coals or the pig unless we wanted to be shot for insubordination.

Everything was going as planned by the commander until she noticed that the coals, apparently cheap and worthless coals, had burned up in about an hour. Which meant we had to jack up the the barbecue grate, plant more coals and fire them up again. We did this three times until One-Hand Walt went up to the gas station and bought some good charcoal. Walt planted the new charcoal in the barbecue and fired it up and lowered the pig down to bake. The new charcoal seemed to do the trick.

It seemed pointless for us all to stay and watch over the pig, so Helen went home to prepare some food for her party which was to take place at the Union Brewery Saloon at six PM sharp. My wife arrived to watch over the pig and I took a lunch break and went up to Tiny Carlson's for a hot dog and dropped in for a drink at Gordon Lane's. I wasn't at Gordon's long when the fire whistle blew and the telephone rang with my wife on the other end. She was frantic and screaming about the pig being on fire, and flames were shooting up to the top of the gazebo, and the fire department had been called and would I get my butt down there before the fireman put the pig out with that chemical stuff they use on grease fires!

I flew down to the burning pig to find the remnants, a miserable heap of tarred flesh smoking on the barbecue. It looked like a sacrificial rite out of the Old Testament. The fireman wagged his head back and forth. "Damn wind kicked up. Shouldn't be barbecuing in this wind," he said disapprovingly as if I should have known better. I was going to tell him it was Helen's fault but instead just looked at her poor blackened pig and thought about my impending demise. "Helen's going to cut my throat, " I said to my wife, "and then she's going to cut her own."

The fireman had raised the barbecue grate and put the fire out. He hadn't contaminated the pig with chemicals. Though the pig was as black and shiny as licorice, the inner meat wasn't spoiled at all, thank God. Helen was at the scene of the crime shaking in horror, this dear old woman with bad eyesight, weeping over what she considered the death of her party and her reputation as the best cook in Virginia City. When the fireman showed up, Helen had screamed at him with a vengeance and made it clear to the innocent that he was to leave her #&*#@*+ pig alone and if he didn't she would kick his #&%, which she would have. The young fireman didn't know Helen—which seemed impossible and radioed a deputy, Bruce Larson, who knew Helen and her reputation. Bruce eventually calmed Helen down to a minor earthquake.

Helen made it clear that the pig had burned up because I wasn't there. "If there had been a man there, " she said, "he would have known how to put out the *damn pig!*" I was about to slit my throat when my wife hugged me and said I would live, even through this. We covered the pig with aluminum foil and got it roasting again.

We sat with Helen through the afternoon watching over her pig and altogether it felt as if we were at a funeral and Helen was moaning and weeping as if she had lost her only friend.

About an hour before we were to uncover the pig and haul it up to the Union Brewery, I went up to Gordon Lane's bar and braced myself for the ordeal. There I related the tale of the flaming pig to Gordon, PSA Jim and Rick Hoover who thought my tragedy was the funniest thing since The Three Stooges. To make matters worse, Rick Hoover ran up to the Delta Saloon where they had this "Your Name In Headlines" print shop where Rick had a special edition printed up. The headline on the newspaper read:

Swine Flambeau at the Union Brewery Tonight.

When Rick showed me the paper, my heart weakened. "Oh, please, for God's sake, don't show that to Helen."

Rick laughed, "All right. Not tonight, anyway."

I needed a hand to get the pig off the grate, so I picked up John, a bartender at the Union Brewery. I told John about Helen's condition and what to expect when we got to the pig's funeral.

We got to the barbecue and lifted the aluminum foil off the pig and when Helen saw that poor blackened creature again, she wailed with a force we thought would bring on the Second Coming. Nevertheless, John and I got the pig off the barbecue, piece by piece, and put the pig on a plywood plank and covered the carcass with aluminum foil. We put the pig in the back of the pick-up and hauled it to the Union Brewery.

There the pig was laid out for her wake alongside other foods Helen had prepared. Helen was chief mourner and sat beside the pig chewing her fingernails as she waited for her guests to view the disaster. We medicated Helen with a few glasses of champagne and assured her the party would go all right, which it did. Only the outer skin of the pig was burned. The inner meat was as tender as a baby's butt. Everybody marveled at what Helen called her "Blackened Pig, " a Louisiana specialty.

Of course, the story of the pig that caught on fire made the rounds in Virginia City. As Helen related it, her pig had burned up because of my neglect. Whenever a fire breaks out in Virginia City, a screaming whistle calls volunteer fireman to the firehouse. To this day, whenever that whistle blows the comment is, "Helen must be roasting another pig."

PART THREE

And the trouble begins

CHAPTER FIFTEEN

Becoming A Writer

The craft or art of writing is the clumsy attempt to find symbols for the wordlessness. In utter loneliness a writer tries to explain the inexplicable. And sometimes if he is very fortunate and if the time is right, a very little of what he is trying to do trickles through—not ever much. And if a writer is wise enough to know it can't be done, then he is not a writer at all. A good writer always works at the impossible. There is another kind who pulls in his horizons, drops his mind as one lowers rifle sights. And giving up the impossible he gives up writing.
John Steinbeck, from *Journal of a Novel: The* East of Eden *Letters*

Writing is hard work.. It's the hardest work in the world. If it was easy, everybody would be doing it...The only reason they pay good money is there aren't many people who can do it.
Ernest Hemingway from *With Hemingway*

After eleven years of self-doubt and frustration, I had become a successful writer. My writing kept a roof over our heads, paid for food and clothes and all the stuff families need with some left over. We were finally living like a normal American family. It had been excruciating getting there. We no longer lived on the ten dollars a day as we did during the early years of our marriage. That ten dollars had paid for food and gas for the car. Every month the mortgage company pounded our door asking for their money and I had to explain to utility companies why we couldn't pay our bills and beg nagging clerks to leave our services on. I cringe when I think of those times. When other couples were buying a new car or a load of furniture, my wife and I were living lean and digging deep for the future. It was severe discipline but it paid off.

I will here kill the romantic notion that being a struggling writer or artist is a wonderful way to live. Contrary to the popular idea that all writers lead romantic lives, my impression is that writers live solitarily and largely bear the burden of their work by themselves. Good writing *is* hard work. It can be one of the most frustrating and difficult processes any human being can put themselves through. You wrestle with a manuscript for months, sometimes years. When the writing goes well you feel terrific. And on the bad days you feel useless and empty. You live with a manuscript like you live with a woman. You love it, you fight it, you sleep with it, you worry over it, you shower with it, you argue with it, you cry and moan over it, and it keeps you awake. And until the manuscript is completed to your satisfaction, which is nearly impossible, you are never free of it.

The difficulty of the work is one reason writers drink. Alcoholism is the occupational disease of the writer. Why? I don't know all the reasons. I think it has to do with the basic personality of writers, loner types, independent, intelligent, self-willed. Most are sensitive and not easily adapted to the world. The struggle and loneliness of the work is nerve racking. When the writer is finished working he wants a lift. Alcohol gives the brain the lift it wants and warms the writer's lonesome insides and convinces him he is a part of the world and everybody in it. Of course, he isn't. How can he be when he is stuck in a room by himself most of the day? The truth is, most people are not writers, and even more exceptional, most people do not earn their livings writing. And that makes writing a very lonesome and hard business. And I suppose that's why alcohol becomes the medication for many writers.

It is more difficult if you are married and have children and the writing isn't earning money yet. A poor writer is no different than a poor ditch digger. All poor people must learn the same things: how to be content with little and how to make your money stretch. You learn poverty is hard and mean and it can kill your hope or make you crazy or angry enough to get off your butt and do something about it. You learn a pint of whisky is the poor man's vacation. You learn what really matters is the people you love and your family. Money can get tight and times can be hard, but if you have each other, you have the best. When we didn't have money we learned to live with less. We eventually earned a kind of freedom from the addiction to material desires many Americans never know, or ever want to know. Now we think we were lucky: we were poor before we had money and independence.

On the bad days the writing always seemed stupid and unrealistic. I had never thought money was that important. Marriage and babies cured that. Money was necessary to buy things you needed. But money was nothing to waste a life chasing after. Building something true and good with words was something to spend a life doing. That's what I believed when my head was clear and my faith held up. And so I stuck with the writing because of a weakness and an asset: God installed a jackass stubbornness in my brain. I don't know when to quit, even when common sense says throwing in the towel is perfectly reasonable.

I became a writer for a lot of reasons, some of it having to do with me. And a lot of it having to do with people who were dead but whose genes and natures I had inherited. Some of it had to do with my father's side, generations of craftsman who worked well with wood and steel. And some of it had to do with my mother's Irish family. They were human, funny, erratic, passionate.

When I was a boy, my father had a work shop in the basement. It was in a corner. Two walls were concrete and the other two walls were two-by-fours with chicken wire stretched from floor to ceiling and a padlocked door to keep me out. I admired my father's work shop. It was as clean and organized as an operating room. The tools hung neatly in rows on nails. My father had a drawer or a box for everything. He had an ingenious way of organizing nuts and bolts. He nailed the lids of screw-on jars to the ceiling beams. Then he put the nuts and bolts and screws into the jars and screwed them into the lids in the ceiling beams. It was so simple, but no one had thought of using jars like that. The jars kept everything separated and you could find anything easily. My father was always inventing things like that. He had a strong need for organization.

Some of my father's need for organization is in me. I need to put things in their place. My father stored nuts and bolts in jars. I store what I learn and feel between the covers of a book. It's sort of crazy when you think about it. But everybody needs a place to store their precious things.

I blame my mother's Irish family for my highly emotional nature that has been a burden all my life. My Irish ancestors fooled around in Ireland, got drunk with leprechauns and played flutes and lutes and made up stories about banshees and pots of gold at the ends of rainbows, sang and danced and talked, talked, talked and lived simply and happily. What terrible, joyous, troubled people!

I know where my tortured brain cells come from because I met the lunatic who gave them to me: "Wild Bill" Dalton, my mother's Irish father. An uncle once told me Wild Bill was related to the outlaw Dalton gang of the American West. I believe it. Wild Bill—trust me, the nickname fit, was meaner than the devil when he was sober or very drunk, and friendly and talkative when he was half or three-quarters cranked up. When he was an old man and half-lit, he used to get the "talkies" and telephoned each of his seven children and was nice and friendly and talked about everything under the sun to the children he had tormented like hell when he was younger and they were younger. Wild Bill didn't mean to be an alcoholic the same way no one means to be an alcoholic. In later years he was sorry for the trouble he caused his children.

Wild Bill's bad luck began being born Irish. He loved Jesus and the Church and he loved his wife and kids when he was sober. And he loved being meaner than hell when he was drunk. My mother's brothers and sisters had the misfortune of being invited to Wild Bill's nightly parties, which meant seeing him pound the walls, pound the kitchen table, pound them and sometimes pound my grandmother. When he drank at night, the kids were so afraid of Wild Bill they avoided going to the bathroom in hopes of escaping Bill's torture sessions. These might include having to bang on the piano so Bill could sing his sentimental Irish songs or listen to him rant and rave about the shortcomings of the human race.

Occasionally Wild Bill shared his wisdom with me when he was toasted. "Do you know why God made whisky, boy," he asked me, and while his eyes floated in their watery sockets he answered himself, *"to keep the Irish from ruling the world, boy!"* Maybe Bill believed it. I think God made whisky to help us bear the pain of living in an often unjust world.

It is a wonder how much pain a child can endure and remain a normal human being. Of Wild Bill's seven kids, my mother, the most sensitive, came out of it the worst. She had nervous breakdowns as a child and breakdowns as an adult. These collapses were not fun to watch. Something sad happens to a boy when he sees his mother become hysterical when asked an ordinary question, or see her suddenly get the compulsion to turn the gas on and stick her head in the oven. It wasn't fun or easy learning to be my mother's caretaker. I blame Wild Bill for my mother's misery and for a lot of mine. The trouble with troubled children, is that they usually grow up and manufacture more troubled children.

The crazy Daltons—they were all a bit off, had a profound good effect on my childhood. They were the funniest and best people. My grandmother Dalton made the most lasting impression on me. Everyone called her "Ma" so I called her Ma. To me, "Ma" was her name, like Nancy or Jane. Ma was stout, grey haired with a cheery pink face and a big, kind Irish heart, a woman who spoke Gaelic on the telephone and a Catholic who committed heresy by watching Billy Graham on television, a Protestant evangelist, who told Ma how much Jesus loved her and all mankind. Her God was a God that listened to the most feeble prayer and sent down angels to protect us from bad men and misfortune. Her God was a friend and a helper, full of compassion and mercy. Her beliefs made Ma kind and simple and loving and trusting. Her Christianity wasn't something she pulled out on Sunday mornings and dressed up and wore to Mass. Her Christianity was living, breathing and real. It wasn't pointing fingers and condemning except in one point: she didn't have much respect for people who declared great love for God and did little or nothing to help anyone, people so full of heaven they were no earthly good. Her God's love was *practical*.

"Whadaya mean *practical*," I asked her.

"Well, like that time after they killed Jesus and he came back alive," she said. "He went looking for Peter and the others. They were down in the Sea of Galilee. They had been out in the boat all night fishing and they hadn't caught anything. Jesus found them the next morning and they were still fishing. He called from the shore and told Peter where to throw his net. And Peter did. And they caught so many fish it nearly broke their net! Ya see, Jesus gave them practical advice. And look what else he did:

"It was breakfast time and Peter and them were hungry from fishing all night. Jesus had made a fire on the shore and had cooked them breakfast and when Peter and them came ashore there was food to eat. Ya see, Jesus' love was practical and sensible. He gave Peter and them good advice. And then he fed them because he knew they were hungry. None of this pie in the sky stuff."

Ma believed in God and her life showed it. She might have gotten mad at Wild Bill and roared at him in a language that was created nearer to hell than heaven, but she was the most loving woman I ever knew. And she loved me. She loved me no matter how rotten I was to her. Peculiar how the troublesome kids can be your favorite. I was my grandmother's favorite grandchild and I knew it. God used Ma to plant in my troubled brain the reality of what real love is.

My grandmother and her grown-up kids gathered several times a month around her big kitchen table, where the mismatched silverware was kept in a big jar in the middle of the table. She slaved over the hot kitchen stove in the summer, boiling potatoes and corned beef and cabbage for her kids and their wives, husbands and children, and laid it all out for us. Everyone sat down and ate and laughed and drank beer and was happy. Ma was the shining heart of that family. Afterward the men went into the living room and watched the fights on television and the women stayed in the kitchen around the table and drank tea as Irish women do, pouring the steaming water into the dainty tea cups over the brown tea bags and adding milk and sugar and then pouring a little of the tea onto the saucers so it would cool faster and the women in the kitchen late at night laughing and giggling about who knows what, sometimes holding their younger children on their laps and I would go in the kitchen and watch them. I didn't know it then, but seeing those people happy and loving each other was going to help me love people and keep my sense of humor and steer me toward a sound mind.

Ma was a cook at the high school because serving others made her happy. So when the doctor told her she had a bad heart and that she would have to stop working it bothered her. But Ma didn't give the Grim Reaper a second thought but kept on working and serving others. And the heart attack killed her just like the doctor said it would.

I remember her death. She was lying unconscious in the hospital bed and it was night and there was a light on her. She was under a clear, plastic oxygen canopy and tubes were stuck in her nose and her face was gray and death was all over her. I loved Ma the way I remembered her. I didn't want to see her gray and sick. I wouldn't go into the room to watch her die. We all went down to the dark, quiet hospital chapel that was lightly lit by the rows of red candles on each side of the altar and the life size, nearly naked figure of Christ hung on the Cross above the altar with His head fallen to His chest. Railroad-sized iron spikes pierced His hands and feet, and the crown of thorns was shoved into his skull and the red blood streamed down His forehead and face and flowed from the wound in His abdomen where they had speared Him and there was the familiar, holy fragrance of burning wax and incense in the chapel. We kneeled down on the hard wooden benches and prayed that my grandmother would get well because if she died the best part of us would die with her. But God had other plans for Ma. He released her into a better world although it broke our hearts and killed a part of us. God not answering our prayers was a hard thing for a boy to understand. But I understand it now.

Ma was the heart of the crazy Dalton family, like mothers are the heart of every family. When she died the heart of that big, wonderful group of human beings died and it was never the same. There were gatherings at the eldest daughter's house, and it was fun, but it wasn't like when Ma was alive. My grandmother's kindness and humor had protected her children from Wild Bill's damage while she was alive. But now it seemed, with her gone, the family could not ward off the infection that had grown in each of them since their childhoods. One brother became an alcoholic; one sister withdrew from the family and the world; my mother became increasingly mentally ill; the brothers developed heart conditions; then the illnesses and the deaths. It was sad as hell; I won't forget it. But I remember them happy once. I remember their humor and their love of life.

Ma taught me being a Christian doesn't mean you are a self-righteous snob. You are not perfect as the rest of mankind is not perfect. You are no better than anyone but you are luckier. You believe that Christ died on the Cross for your sins and the penalty of eternal damnation has been lifted by God's sacrifice, grace and mercy. *Mercy.* What was it that Ma taught me about mercy? Mercy is not giving people what they deserve for screwing up. When we make a mistake we admit it to God, apologize and trust God to forgive us. It's as simple as that. I am certain that Ma, knowing the marital troubles my parents were having, often said prayers for me. I am convinced that it is those prayers that have followed me all my life and helped me to believe that God is my friend and will always be my friend no matter how badly I behave.

When I was eleven, we moved away from the Daltons. It was a terrific loss for me. My father was a lifer in the Air Force and we moved around. We lived in Massachusetts, Louisiana, Montana, Bermuda and California. When Edie and I were married and started having children, it was our turn to reduplicate the families we had come from. Many of them were dead or scattered across the country. Now we wanted to find that group of people we could call family and feel we belonged to. But where were they?

In the heart of every serious writer there is a seed of pain. Children from normal families usually do not become writers. I was an only child and I grew up in a home where I saw the two most important people in my life wreck each other's lives. You do not come out of such a home life whole. You carry a wound in your head and heart nothing but time and understanding and God's power can heal. My parents didn't plan on hurting each other when they were young and wanted to be married. No one does, I suppose. They made a mistake.They suffered. I suffered. But it has taken me most of my life to understand and forgive them.

I learned things as a boy I would have rather not had to learn. You need people and yet you do not want to need them because your need makes you vulnerable. You balance precariously between your need for people and the fear that they will carve out your heart if you give them the chance. You learn to be cautious and think for yourself.

There were times when I felt, and occasionally still feel, that I was sort of like my pal the coyote, who slinks around the outskirts of human habitations, always wary of humans but sometimes needing the left overs from their trash cans, and always careful not to be caught scrounging through them in the night. A part of me has always felt a part of, and a part of me has always felt in left field. That's just the way it is when you grow up in a troubled family. You would like to blame somebody for the pain and put the pain on them rather than carry it in your head and heart the rest of your life. But that's impossible, of course. The pain is no one's fault, really. People don't mean to make mistakes; they just do. And then you are left with the problem of forgiving them. Forgiving is always hard and sometimes impossible. Feeling a part of and feeling this strange, clinical distance from others can be a good combination for a writer.

Pain has the power to make us very bad or very good. It is easy to be bad; we all have great capacity for doing terrible things. A child can believe he is bad because he got a raw deal from adults he trusted. And when he believes he is bad, he behaves badly. A committed writer must have an unwavering sense of justice and injustice. Without it, he is as impotent as a human without a heart. My family life taught me all I needed to know about injustice. A child blames himself for his parents' troubles. Maybe I had been bad because I was made to believe I was bad. But now I wanted to be good and to do good. Writing could be a way to achieve this.

True writing takes honesty and honesty is the writer's burden. First he must be honest with himself and that is nearly impossible. And then he must be honest with others and that means he must tell the truth. And telling the truth is the best way to get into trouble. It should not be so, but it is. There is nothing we can do about that. Truth is the bottom line. And as hard and painful as it is to keep the bottom line straight, someone must do it. Writers are usually the ones who are idealistic, caring and foolish enough to try to do it.

I had worked hard and become successful. I had been given much. I felt responsible to give back some of what had been given to me. I was, after all, my Irish grandmother's grandson. I couldn't stand lamely aside when something terrible was being done to people I cared about.

CHAPTER SIXTEEN

The *Virginia City Voice*

So there in this wacked-out former mining town hanging high on the steep face of a mountain, in a county where prostitution and gambling were as ordinary as eating pie and the crookedest creeps were elected to the highest offices, where houses and saloons were haunted by spooks from a world that was dead and buried, amongst a crowd of endearing and insane characters no novelist could invent, I deposited myself and began working through my mid-life crisis. I had dragged my wife and children along for the ride. I couldn't help myself. I thought I belonged there. I was in love. I was half mad. I had fallen for Virginia City as hard as an adolescent boy for the wrong girl. I wanted to do something for somebody else. I wanted out of my isolation as a writer. I wanted—dear God, I didn't know *what* I wanted. I had this half-baked idea that I could write something that would help the community and make a difference. I was as naive and trusting as a turnip. Believing you can change anything in Storey County is sort of a disease newcomers are slayed with. The illness lasts for an indefinite period depending on the individual. The sorry soul who has been a nobody in the big city, who has felt neglected and lonesome and pushed around, now discovers he can win friends and influence people in a small town. And this leads them down the road to ruin.

I went in search of something to do and found it. I volunteered to help the local newspaper establish a better relationship with the townspeople. The paper was run by a group of young homosexual men who had infuriated the community by publishing articles which advocated their sexual preferences and by their blatant, unashamed lifestyles. I was not prejudiced. However, since God has created two sexes and only one has the ability to bear children, I assumed He had a good reason for inventing the woman.

This sorry newspaper was the only newspaper in Storey County. I felt having something was better than having nothing and thought I would try to help make the paper better. So I volunteered to write a series of articles to spotlight local business people. The newspaper needed local advertising to pay its way and it was having trouble selling ads.

Giving attention to local businesses would put the newspaper into better graces with the town and hopefully bring in more advertising dollars.

I wrote several articles for free and all went well until Deputy Heartless gave me a ticket for parking my truck in a loading zone. I had parked to unload our books for stores along C Street. There was no time limit on the loading zone sign. Thinking the ticket was a simple mistake, I went up to the courthouse to speak to Heartless and have the ticket voided. Heartless was himself. He said, "Take it up with the judge."

"You bet I will," for if convicted this trifling ticket would cost me forty dollars! Having once been poor, I had developed a deep regard for my hard earned money and I didn't like being robbed.

I pled innocent, asked for a trial and got it. Deputy Heartless did not appear for the trial. I asked for the charges to be dismissed. This would have been done by any reasonable judge in America. But this judge, who had been imported from Lake Tahoe, would not. In fact, he wanted to go ahead with the trial right then. I told him that would be impossible. I needed to cross-examine the officer. The Constitution says we have the right to confront our accuser.

"You do not," Judge Yahoo from Tahoo said.

"I do," I said.

"You do not," he said.

"I do."

"You do *not*."

"*I do!*"

"I said *you do not!*"

Finally District Attorney Bill Wright—someone had renamed him Bill *Wrong*—Joe Pastrami wasn't reelected yet, stepped in and said, "Let's give Mr. Williams what he wants, a trial with the citing officer present."

To make a long story short, I lost my case and Judge Yahoo and Bill Wrong separated me from my money. Then they went to lunch together and my money paid for it!

For retribution, I wrote a satire and published it in the newspaper. I recall saying the Judge and the District Attorney, "wouldn't know justice if it ran over them," and that Judge Yahoo and Bill Wrong had "received their legal training at Screw U."

Judge Yahoo threatened to have me arrested for contempt and thrown in jail. District Attorney Bill Wrong came blazing into the Union Brewery Saloon and there before the Human Beings shouted, "I'm going to sue your ass for libel, Williams." I took Bill outside and told Bill about the First Amendment.

"I don't give a damn.What you wrote was libel because it was malicious," Bill whined.

"Oh no it wasn't Bill. I was just having fun."

"You said we robbed you."

"Well, you *did* rob me."

"We did not."

"Did too."

"Did not."

"Did too."

"We did not! "

"You did too! "

"I'll see to it that you're fired from that paper," Bill yelled.

"I can't be fired. I've never been hired."

"I'll see to it that you never write another word for that paper!" And Bill did. He stormed up to the newspaper office and scared the editor by threatening to sue if a retraction was not forthcoming. The editor published a retraction and fired me from my voluntary position on the paper. I was going to kill Bill Wrong and the editor. But I was merciful and gave up that idea.

Instead, I threw together a little newspaper, called it the *Virginia City Voice*, and with a tongue molten with a righteous cause, went thundering after Bill Wright, Judge Yahoo and the newspaper. I printed several hundred copies and spread them around town. The Human Beings laughed; I wagged my tail like a puppy whose discovered a new trick. All the while I had second thoughts about what I was getting into.

For all the eventual trouble the *Virginia City Voice* caused me and my family, initially I meant it to be silly and blow off some steam. It was never meant to be a real newspaper as some later took it. The *Voice* was an underground newsletter. It was a wise guy publication that followed a Virginia City journalistic tradition that was in Virginia City long before me. Mark Twain had started it in the *Territorial Enterprise.* From time to time he concocted fantastic, grizzly stories which he led readers to believe were actual events. One in particular, "The Massacre at Dutch Nick's," told the savage tale of a man who went insane because he was duped by crooked stock brokers, murdered his family with an ax, slit his throat with a razor, and spewing blood from his jugular, leaped on his horse and galloped six miles to Carson City where he finally dropped dead! Such hoaxes had gotten Twain into considerable trouble with the public. The *Virginia City Voice* followed Twain's twisted example.

I published the *Voice* whenever I got the urge and handed out several hundred copies at my expense. Finally, a businessman asked if I would publish the paper each week.

"Will you support the paper with advertising dollars," I asked him.

"You bet I will. I'll advertise for a year." But after the first controversial issue he pulled out without a word. A couple of businesses advertised and a handful of subscribers essentially paid for the printing. I did the writing for fun and for the trouble it caused.

The one serious intent was to publicly roast incompetent local politicians and public servants who took themselves very seriously. Storey County was full of them. They infested the courthouse, the School Board, the schools, the District Attorney's office, the sheriff's department, the fire department, the television board. I began an assault on these guys they would not soon forget. They needed lessons in humility; I volunteered to help. The People seemed to agree. The *Voice* became more notorious with each searing issue. I dropped off a pile at the Union Brewery Saloon and Markham's Virginia Market. The papers were grabbed and read and talked over at the bars in C Street. Some laughed; others scorned. In time the *Voice* replaced the effeminate newspaper. For all its faults—and there were many, the *Voice* told things as they were, at least tried, and the Human Beings seemed to appreciate the honesty and exaggerated humor. On the other hand, there were others, primarily my victims and their crews, who would have liked me hanged from the nearest telephone pole.

Under its heading was this: *Editor, chief reporter, heterosexual, janitor: George Williams III.*

To protect myself from libel suits, I followed with this disclaimer:

Note to readers: Some of the stuff printed in this paper is true. Then again, some of this stuff is a pack of lies. You'll know when you read a lie because I'll say, "OK, I lied," or "That's a lie." Otherwise, you can believe what you read unless I change my mind about the above.

If I was going to lampoon others, it only seemed fair that I start with myself. I played the fool. I wrote little pieces which portrayed me as a sort of innocent lunatic writer. Like this one, "Author Arraigned:"

Thursday morning, author and publisher George Williams III was arraigned in the Justice Court for drunken and disorderly conduct. Williams was arrested during the Christmas holidays at the Wagon Wheel Restaurant after a wild night out on the town. Apparently he had been ranting about burning down a certain infamous house on A Street [the offices of the homosexual newspaper]. Our reporter was at the court and gives us the following:

"Mr. Williams, you were arrested for drunken and disorderly conduct. How do you plead," the judge asked.

"Guilty with an explanation your Honor."

"Let's hear it."

"Well your Honor, it was the holidays and I was kinda depressed about everything. You know the homosexuals who run the other paper are suing me and it didn't snow for Christmas. I was depressed."

"So?"

"So I got to celebrating with Doug Kick and Gordon Lane."

"Oh those two are bad, very bad."

"Yes, your Honor they are very, very bad. So Doug and I started out at the Silver Queen Saloon with Gordon, migrated across the street to the Union Brewery and ended up at the Wagon Wheel."

"And that's where you got into trouble?"

"Yes, your Honor. I was toasted by the time we got there."

"The arrest report says you were carrying a red can of gasoline and you were ranting about starting a bonfire on A Street. Something about burning down that 'den of iniquity.' Is that true?"

"Well, I guess. I can't remember."

"Report says they tried talking you out of it but you wouldn't listen. Says here they were afraid you'd get yourself into trouble."

"Well, it was sorta Rick Wegman's fault. He was the one who started talking about burning down that—that, well, infamous house."

"Now George, you're fairly intelligent. You ought to know you can't go around burning down buildings."

"Yes, your Honor. Sometimes I get all excited about something and just can't get it out of my head."

"Like burning down that 'den of iniquity.' "

"Yeah. I was pretty excited about that."

"Now George, I don't want you going around threatening people and burning down their houses."

"Yes, your Honor."

"And I know how much you enjoy supporting the local saloon economy, but perhaps a little restraint is in order."

"Yes, your Honor."

"And maybe you should stay away from Doug Kick and Gordon Lane. They are very bad."

"Yes, your Honor."

"Now promise me when you visit the natives in the saloons, you'll leave that can of gasoline home."

"Yes, your Honor."

"Scout's honor?"

"Scout's honor Judge."

Williams received a small fine and was allowed to go.

District Attorney Bill Wrong was so easily offended by anything negative written about him, I couldn't help myself. For several issues I hounded him. Like this:

Williams was down at the Union Brewery Saloon Tuesday night, drunk as usual, with a loaded .38. Julie Hoover, the bartender, said Williams was acting very strange and had a glazed look in his eyes. With his pistol in his right hand and spinning the chambers with his left, Williams kept asking Julie if she thought he ought to "put Bill Wrong out of his misery." Julie attempted to talk Williams out of it and finally called in deputies Heartless and Bruce Larson. The two took Williams out to the back porch of the Union Brewery where they appeased Williams' thirst for blood by letting Williams shoot jack rabbits and headlights. Williams bagged about thirty rabbits. Apparently after that, and the fact that all his ammunition was gone, Williams' settled down, saying that he would show mercy to District Attorney Bill Wrong and "let him live."

I was joking of course. But the day this was published Bill Wrong asked Sheriff Dick for a guarded escort out of town. Some people have no sense of humor.

CHAPTER SEVENTEEN

Doug Kick and the Space Aliens

I was having lunch at Calamity Jane's Saloon when Doug Kick came in and sat down beside me. I had seen Doug lots of times in the Union Brewery but he was quiet and I didn't force myself on him. He was about sixty-six and had the calmness and peace of God in his blue eyes. He would lay those eyes on you as if you were a newly invented creature and take your whole being into consideration. Doug's eyelids were wrinkled and drooped half-shut over his eyes like lizard eyes. Doug always wore a baseball cap that hid his thick head of white hair. He had a hundred hats to choose from. Doug walked up the wooden boardwalks rocking side to side like Charlie Chaplin, with big heavy black shoes the kind cops wear.

Doug Kick is the most disarmingly friendly man in the world. Doug could talk the Devil in Hell out of a glass of ice water. Youthful beyond his years, he makes young men seem old. Doug Kick is Huckleberry Finn fifty years afterward. He often has this cunning mischievous twinkle in his kind blue eyes.

When I first met Doug he was retired and recently widowed. Married for forty-four years, his wife Katie was sitting in a chair in their bedroom one afternoon. She said to Doug, "I don't feel so well," closed her eyes and was gone. Her heart just stopped working. They did not have children and that made her going away worse.

Katie was tiny, dark haired and pretty. She held herself with a kind of dignity that immediately drew respect, but it was not an austere dignity. She was kind and thoughtful and strong and would sacrifice whatever was necessary to help an injured animal. She was popular and very well liked in Virginia City. She looked after Doug as if he were a puppy.

Katie stopped by Gordon Lane's saloon each afternoon for a beer on the way home from work. Katie was tough and demanded respect. On one occasion an intoxicated patron persisted in using foul language. Katie warned him to watch his tongue. He ignored Katie's advice and the next time he swore, Katie punched him square in the face and knocked the man off his stool to the floor.

One evening Doug arrived home late. Doug always called when he would be late. Katie had worried.

"Why didn't you call me. Don't you know I'd worry?"

"Oh, don't give me that," Doug said, and mentioned something about Katie being stupid. Boom! Katie slammed Doug between the eyes and the next day he had two blackened eyes. Doug never called Katie stupid again.

Doug and Katie were from southern England, around Cornwall where my grandfather was born. They met and married during the War. After the War they immigrated to Ottawa, moved west to Vancouver, British Columbia, and then moved to Las Vegas in the 1950's when Las Vegas was a good, friendly small town. Doug and Katie enjoyed the desert and visited Death Valley often and started visiting Virginia City where they met Gordon Lane the Terrible. Gordon was seductively friendly, as were Pat Hart and Bill Marks, "Chief" Frankhauser and all the saloon keepers in town at the time. Katie, Doug, Gordon and others became friends.

They were in Gordon Lane's bar one evening when Doug had had several too many. Someone at the bar mentioned that they were trying to sell their cottage in Virginia City. Doug immediately offered to buy it. The seller took Doug and Katie down to the cottage. They liked the place and Doug made a cash offer.

The next morning Katie said to Doug, "Do you remember what you did last night?"

Doug massaged his forehead. "No, what."

"You bought Sam Salani's house for cash."

"I did *what!*"

"You bought Sam's house. Now what are we going to do with our house in Vegas?"

"Well, Katie, do you like it here?"

"You know I like it here."

"Then let's sell the house in Vegas and move."

"Good," Katie said.

They went back to Vegas and sold their house, piled their belongings into the pick-up truck and moved to Virginia City.

Doug was a machinist and a mechanic. He rented a stall in the Virginia City garage and went into the auto repair business. He did good work, kept his word and his business prospered. Katie went to work at the Virginia City Visitor's Bureau. The two quickly fit into the town. They had lots of friends and there was always something doing in one of the saloons.

One day Katie learned about a local who was sick and didn't have money for medical care. Both Doug and Katie rode motorcycles for fun. To raise money to help the woman, Katie suggested they start a motorcycle marathon from Tonopah—which is two hundred miles south of Virginia City—and ride back on jeep trails to Virginia City. Each rider would recruit sponsors who would pay so much per mile or whatever they felt like contributing. All the money would go to help needy townspeople.

Doug and Katie knew a lot of dirt bike riders. They invited riders from as far away as Southern California to help with the cause. The first year there was a good turnout. All the boys piled their bikes into pickups and hauled them to Tonopah, had a party, and the next morning rode the two hundred miles to Virginia City across the desert. It took the riders all day to make it back to town. And when they arrived they were given a big dinner and drinks at the Bucket of Blood Saloon. The Virginia City Motorcycle Marathon has been a tradition ever since and the group has raised thousands of dollars and helped many people over the years.

So as Doug and I sat together at Calamity Jane's Saloon—I don't remember how it happened, we just started talking. Doug was immediately very likeable. Very funny, clever and honest. We became friends that day.

Doug lived by himself with six fat cats that lined up each evening beside their bowls and stared at Doug and seemed to say, "Well, it's time for dinner. Get to it."

"Oh, all right," Doug said to the staring cats. "You keep this crap up and I'm going to kill each of you." He would never do it. They were Katie's cats, all strays she had brought home.

It had been about three years since Katie's death. And like all grieving souls, Doug had withdrawn. He would go out and have a beer but he was still very much inside himself. We sort of helped bring Doug out of it. "You never get over losing someone like Katie," Doug said, "But you go on. You have to." Often after writing I'd call Doug up and we'd meet for coffee or lunch and a drink at Gordon Lane's bar.

From time to time Doug would get feeling bad about Katie being gone. He always talked of Katie as if she were still alive. And I believe to

Doug, Katie was still alive. Katie was buried out in the Virginia City cemetery. Doug walked out there each day to make certain the grave was not disturbed and said hello to Katie and told her how he missed her.

Taking a vacation and getting away from Virginia City would have been good for Doug. But getting him out of town was impossible. He just wouldn't do it. I think he didn't want to leave because he didn't want to leave Katie out in the cemetery by herself.

I was in the grocery check-out line in Carson City when I figured out how to get Doug Kick out of town for a vacation. The headline in one of those pulp newspaper rags read: I WAS RAPED BY SPACE ALIENS, or something like that. It gave me an idea.

The next headline in the *Voice* read:

SPACE ALIENS KIDNAP DOUG KICK

and commenced with the story. It was allegedly reported by Louie Beaupre one of the town's glorious characters. Beaupre looks like a Canadian woodsman, with a thick, salt and peppered beard, well worn Levis, black cowboy hat and cowboy boots. He drives around town in a gray primered 1963 Ford pick-up without a muffler. Strapped to the top of the cab is a real dried up alligator head, jaws wide open, gripping a female manequin's leg. Snow shoes are mounted to the sides of the truck. Louie Beaupre is the well of a thousand jokes. Louie was never a reporter for our paper, but I made him one for this story:

Doug Kick, co-founder of the Virginia City Motorcycle Marathon (VCMM) was kidnapped by space aliens Tuesday evening. Louie Beaupre, an eyewitness who never exaggerates, gave us the following account.

Apparently, Doug Kick was at the Silver Queen Saloon drinking with Gordon Lane and Beaupre late Tuesday evening. It was about 10 PM and Gordon was ready to close when two large green creatures, about seven feet tall, entered the Queen and sat down next to Doug Kick. Doug at that moment had his head bent down and was contemplating his half-empty glass of Bushmills Irish Whiskey and didn't notice the creatures at first.

Beaupre says the aliens had bright glowing red eyes and large pointed ears not unlike those of a donkey. Their faces reminded Beaupre of a dog's; both creatures had long snouts.

The aliens were entirely naked except for a red loin cloth which covered what appeared to be monstrous genitalia. Their green skin was smooth and hair-

less and reminded Beaupre of lizard skin. Each alien had seven fingers on each hand. The aliens did not wear shoes. Each of their feet had seven toes. The aliens spoke English fairly well but with a slight lisp, sounding something like Daffy Duck.

Gordon Lane, who has seen everything, didn't even blink when the aliens sat down at the bar, but simply asked the two what they wanted to drink.

"Thu club thodas," one of the aliens replied.

"What," Gordon asked.

"Thu club thodas," the alien repeated.

"Two club sodas," Gordon asked.

"Yeth," the alien answered.

"Hoo, hoo, hoo," Gordon laughed. "Whatya nuts? Club sodas? If you can't drink, stay home." The two aliens looked at one another and appeared to smile. "All right then, double Hothey Cuervosth tequilasth on the rocksth, and leef the bottle."

About this time Doug raised his head and noticed the two space aliens on his left. His eyes opened like saucers when he took in the sight: two green seven foot monsters, with bright red eyes, donkey ears and long dog-like snouts the creatures eyeing Doug as if they had just discovered gold.

"I say, you boys aren't from around here," Doug said.

The space aliens turned their heads toward Doug and appeared to study him with extreme interest.

"No. We're from Frethno."

"Arrgh, Fresno. I say, you wouldn't happen to have an old rind of cheese on you, would you mates," Doug asked.

The creature beside Doug reached into a slit in his skin where his right rear pocket should have been, and pulled out a greenish, moldy hunk of cheddar cheese and handed it to Doug.

"Arrgh matey, thank you," Doug said and bit off a chunk.

Meanwhile, the two creatures began chugging double shots of tequila with astonishing regularity all the while jabbering in a strange language that sounded like pig-Latin. And the more they drank, the more they laughed in a yuk-yuk sort of way.

After about a half hour, the aliens, who had told Gordon and Beaupre that their earth names were Sam and Dave, were drunk. Every so often Sam and Dave turned their heads toward Doug and watched him eat his cheese, then looked at one another and yukked-yukked with extraordinary delight.

Beaupre said the aliens then began buying drinks for him, Gordon and Doug. They appeared to have terrific senses of humor. They yukked-yukked at Beaupre's jokes but were absolutely astonished when Doug began to tell the aliens limericks he had learned in his youth in the English pubs. *Pulling himself up, head held high, arms crossed, elbows on the bar, Doug quoted limericks in a deep, baratone voice:*

> *There was a young lady called Hilda,*
> *Who went in the woods with a builda.*
> *She said that he could,*
> *He said that he would,*
> *And he did and bloody nigh killeda.*

And then another:

> *There was a young lady called Maude,*
> *A sort of society fraud.*
> *In the parlour tis told,*
> *She was distant and cold,*
> *But on the veranda by God...*

Doug quoted limerick after limerick and with each Sam and Dave roared with laughter. In fact, Sam and Dave were so taken with Doug's limericks, they decided to take Doug with them.

"Lithen," Sam said to Doug, "we're flyin' to Vegasth. There'sth a hell of a party at Wayne Newtonsth tomorrow night. Why don't ya come with usth?"

"Vegas, why I used to live there. Arrgh mateys, I'd like to go but I have the cats to feed and..."

"We won't take no for an ansther. Come along. We'll have a great time," Dave said.

The two, green seven foot aliens, somewhat wobbly from the liquor, rose from the bar. Each put an arm around Doug, lifted him off his stool and the three, with Doug in the middle, arms around each other staggered out the Silver Queen Saloon and down C Street. Doug could be faintly heard in the distance, fading away as the three weaved down the C Street boardwalk,

> *There was a young lady named Mable,*
> *Who would %#&* on the floor or a table...*

Beaupre said he saw a bright silver saucer rise from the parking lot on E Street and speed in a haphazard, zig-zag pattern south toward Las Vegas. Doug Kick is believed to be with the space aliens somewhere in Vegas.

For the next several weeks whenever the local characters ran into Doug they asked, "So how was the trip Doug?" or, "How are Sam and Dave?" or, "Where are the space aliens, Doug?"

"Oh, they're down at the house feeding the cats," Doug said.

CHAPTER EIGHTEEN

Doug and Gordon's Game

Then it was winter and very cold in the late afternoons when the sun slid early behind Mt. Davidson and the mountain's shadow fell and darkened the town. It was quiet along C Street and there was the sweet, friendly fragrance of the pine nut fires from the chimneys and stove pipes. The mountains were salt and peppered now with the snow. They looked as if they had been dusted with powdered sugar. Pogonip lay soft and gray on the mountains below Virginia City like cotton candy and hid the usual hundred mile view. In Virginia City above the pogonip it could be bright and warm in the sun. But down in Dayton Valley it was fogged in, damp and gray.

The tourists left town early to escape the cold and the boardwalks were nearly empty and the town was gray and slow. Long icicles hung like spears from the ends of the overhangs above the gutters. If the day was warm, the snow melted on the overhangs and dripped down the icicles into the gutters that ran with water. The careful shop keepers knocked them from the overhangs with shovels or brooms in the mornings but the others let them hang and when the afternoon sun warmed them, some fell and dented cars. One day I expected to hear an ice spear had nailed a tourist but none ever did.

After I finished writing I called Doug Kick or he stopped by the morgue and we went up to Gordon Lane's bar. Work was done and it was time to meet with friends, have a drink and relax before dinner.

Doug Kick is an amiable man sober and a more amiable after several shots of Bushmills Irish Whiskey. Bushmills was known to sometimes get Doug into trouble. Not real trouble. The sort of trouble that is mischievous and makes good stories. Like the time Doug left a saloon one winter night feeling little pain and walked home. Unable to find his house keys, Doug laid down near his door and fell asleep in the snow. It could have killed him, but he told me, "Couldn't get any sleep. The snow got my clothes all soaked." Doug woke up, got in the house and slept it off. After an event like this, Doug periodically repented and kept away from the Bushmills. He drank Coke or maybe a beer instead.

I usually got to Gordon's before Doug. The long golden wood bar was clean and empty. Gordon and I had a drink and talked about the latest town nonsense. There were one or two playing the slots and you heard the pull of the lever and the dropping of coins. When Doug came through the high swinging doors of the Silver Queen Saloon, Gordon smiled and laughed, "Hoo-hoo-hoo." The two men, both in their late sixties, had been friends for about thirty years. They liked each other and made each other laugh. Doug lived by himself with a half dozen cats now that Katie was gone. It was good for Doug to get out of the house each day and visit friends up town.

"Hello Doug. Whataya have," Gordon asked.

"Oh Gordon, I'll just have a Coke."

"Coke?" Gordon winked at me, "Sure that's all you want Doug?"

"Yes Gordon, just a Coke."

"Hoo-hoo-hoo. A Coke huh?"

Then they began their game. They had played it many times, but they began as if it was the first time and neither knew what the other would do. Gordon and I had a drink; Doug sipped his Coke. The three of us talked, joked, laughed. Gordon and Doug told stories about characters who came into the Brewery or had lived in town who were dead now or gone away. Their stories were always good, warm and funny.

After a half hour, Doug's Coke was gone.

"Have a beer Doug," Gordon asked.

"Better not Gordon. Got myself into a bit of trouble the other night. Better just have a Coke."

And Gordon winked at me and laughed, "Hoo-hoo-hoo," and gave Doug a Coke and made a Scotch and soda for me and made himself a drink. We went back to talking and telling stories and laughing, I doing most of the listening. This went on until Doug's Coke was gone.

"Wanna beer Doug," Gordon asked.

"Well, Gordon, I don't know if I oughta."

"Well, maybe just one."

"Well, maybe just one Gordon. But that's all."

Gordon turned to the cooler, reached for the dark neck of a beer, opened it and slid the bottle and an empty glass across the old oak bar to Doug. He poured the golden bubbly beer into the cold glass and the white foam slid over the lip and made a little puddle on the bar. Doug reached for it and sipped his beer.

The three of us went back to talking and the time seemed to pass very fast. Doug's beer was gone, I was empty.

"Another George? It's on me."

"All right Gordon."

"Doug?"

"Well..."

"Little touch, Doug," Gordon asked.

"Now Gordon, don't start that. I better stick with this."

"Just a little touch Doug. It's on me."

"Well, Gordon," Doug rubbed his throat, "I don't know..."

That was all Gordon needed. He turned to the back bar and grabbed the Bushmills, poured a shot and slid the dark whisky to Doug and grabbed another beer from the cooler, opened it and slid it across the bar. Gordon did this so matter of factly it almost went unnoticed to Doug who has gone from two Cokes, to a beer, to a boiler-maker. Doug sipped the Bushmills, had his beer chaser and we went back to talking.

After a little time, the Bushmills loosened Doug's tongue and he told us stories about the War and his family back in England and the misadventures of his youth. We felt warm and the talk was very funny and we were laughing and the sun had gone down and night had fallen across Virginia City.

Then it was after six and time for me to go home for dinner. "Well guys, I've got to get home."

"Now George, you get me down here to Gordon's, and you're gonna leave me *alone* with this terrible man," Doug said.

"Edie's expecting me." I put my hand on Doug's shoulder, "I'll see you tomorrow. We'll have lunch together. See you guys tomorrow night."

"Oh, all right," Doug said.

"See ya later," Gordon said.

I pushed open the tall ornate door of the Silver Queen Saloon, and looked back through the windows and saw the two old friends alone at the bar talking and keeping each other company. The next day Gordon said, "Doug stayed until I closed. Drinking Bushmills. Hoo-hoo-hoo."

And then Doug said to me, "Gordon Lane's the rottenest man I know. Absolutely, undeniably rotten. He's a detriment to the community. Why, I never drank until I met Gordon Lane. You know he's *always* trying to get people drunk. Always. He has no conscience. He *can't stand* to drink alone. He's terrible, just terrible. Someone ought to put him to sleep." And we laughed.

That evening we were back at Gordon's and the game began again.

CHAPTER NINETEEN

Election Year

It was election time in Storey County. Several county offices were up for grabs including County Clerk, District Attorney and Justice of the Peace. County offices were sought after positions. Not only did the office holder win the prestige and power of political office, the elected got health insurance and the possibility of a state pension. Providing a candidate lasted long enough in office. That usually wasn't a problem unless an office holder did something really stupid or crooked to get ousted.

The Justice of the Peace of Storey County was the most coveted political office that election year. The term of office was four years. In that job-poor county, having employment for four years was a luxury. Once elected, the Justice of the Peace was likely to be elected indefinitely. Former Justice of the Peace Ed Colletti held the office twenty years.

The Justice of the Peace presided over misdemeanor complaints. Once elected he had the honor of being called "Judge" by the townspeople. It was a lofty position for an ordinary citizen to wake up the morning after the election to discover he was now judge of his peers. But the real attraction was the extra money that could be earned performing marriages. Virginia City was a favorite place to get married and the usual site was the chapel in the Silver Queen Saloon. When a couple showed up, the call went out over the sheriff's radio that the judge was needed. The judge was rounded up, usually at some saloon on C Street, appeared at the Silver Queen chapel, married the couple in ten minutes and put his earnings in his pocket, minus what went to the county. Unlike most judges, an ordinary layman could be elected Justice of the Peace; you didn't have to be a lawyer or even have considerable knowledge of the law. Once elected, the Justice of the Peace was sent to school where he learned everything needed to run a court properly.

The Justice of the Peace in Virginia City traditionally did business rather casually. Which meant you could normally find him at the nearest saloon. If you were from out of town and wanted to appear on a traffic ticket, you were directed to the saloon, asked the bartender for the judge and the two of you negotiated over a beer. The judge usually settled for half the fine; the two of you had some laughs; he wished you good day and that was the end of it. Life was simpler that way.

A pile of contestants lined up for the Justice of the Peace race that year. The primary whittled them down to two candidates. One was a Storey County deputy; the other operated a wedding chapel in Reno. Independent polls showed the chapel operator was likely to win.

The fruit of a man's life turns up in the oddest ways when he runs for political office in a sparsely populated rural county. And those whom a candidate has wronged are first to make known the candidates' sins. In this case, an informer came to the morgue and told me the wedding chapel operator had been caught shop lifting in Reno. He was prosecuted, convicted, appealed his conviction and was convicted again. The informer showed me the court papers.

The other newspaper was still in business. The editor had declined to publish the information. I couldn't understand why. The court papers were public documents. The people should know the sort of man they were about to elect for Justice of the Peace.

I published the candidates' court record in the *Voice*. The candidate was furious and threatened to sue me and every business where the *Voice* was distributed. Caught with its pants down, the other paper permitted the candidate to defend himself in its columns. The candidate denied the charges.

In response, I told the public where they could find the information for themselves. The wedding chapel candidate settled down after that. And he lost in the general election. Sometimes truth makes a difference.

The second best office that year was District Attorney. It was open now because Bill Wrong wasn't running for reelection. Bill wanted to go off and write a book. I could have warned Bill about the hell and torment he was about to embark on. But I didn't. He had robbed me and he could do without my advice. He wouldn't have believed me anyway. Let Bill spend two or three years wracking his brains at a typewriter in a room by himself, tormented by loneliness and self-doubt, and Bill would discover the paradise that is a writer's life.

Instead, Joe Pastrami, who had been Storey County District Attorney for two terms and had left office to run for judge but lost, was looking for his old job. In 1970 Joe Pastrami had teamed up with the pimp , the man who operated the largest brothel in the United States in Storey County, and ran for District Attorney and won. The pimp was a big help.

He held captive two hundred votes down in the brothel district. One hundred votes were prostitutes who weren't legal residents or prostitutes who had registered to vote under several assumed names. Another 100 votes were residents of the pimp's trailer park; in exchange for cheap rent they voted as they were told. They would have chopped off their left foot if the pimp asked them to. Storey County had a mere 500 registered voters. With 200 votes in his pocket, the pimp held 40 percent of the vote which determined elections.

If you wanted to get elected in Storey County you paid a visit to the pimp, bowed down and promised to do whatever he told you. Not every candidate did this, of course, and those who didn't usually were not elected. Which meant some of those candidates elected were considered questionable characters. This ring of corruption had been in force for about sixteen years when we were in Storey County.

In 1971 Joe Pastrami rewrote the ordinance that had legalized prostitution in Storey County. Now after an eight year hiatus Joe Pastrami was back looking for his old job as Storey County District Attorney.

Joe Pastrami laughed when he came up with his reelection slogan:

Bring Back Old Time Corruption
Vote for Joe Pastrami

Joe Pastrami and Nancy Ann Leeder were the leading candidates for District Attorney that year. The pimp instituted one of his private polls to see how Joe Pastrami was doing in the race. The pimp did a poll every election. Joe Pastrami was ahead but not by much; Nancy Ann Leeder was running close. The last thing the pimp wanted in Storey County was a diligent prosecutor.

One night Nancy Ann Leeder was driving alone down steep and dangerous Geiger Grade when someone found her and ran her off the road. Nancy Ann Leeder went to the hospital. She was shaken but all right. Everyone knew who was responsible. The pimp and the Storey County boys had sent Nancy Ann a message. Nancy Ann was less enthusiastic in her candidacy after that. And Joe Pastrami was elected for a third term as Storey County District Attorney. Joe brought back old time corruption just like he said he would. Joe always kept his promises.

Bad things happened to good people in Storey County. The FBI knew it. The Nevada Attorney General knew it. The Governor knew it. Congressmen and senators knew it. Every Nevada politician who could have intervened knew it.

There were many people in Storey County who knew about the payoffs and wanted to get rid of the men who accepted them. But who could they turn to for help? Their Sheriff was a crook. Their District Attorney was a crook. The Commissioners were pawns. The Governor and Attorney General looked the other way. The People's helplessness made them angry. They needed help. And I stupidly thought I was it.

CHAPTER TWENTY

Ol' Al and the Pharaoh

In the first place God made idiots. This was for practice. Then he made school boards. Mark Twain, *Following the Equator*

Al Ricardo was the handsome psycho case and Superintendent of Storey County Schools. He had been recently hired to educate, encourage and enlighten. Instead, Al made life hell on earth for anyone with a brain in their head.

Al grew up in a burrow in New York City. For some unknown reason— probably because someone wanted to kill him, Al came to Nevada and went to college. He applied for the Storey County Superintendent and the School Board, trusting human beings who had never met anyone like Al, made a mistake and hired Al.

Al's problem was simple: he belonged behind a desk shuffling paper deep inside an obscure bureaucracy. He did not work well with people. He had all the education a college could cram into his head and not enough sense to use any of it. In his hands Al's education became a weapon.

We know that there are ways to work with people to get results. One, is to inform your people of the objective, consult with them and together press toward the common goal. Another less effective method is to take control like a battling ram, force people to do what you want, not listen to their ideas and thoughts, not inform them of the objective and whip them into submission like Attila the Hun. Al chose this second method. That's how Al's troubles started.

Al was new to Virginia City and didn't know squat about the people and apparently didn't care to learn. He no more cared for his staff and students than a tuna would have. Being from the big city, Al thought he was in the backwoods wilderness. Storey County was a stepping stone in Al's career, and Al said so. Al really wanted to be Superintendent of Schools down in Carson City.

I began to hear horror stories about Al at the Union Brewery Saloon. Al was continually brow beating teachers, insulting students and secretaries and dreaming up all sorts of unnecessary tortures. If anything was fun or enjoyable, Al was sure to kill it. Like the annual school picnic, a tradition in Virginia City for decades. Al annihilated the picnic with one swoop.

Perhaps the most insensitive thing Al did is what he did to the high school basketball team, the pride of the community. These boys had won the state basketball championship for five years. The team had won ninety-three games straight. And they might have won for another five years if it wasn't for Al. All the championship basketballs were kept up at the Crystal Saloon, Bill and Margaret Marks' saloon.

Although Bill Marks is in his seventies, he looks like the Pillsbury Dough Boy. He has the cleanest, friendliest pink face, big wide blue eyes with a shock of lovely white hair, parted and combed neatly to the side and back. He has the face of a boy on the body of an old man. Bill always wears casual dress slacks, a plain white shirt and a knotted tie. He is as neat as a whistle. Bill takes pride in being an old time saloon keeper.

Bill and Margaret Marks run the Crystal Saloon on the corner of Union and C Street across from the old California Bank Building. They have been running it for about thirty-five years and the saloon has been in the family for nearly a century. It is a well lighted saloon with a long dark bar, a huge back bar with a great big mirror and several crystal chandeliers dangle from the ceiling. Bill and Margaret and their customers are good natured and friendly. The Crystal Saloon is right up the hill from the high school. The Crystal is the local hangout before and after basketball games at the high school gym. All the balls from the championship games are displayed on the back bar of the Crystal Saloon. All the players signed their names on the balls with black markers. The balls seem to belong in the Crystal Saloon. Bill and Margaret were raised in Virginia City and their class was the last to graduate from the old Fourth Ward School. There were seven in the graduating class.

Anyway, the worst thing Al Ricardo did was to start making the championship basketball team practice in the mornings before school! The boys were off to practice before sunrise. The team lost its spirit and there were morale problems. Then the team started losing games. And the talk turned sad at the Crystal Saloon. Surprisingly, no one asked Al what he was doing by making the championship basketball team practice before dawn.

The more bad things I heard about Al, the more I felt it was my moral responsibility to do something. Al would have been hanged or murdered in the Old West. But we have sadly done away with those happy, quick forms of justice. This is a rotten shame.

Before I embarked on my mission, I thought I would try to talk to Al. That seemed fair and decent. A lot of people tried talking to Al. But he wouldn't answer anyone's questions about his actions. You'd ask Al, "Hey, Al, why you making the boys practice before dawn?" And Al just looked smug and said nothing.

And you'd say, "Hey Al, why you giving Ed the principal such a sorry time?" And Al just looked smug and said nothing.

And you'd say, "Hey Al, how come you won't let Joe Verant, who lives right here in town, substitute teach, when he subs everywhere else?" And Al folded his arms, looked smug and said nothing. Al was the sort of iron-headed bureaucrat you'd like to club with a two-by-four just to get their attention. But you couldn't do that, even in Virginia City without getting into trouble, which was another rotten shame.

Finally things got so bad, Ed Murkovich, who was the high school principal, quit. Ed was absolutely fed up with Al. When I learned about Ed's decision, I thought maybe if I embarrassed Al badly enough in my paper—peer pressure can be a useful persuader—Al would get the message and be normal. Maybe that would do it. So I sat down and happily composed *Ol' Al and the Pharaoh*: In part it read:

There once was a man called Ol' Al who came to Virginia City to run the school. Ol' Al thought he was better than everyone. You knew Ol' Al thought he was better than you because he would come right out and tell you so. If you said, "Ol' Al, are you better than me," Ol' Al would say, "Yeah, I'm better than you and I'm smarter too."

And you'd say,"How come Ol' Al?"

And Ol' Al would say," Because I'm from New York City and you're from Nevada. Nevada people are stupid."

And you'd say, "How come Ol' Al?

And Ol' Al would say, "Just because."

Ol' Al was like Pharaoh who gave Ol' Moses a hard time. You remember how the Lord told Moses to tell Pharaoh to let his people go. Ol' Moses told Pharaoh if he didn't let his people go, the Lord would fill Egypt with frogs and insects and stuff. First Pharaoh said he would let Moses' people go, and then he said he wouldn't. So the Lord sent plagues of frogs and insects and turned the river into blood and killed off Pharaoh's kid. Finally Ol' Pharaoh got the message and let Moses' people go.

Ol' Al was like Pharaoh. Al was mean to his teachers and secretaries. He was mean to the students, too. Nobody liked Ol' Al much but it was Al's fault. He tried real hard to be dislikable. People tried to talk to Al to make things better, but Al wouldn't listen to anyone.

Then one day the Lord really got mad at Ol' Al because Al got Ol' Ed so mad—Ol' Ed was the high school principal—that Ed said to himself, "I'm really tired of Ol' Al making my life miserable. I'm gonna quit being principal and get away from Ol' Al"

So the Lord said unto his servant Moses, "Yo, Moses. Behold Ol' Al. He has offended My people. He has hurt his secretaries' feelings. He has troubled Ol' Ed. And he has been mean to his students. My anger is kindled against Ol' Al.

"Go unto Ol' Al and tell him, stop being so mean and nasty to My people. Go and apologize to your secretaries. Go make peace with Ol' Ed. And if Ol' Al will not listen to you, tell him I will roast him in hell for a million years! And I will see to it that he does not get that Carson City Superintendent job he covets. Go Moses, and tell Ol' Al what I have told you."

So, Moses went unto Ol' Al and told him what the Lord had said. But what do you think Ol' Al did?

Al didn't do anything. He stayed just as stubborn and mean as he always was. But after a few weeks of ragging on him in my paper, he didn't look so smug. And he was real worried about keeping his job.

Then I made an appointment and met with the School Board and told them what I thought of the monster they had unleashed on this undeserving community. In a closed personnel session the Board sat quietly and patiently for an hour and a half while I pounded the table and ranted about Al's atrocities. Again I asked Al questions, and again he wouldn't answer. I warned the Board that Al would embroil them in all sorts of lawsuits if they didn't do something.

It went in one ear and out the other. The Board thought I was the crazy one. They had been reading my paper and took my invented stories seriously. They didn't give me the time of day.

Then the lawsuits began. A teacher who was fired by Al for no good reason, took Al and the School Board to court. The teacher was awarded a large settlement, all his back wages and got his job back.

And then there were more lawsuits.

After the lawsuits, the School Board saw the light and some of them quit and went into hiding. Al read the writing on the wall and got a job in another state. Al never did get the Carson City Superintendent job he wanted just like Ol' Moses warned him.

I really wish people would listen when you try to help them. My father always said, "Good advice is the hardest thing in the world to give away." And he was right.

CHAPTER TWENTY—ONE

The pimp

When a man is getting better, he understands more and more clearly the evil that is still left in him. When a man is getting worse, he understands his own badness less and less. A moderately bad man knows he is not very good: a thoroughly bad man thinks he is all right...Good people know about both good and evil: bad people do not know about either. C.S. Lewis

The real trouble in Storey County was the pimp. He was a pushy big mouthed habitual criminal who ran the biggest legal whorehouse in Storey County and controlled Storey County by bribing local politicians and defrauding county elections. He was a pimp who wanted to be a king. I would publish his name here except that he gets so much pleasure from seeing it in print.

Let me be perfectly clear what I mean by *pimp*: I mean specifically a man who procures women to have sex with other men for money and who earns part of his living from prostitutes. The pimp emphatically denied he was a pimp although he had been convicted of the crime twice in California and was a well known pimp by his own notorious activity. The pimp said he was a businessman. Nothing but an everyday businessman. A businessman who had been convicted of pimping, extortion, federal tax evasion, bribery, attempted murder, perjury, been sent to prison and was a suspect in several murders. Although he said he was not a pimp and threatened to sue newspapers who called him one, journalists and judges never let him forget what he really was. The pimp hated being called a pimp.

The pimp was short, dark skinned, paunchy, receding hair line and had these big brown sad eyes that convinced the foolish he had been victimized all his life. He was nothing you would call handsome. He looked and acted every bit of what he was. And yet the pimp had this little boy charm. He could turn on the charm and make people feel comfortable. The truth is, many were intrigued by this man who could be so evil and yet so charming. And generous. His superficial charm, his contributions to local charities and his constant reassurances that he was just a businessman serving mankind was what eventually made some people like and accept him. They even sent fan mail. They saw the pimp as a sort of Robin Hood folk hero. For the pimp's talk was as slippery as an oyster. He could make the innocent feel he was their best friend while he slowly carved out their soul with a dull butter knife. He had a radar-like instinct that could detect human weakness and use those weaknesses against his victim for his benefit. He enjoyed corrupting good men. Everything Midas touched turned to gold; nearly everything the pimp touched he defiled and destroyed. The Nevada Attorney General said he was "capable of anything." The pimp would do wrong when it was just as easy to do right. He may not have been thoroughly evil, but he was as close as a man gets without being obvious.

There were some in Storey County who spoke familiarly of him and used his first name in their conversations as if he was their best friend and one of the finest human beings God ever made instead of seeing him for what he was. They thought the pimp was a humanitarian because he gave away turkeys and bottles of whisky around election time.

His story shows how poverty and misfortune can destroy a human being and turn him into a monster. He was born in Italy to poor parents. The father left the family and went to America to make a place for his family. The pregnant mother was left behind with her children. The boy was born while his father was in America. When he was four, his mother was stricken with cancer and died. The boy was taken in by relatives. They were poor and the boy stole food to feed the family.

Because of his own poverty in America, his father did not return to Europe until the boy was eleven. By then poverty, the early loss of his mother, not having a father to teach him right values, and a feeling that he had been betrayed, had shaped the boy's ideas of the world. The father brought the boy to America where he lived with his father and stepmother in the slums. Always small, semi-literate, he learned to take care of himself by stealing, lying and using violence. The boy was rejected by his step-mother. The feeling he had been rejected by his mother's death, and the subsequent rejection by his step-mother caused him to mistrust women. He was angry for having been cheated out of the love and nurturing every child deserves. He hated women; he would find ways to make them pay for his pain.

Such are the beginnings of a psychopath.

The psychopath is a curious creature. He is, as the psychiatrists tell us, antisocial, absolutely amoral, incapable of making complete emotional commitments, aggressive, often violent, has complete disregard for the rights of others and feels no sense of guilt even when he commits horrendous crimes. Not all criminals are psychopaths; not all psychopaths are criminals. Some psychiatrists consider the psychopath mentally ill. Others consider him "morally insane." Some believe the psychopath is evil incarnate. Most agree that the psychopath is an abnormal person.

The psychopath is created by people and environment. There has usually been a break or absence in parental care, principally maternal care. The mother leaves the home, dies or the child is in some way separated from the mother. The child is deeply hurt by the mother's absence, and deeply angry. If both parents are missing and there is a lack of affection from the child's caretakers, the child does not learn how to identify with parental figures and thereby assimilate normal social values. The child becomes what he has experienced: cold, affectionless, unable to sustain meaningful loving relationships for any substantial length. He has difficulty feeling for others; though he may act like he understands other people, he does not; he cannot. He has closed down all normal feeling; to feel is to feel pain.

To protect himself from his utter sense of helplessness, the psychopathic child promises to never need anyone again. It is an impossible goal of course. He becomes detached from his true feelings. He sublimates his need for love, affection and his deep seated anger. He seeks a painless freedom from people and his intolerable helplessness. He sees love and human attachments as impediments to his freedom.

To the psychopath, people are important and useful to the extent to which they meet his needs. The psychopath is a parasite who uses and disposes people as if they are candy wrappers. Paradoxically, the psychopath can be remarkably charming, exciting and fun to be with. He is particularly successful with women who are impressed with his straight forwardness and his seeming utter self-reliance. He is often an incredible ego-maniac. He cannot get enough of himself; he loves to hear himself talk. This amazing self-confidence is a successful barrier to the truth of himself. He makes friends quickly but usually is unable to maintain friendships for any length. Friendships require intimacy. The psychopath cannot let anyone get close enough for intimacy; for in so doing people would discover the cold and indifferent person he is beneath the smooth exterior.

The psychopath of course is a bad actor. To defend himself from the truth of himself he creates elaborate, paranoid rationalizations. He is an incredible pathological liar; he will continue to lie and rationalize even when the truth is proven by facts and evidence. It is not he who is wrong; the world is wrong. He determines to shape the world to fit his shoes. And this invariably leads the psychopath into conflict with society. In short, he often breaks man's laws. For he sees man's laws as an infringement upon his rights to freedom. Laws are oppressive. When they frustrate his desires, they are to be broken. Ironically, the psychopath finds it difficult to understand why society makes such a bother about breaking the law. To him, it is a trifling. No matter if it is murder, robbery, theft or rape. People and society are there to serve him. Unlike the neurotic who is in constant mental conflict, the psychopath does not feel conscious guilt. If you do not feel, you cannot feel guilt.

To the sane and normal, the psychopath is an aberration, evil incarnate. To the psychopath, normal people are fools who don't understand how the world works.

No human being is entirely psychopathic. An individual is more or less psychopathic. Fortunately, periods of purely psychopathic behavior are short and infrequent. The psychopath's deep need for love and affection and his helplessness prevent him from operating psychopathically for any great length. For underneath the cold exterior, the psychopath has a deep, sublimated need to be punished for his wrong doing. This often causes him to commit a crime in order to be caught and punished. Once imprisoned he is taken care of by others. He who has felt entirely helpless, and has rebelled from feelings of helplessness, has now gotten what he has wanted all along. The tragedy is that the psychopath's irrational and often unlawful behavior is ineffectual. He has gotten the help and attention he's craved, but at great expense to others and himself. If society were filled with psychopathic personalities we would have complete chaos.

It is easy to have sympathy for an individual who as a child is deprived of the love and affection each of us needs to grow up whole. But our sympathy is usually replaced with hatred and anger when a psychopath carves up our lives or our loved ones or causes such incredible difficulty and pain through his criminal activity that we want nothing more but to imprison him or hang him from the nearest telephone pole.

At the age of fifteen the pimp ran away to New York City and worked in the slums for a fruit and vegetable peddler. He stole money from his boss who discovered the theft. The boy quit his job and eventually enlisted in the military. He got married and divorced a couple times and had some kids.

He ended up in Oakland, California as a cab driver. Always looking for a way to overcome his sense of inadequacy and powerlessness and a way to make easy money, he started running girls. In 1952 and 53 he was convicted of running a disorderly house, an illegal brothel. For his second conviction he was fined $350 and chose to pay it off by spending it in jail at $5 a day. Since his whorehouse wasn't appreciated by the Oakland police the pimp decided to move it to Nevada where prostitution was legal in some counties.

The pimp arrived in Reno in 1955. He wanted to open a brothel in Reno but wide open prostitution had been outlawed during the War. The pimp learned he could operate a brothel just outside Reno in the Triangle, where Washoe, Lyon and Storey counties converge just past a hole in the wall called Wadsworth. The pimp opened his "ranch" in two small wooden buildings. He immediately made a lot of money. He enjoyed driving to Reno in his big car with a couple of his girls beside him. He paraded through the casinos in tailored suits and a busty, beautiful young girl on each arm. Some men admired his money and his audacity. The pimp thumbed his nose at the Reno District Attorney with whom he was angry. The District Attorney had refused to allow the pimp to open a brothel in Reno.

The Reno District Attorney was a tough law and justice kind of guy. He didn't like the pimp making fools of honest folks who worked for a living. He didn't like the pimp flaunting his ill-gained wealth around Reno. There is a Nevada law that says that any man who persistently hangs around a house of prostitution is a vagrant and can be arrested. In 1958 the District Attorney ordered the pimp to stay out of town. The pimp refused to obey the order and went to Reno in his big car with his girls and was arrested and convicted of vagrancy. These arrests continued and the feud and the bad blood thickened. It really went bad when the District Attorney burned down the pimp's whorehouse because he considered it a public nuisance.

Finally the pimp conjured an idea to get the District Attorney off his back. He would entice the District Attorney with an underaged girl. The girl would seduce the District Attorney. Then the pimp would threaten to expose the District Attorney if he wouldn't let him run his brothel in peace.

The underaged girl seduced the District Attorney and the pimp tried to blackmail him. The pimp's plan bombed. Instead of giving into the pimp's threat of blackmail, the District Attorney charged the pimp with attempted extortion. In 1962 the pimp was convicted and sent to the

Nevada State Prison at Carson City for two years. And then he was shipped to prison in California for six months for tax evasion. After he got out of prison he went back to running his brothel in Storey County.

In 1963 he was convicted of federal tax evasion, spent time in a California prison and given a three year parole. As soon as the parole was up in 1966, he was convicted in Storey County of assault with intent to commit murder and spent time in the Storey County jail. In 1977 he was convicted a second time for tax evasion; he was sentenced to twenty years in federal prison, four, five year terms to run concurrently. He appealed the sentence which later was reduced to eighteen months.

July 5, 1979 he was indicted in Washoe County for bribing the Lyon County District Attorney in an attempt to obtain a brothel license in Lyon county. Because the actual bribery took place in Washoe County, the pimp was indicted in Washoe County. To add to his troubles, Washoe County District Attorney Calvin Dunlap charged the pimp with being an habitual criminal. Under a new Nevada law, an habitual criminal could be sentenced to life in prison. Facing life imprisonment, December 1980 the pimp fled to Rio de Janeiro and hid for three years. In Brazil he was immune to extradition.

During this time his former attorney, Harry Claiborne, who had become a federal judge, was indicted for committing various criminal acts. The pimp returned to the United States in December 1983 and made a deal with the feds to testify against his old friend, Harry Claiborne. Testifying before a federal grand jury, the pimp lied and was convicted of perjury. Still, he managed to cut a deal with the feds: he agreed to plead guilty to the 1979 Washoe County bribery indictment and accept eighteen months in jail and a $10,000 fine, and pay $200,000 which Washoe County forfeited for his bail jumping act. The bribery sentence was to run concurrent with his 1977 tax evasion sentence. Thereafter the pimp was protected by the federal witness protection program and spent eighteen months in a comfortable California prison.

When he got out of prison in December 1984, he went back to running his brothel in Storey County. A year later December 13, 1985 he was arrested in Reno for contributing to the delinquency of a minor. Now fifty-nine, the pimp had brought a seventeen year old girl into a casino and bought her drinks. The pimp was arrested by the Reno police. The pimp's attorney intervened, cut a deal with the Reno City Attorney and charges were dropped. The Reno Police were furious; the City Attorney was barraged with allegations of bribery and obstructing justice.

Through all the ups and downs of his career as a notorious Nevada criminal, the pimp had a partner, his wife. She was the nuts and bolts of the operation. While the pimp was out bragging and showing off his girls and winning notoriety and spending time in prison, his wife ran the brothel and kept the place in order. She had operated brothels before she married the pimp. The two recruited hundreds of vulnerable young girls and gave notorious parties to publicize their business. The pimp and his bride were shortly the toast of the Nevada underworld and infamous for having the biggest whorehouse in the United States. This apparently gave them great satisfaction.

Like all pimps, the pimp saw himself as a sexual prophet. His lone voice cried out in the wilderness that indiscriminate sex is beautiful and normal. He didn't think having sex with a prostitute was wrong or immoral or sin. Humans were sexual machines. Sex was sex and there was no reason a clever fellow should not make money from it. He didn't think he used his girls or his customers. He did his customers a favor and he helped his girls by giving them a job. He was a great guy and he wanted the world to know it.

He was determined to use modern marketing techniques to sell sin to America. Instead of running his whorehouse quietly as whorehouses are usually run, the pimp sought out publicity. He sold his whorehouse like Barnum and Bailey sold their circus. He created publicity stunts and gave interviews to journalists and used newspapers, radio and television to attract attention. The media and the public ate it up.

The pimp repeated his message until the repetition of it dulled the senses.

This was his subliminal message: *sex with a whore is good.*

And he repeated it: *sex with a whore is good.*

And he repeated it: *sex with a whore is good.*

First the public was outraged. Then it was curious. Then it was entertained. And after hearing it long enough, many in Nevada accepted the message: sex with a whore *was* good.

The pimp wanted the world to believe that running a whorehouse was perfectly normal. He wanted society to accept him as if he were any professional. To win acceptance, he gave to charities and spread around turkeys at Christmas time. He did not give quietly as truly generous people do. He made spectacles of his giving. His notoriety grew with each million dollars his whorehouse earned. Some have estimated he made 15 to 25 million dollars each year from his brothels in Storey and Lyon counties and various businesses. He courted and financially

backed Nevada politicians. Some considered him one of the most powerful men in Nevada because of his wealth and political influence. As for
Storey County, this sparsely populated land of rock and dirt, the pimp
was a king. Storey County wasn't much of a kingdom, but it was his
kingdom. His success and power went to his head. He thought he could
get away with anything. No one stopped him. For years Governors and
Attorney Generals turned their eyes from Storey County and the crimes
being committed there, bribery and murder among them.

Perhaps if these men had known the depth of the pimp's depravity
they might have taken greater interest in his activity and done something about him. But I wouldn't count on it.

The pimp's twisted brain understood legalizing prostitution would
be the ultimate seduction and mockery of society's values. He longed for
this as he longed for nothing else. And where could he legalize prostitution? Where else. Right in Storey County where he had illegally operated
his business for fifteen years.

And that's when he began to corrupt Storey County.

Prostitution had been legal in Virginia City and Storey County from
the early 1860's until 1947. What got rid of it in 1947 was a murder. A
"D" Street prostitute became involved in a love triangle. One of the male
sides of the triangle got perturbed one day and killed the prostitute, buried her in a basement and hanged himself from a rafter in the same
basement. That's what some believed. Others thought the surviving
lover had killed the woman and her lover and made it look like a mur-
der-suicide. He was never charged with the crime. Authorities thought
it was too expensive to try him for the murder of an ordinary prostitute.
I used to see this man on C Street; by then he was very old, crippled up
and very sad. It was hard to believe he had once been a sensation in the
newspapers.

During the twenty-four years prostitution was outlawed in Storey
County, Virginia City prospered. The "Bonanza" television show became an international hit in the 1960's and caused tourism to boom;
times were good. Then the pimp showed up with his deceptive plan for
the county's prosperity. It was really a prosperous plan for himself and
a few politicians.

Storey County was controlled by a three member Board of Commissioners. Unlike Virginia City in the 19th century, the town was without a Mayor and a Board of Aldermen, which had acted as a Town

Council. The town had been divided into districts and the people in each district elected their town representative. But when the mines closed and the town dwindled from a high of twenty-five thousand to a few hundred residents, the Mayor and Board of Aldermen were done away with and the three member county Board of Commissioners was adopted. Virginia City was reduced to two county electoral districts.

As the town re-populated in the 1960's, the loss of a Mayor and a Town Council denied the people the direct representation that is needed to keep government honest. The fewer elected representatives and their low pay made their seduction easier by the pimp.

Off and on for about fifteen years, the pimp had essentially operated his brothel in Storey County illegally. Legalized prostitution had been outlawed in 1947. The District Attorney and the Sheriff allowed the pimp to operate his business anyway. The pimp wanted no more trouble with district attorneys and cops. He wanted prostitution legalized in Storey County. And he was willing to pay politicians before and after their elections to get what he wanted.

In 1970 tiny Storey County had less than a thousand residents, no industry and no resources except for silver mines that had gone bust. It needed money badly. The pimp had lots of money. He would give some to the county and the Storey County boys if they would legalize prostitution. The pimp would take care of them. They should play along. There was a lot of money to be made, millions. The pimp would gladly pay a $25,000 brothel fee every year, even $30,000 to help the county, just because he was such a good guy. And there would always be something in it for some of the Storey County boys. The ones who would take his money.

Two of the three county Commissioners wanted to legalize prostitution. But only one would vote for it publicly. The Commissioners needed two of three votes to pass the law.

Commissioner Bill Marks was in favor of prostitution but was against the pimp operating his whorehouse legally. Marks refused to vote for the pimp's operation. One evening the pimp sent two goons to Virginia City to change Marks' mind. They shoved him against the wall of his Crystal Saloon. They threatened to kill him and his family if he didn't go along. Marks went to the FBI. The FBI told the pimp to lay off.

About this time, Marks was forced to resign as Commissioner in order to serve on the Selective Service Board. He spoke with Governor Paul Laxalt—later Senator Laxalt and President Reagan's right hand man—and recommended a specific individual to replace him. Governor

Laxalt listened to Marks' request but in the end appointed his own choice, Lowell "Buzz" Goodman. Two days after Marks' resignation, Commissioners Buzz Goodman and Martin Rosso legalized prostitution in Storey County. They had no idea of the evil they had unleashed in Storey County.

Preceding county elections in 1970, the pimp made a deal with several candidates running for election for the first time. He agreed to pay their campaign costs. When they were elected he would pay each of them various sums if they did as they were told and left him alone. The candidates were naive and unsuspecting. It seemed simple and harmless. The pimp had money; the candidates needed the money; they made a pact to get the money.

Storey County had less than five hundred registered voters. A candidate could win election with a mere two or three hundred votes. Most residents and voters lived in Virginia City. However, the pimp did two things to acquire forty percent of the county vote.

First, he built a trailer park in the River District where about one hundred occupants rented spaces for sixty dollars a month. In exchange for the cheap rent, the pimp made it clear they were to vote as he commanded.

Secondly, he registered his prostitutes to vote in Storey County although Nevada law specifically states a prostitute cannot claim her place of business as her residence. The prostitutes were told how to vote. Prostitutes also falsely registered to vote under assumed names. Between his new renters and the illegal prostitute votes, the pimp had rounded up two hundred votes. These became the deciding votes in races for county offices.

If you examine the Storey County voting tallies from 1970 through 1990, the voting record of District 3, the brothel district, is curious. Large number of votes for Sheriff, District Attorney and county Commissioners bear a remarkable similarity from election to election. The District 3 votes are always fantastically slanted toward the winner. Sometimes one hundred percent of the vote went to a particular candidate. And if you compare the District 3 votes with other districts, it is obvious, without the votes from the brothel district, certain county candidates either would not have been elected or the races would have been close. Those politicians suspected of being under the pimp's influence, both county and state, received large numbers of votes from District 3. The pimp's brothel district often provided candidates with one third to one half of the total votes they received in Storey County elections. However, in election years when the pimp was absent from Storey County, say 1982, District 3 votes appear normal.

The pimp's vote not only went to county politicians but to candidates for Justices of the Nevada Supreme Court, Attorney Generals, Secretary of State, Governors and U.S. Senators. Because of this, some said the pimp's money had managed to compromise county, state and even federal officials. It was common knowledge that politicians were given free sex at the pimp's whorehouse.

After his election in 1970, District Attorney Joe Pastrami re-drafted the original prostitution law, Ordinance 38. Ordinance 39 A, passed by the Storey County Commissioners September 7, 1971, limited brothels to the River District just outside Reno. The Storey County boys had put the pimp's whorehouse in a hidden, sparsely populated part of the county. Out of sight is out of mind. The measure never went on a ballot before the voters.

Legalized prostitution was back in Storey County and the pimp's infamous reign began. His influence would kill whatever democracy had existed in Storey County and compromise some of the county's and the State's highest elected officials. Big money has a way of winning small friends.

It may have been all right if the pimp had stayed at his end of the county and ran his business quietly. He wasn't content earning millions of dollars each year. All his life he had weaseled around and cheated and lied and been sent to prison. All his life others had controlled him. But now this was his time. He had made money and money made him powerful. Now he would make people respect the short crook people called a pimp. He was a sociopathic megalomaniac who liked people under his control. He bragged about the hundreds of women with whom he had copulated; he had sex with any of his girls any time he felt like it. He gloried in the power he felt by controlling the Storey County Sheriff, District Attorney and Commissioners. He was a tyrant, but a benevolent tyrant some said. He was happy as long as people did what they were told. And when they didn't, they were threatened, beat up or killed.

After the pimp's operation was legalized in Storey County, he went to the trouble of committing various felonious acts for no good reason. First, he bribed elected officials and public servants. He gave rolls of cash to Sheriff Dick who became the bag man; everyone was paid in cash.

Bribing public officials is a felony in the state of Nevada punishable by ten years in prison.

He defrauded county elections by ordering non-resident prostitutes to register to vote in Storey County. According to Nevada law, a prostitute cannot claim her place of business as a residence. Prostitutes live in brothels; by law brothels are not considered a residence. Therefore a prostitute cannot legally vote in the county where she is employed as a prostitute. The pimp ignored the law and gave his girls a list of candidates and told the girls to vote for the men on the list. When election time came around, he ordered all his girls who had worked at the brothel and gone elsewhere, to return to the brothel for the county election. The girls piled into the whorehouse a few days before the election. On election day he carted them to the local polling place where they voted as they were told.

He threatened public officials who didn't act in his best interest and he threatened and harassed journalists who wrote the truth about his activities. He threatened citizens who spoke out against him. He had opposing county candidates threatened and harassed.

He used underaged girls at his whorehouse. Some girls were as young as fifteen. Using underage girls in a brothel is a felony in Nevada.

He conspired to extort and blackmail public officials in Lyon County where he was attempting to get a brothel license in his own name.

Though he was astronomically wealthy, he either would not pay the required federal income tax or would fight the IRS tooth and nail. The federal government wasted millions of dollars investigating and prosecuting the pimp for numerous counts of tax evasion.

The People of Storey County might have thought legalized prostitution was all right. But they hated the pimp for paying-off their local politicians and interfering with their elections. Some of the people tried to stop the corruption but always met with defeat.

Who do you turn to for legal help in a tiny rural county when your Sheriff, your District Attorney and your county Commissioners are crooks?

You go to the Attorney General and the Governor.

And what did those good ole boys do?

Nothing.

It was a pitiful situation in Storey County. Much worse than people knew.

CHAPTER TWENTY–TWO

Murder in the pimp's kingdom

I had prejudiced feelings about prostitution. I had studied prostitution for ten years and written two books on the subject. I knew why women became prostitutes and knew that prostitution most often destroyed them.

Contrary to the accepted but false notion that women become prostitutes because they are over-sexed or immoral, women usually become prostitutes because they have been abused as children. I tried to point this out in my first book, *Rosa May: The Search For A Mining Camp Legend*. In that book I wrote about the causes of prostitution:

> *In an effort to discover the major causes of prostitution, Harold Greenwald, a psychoanalyst, conducted intensive interviews with twenty call girls. His findings differed only slightly from Polly Adler's [a New York madam.] Emotional impoverishment seemed to be the greatest cause of prostitution today.*
>
> *Of the twenty prostitutes Greenwald interviewed, not one came from a home where there was a permanent, well adjusted marriage. Not one admitted growing up in a happy home where parents got along well. In seventy-five percent of the cases, homes were broken up by adolescence. In the remaining cases, the girls never saw any evidence of sympathy or affection between parents. Two girls had parents that went through three divorces; three girls from families where there were six divorces, and six girls saw their mothers living with men to whom they were not married. Because of the absence of warmth and permanence in their families, these girls had not been able to form an attachment to either parent, and hence, were not able to absorb the values of society which we most often learn from parents to whom we feel close.*
>
> *The general attitude of such parents toward their children seemed to be one of complete rejection. The girls were rejected by fathers who didn't care about them, left home or died; and by mothers who never let them forget how much they had sacrificed for them. Nineteen of the twenty girls admitted feeling rejected by both parents.*

In addition, many of the girls were thrown from one home to the next. Three girls passed from family to family; three girls from one foster home to another; four lived in a succession of boarding schools.

It was from such a background of neglect and rejection that ten girls reputed engaging in early sexual activity for which they were rewarded. They learned early that they could barter sexual favors for affection, interest and attention. By providing sexual gratification, they were temporarily able to overcome their feelings of loneliness and unworthiness—while at the same time expressing their hostility toward parents for having neglected them.

— from Chapter 11

The young woman who chooses to become a prostitute is a confused, emotionally damaged, vulnerable victim. Very often she has run away from home to escape physical, psychological or sexual abuse. She drops out of high school. Young and uneducated, good jobs are hard to come by. She is a perfect victim in our society. Prostitution becomes an easy way—sometimes the only way for her to pay for food and shelter. Likely she has been abused and rejected all her life. She wants to belong and will do nearly anything to be accepted. The prostitution underworld with its easy money and immediate acceptance is hard to reject. Here she finds others who bear the same wounds and feel the same anger. She learns to adjust to prostitution by sublimating her feelings. She cannot see she is a victim used by customers, pimps and madams; at least she is a part of something. She likes the attention she gets from customers and pimps. It's like being in show business. She feels she is good at something. She feels attractive. She gets addicted to the excitement and the fast money. There is no future; there is only now. She cannot see the dangers.

Like alcoholics and drug addicts, she denies she has a problem. She does not understand what motivates her. She does not understand she uses her sexuality as a weapon against forces she cannot control. She uses her body to get back at parents who have rejected or abused her, and people and society. She needs acceptance on some level, no matter how low and self-destructive. She has little or no self-esteem and accepts the "sick love" from her pimp who trades insincere love and affection for money. As strange and as abnormal as it may seem, the pimp is the most important person in her life and she will do almost anything to win and keep his attention.

If she is honest, usually she cannot say why she became a prostitute and stays one. Some say they do it for the money. Some say they do it for the power they feel by controlling men with sex. Some say they do it for the pleasure of having sex with many men. But for most prostitutes, having sex with customers is an unpleasant experience. Only the crazies do it for fun and they don't last long in "the life." A prostitute is usually only able to reach sexual gratification with her pimp or lesbian lovers. Some girls get hooked on the excitement and strangeness of the life. And there are always lazy women and evil women or women who lack the intelligence or education to do anything else. It is because of the prostitute's troubled state of mind and her low self-esteem, that she is easy prey to any man or woman who even pretends to care for her. Their ends are nearly always tragic. Many kill themselves or become drug addicts or they are murdered by pimps.

I personally consider the act of prostitution a form of mental illness not unlike alcoholism and drug addiction. Like the alcoholic, the prostitute suffers from denial; she claims she has no problem. And like the alcoholic and other forms of mental illness, the prostitute has a similar family history of child abuse, neglect or lack of affection. There is the same lack of self-esteem, neurosis, guilt, anger. When we have been injured as children, as adults we try to fill the hole in ourselves with substitutes. Unfortunately, there is no substitute for love.

The pimp's brothel was a collection of mobile homes crammed together surrounded by a ten foot fence, a locked gate and a guard tower. Armed guards looked down from the tower and patrolled the brothel's grounds. The place looked like a prison; the pimp called it a "compound." The girls called it a prison and grew to hate the place and its regulations.

Thirty to fifty girls worked at the brothel at one time. The pimp laid down the rules of his house as if they were the Ten Commandments carved in stone. Each girl was required to work twelve hours each day without a break. Each girl was required to work seventeen days straight; if the girl left before her time was up, she was not paid. If a girl's period appeared during the seventeen day sentence, so be it. Girls worked during menstruation, pelvic and back cramps or not, by using a small sea sponge which was inserted into the vagina. After each customer, the blood and semen soaked sponge was removed from the vagina, washed out and inserted into the vagina for the next customer. It was all quite sanitary. And thoughtful.

Each girl's name was daily written on a large piece of white paper which was kept in the kitchen and lorded over by the female manager. With each customer, the girl first obtained the customer's money and then walked to the kitchen. The girl gave the money to the manager who wrote the amount down in the column below the girl's name. Each girl was given a 3 by 5 inch pay card where the manager punched holes in the card for the various amounts written on the white sheet of paper. The girl carried the pay card with her at all times during her shift; if she lost the pay card, she would not be paid for that shift.

Girls were told not to share their personal lives with other prostitutes; they were not to encourage friendships. All the girls used phony names; most of them were afraid former friends and family would learn what they were doing. The girls gave their drivers licenses to their pimps when they were dropped off at the brothel. Girls were not permitted to visit each other in their rooms.

Each girl was given a room about eight feet by ten. At one time, most of the rooms were without bathrooms. Here the girl worked and lived for at least seventeen days. The girls were permitted to leave the brothel only to visit a neighboring bar, where most girls got drunk to forget their lives. If a girl wanted to leave the brothel for any other reason, she had to buy herself out—at one time the fee was $40 per hour. Some girls were willing to pay the fee just to get away from the brothel.

Of each girl's daily gross income, ten per cent off the top went to the brothel for the room and food. The remaining ninety per cent was split with the house. That left the girl with forty-five per cent. From this she paid for supplies: towels, soap, petroleum jelly for intercourse, paper towels, birth control pills, and visits to the doctor for weekly inspections for disease, preventative shots of penicillin and alleged "vitamin" shots, which were given to the girls to keep them from getting too tired to work. The pimp required the girls to go to a particular doctor whom some called Dr. Death. Several girls died following his mysterious injections. Dr. Death's office was dirty, the linens, walls and floors spotted and stained with blood, probably from giving D and C's and abortions.

All this left the girl with maybe thirty-five per cent of her daily earnings. The pimp considered this excessive. He seduced some of his prostitutes into his personal stable by taking them on luxurious trips, taking them to dinner and buying them gifts. After the seduction, the girl became the pimp's exclusive property and gave him the rest of her money. This left these chosen women with nothing but the pimp's promise that he would do them right. Sometimes he did. He paid for the college educations of some girls and bought others houses.

Those girls who were not chosen by the pimp, had pimps who demanded the rest of their earnings. The girls forked-over their money in exchange for a pat on the head and a pimp's comforting lies: "There's no one like you, baby. After we get a good nest egg, we'll quit this, start our own business and be happy ever after." Some pimps had several girls working for them.

The girls generally blew what was left of their earnings on jewelry, booze, dinners and clothing. They didn't save for the future; there was no future; there was only NOW.

The pimp allowed the other pimps to visit their girls at the brothel on Sundays. He charged each pimp $20 an hour to visit his girl. Sort of funny, one pimp paying another pimp.

As the required seventeen day brothel sentence neared its end, the girls grew testy, mean and impatient. They wanted out; they couldn't wait for their required term to end. Twenty-five to fifty men a night really gets on a girl's nerves.

As if this humiliation wasn't enough, the pimp at one time invited girls to participate in a scientific program. The girls were to volunteer to use a new drug, *progonosil*, several drops of which was placed in the vagina. The drug was supposed to prevent venereal disease. Or rather, kill the bacteria and viruses that cause venereal disease. Of course, the girls were not paid for participating in the pimp's experiment. Wouldn't want to spoil them.

The girls were required from time to time to contribute a portion of their earnings to various local charities. Prostitutes as a rule are generous. But they didn't like being ordered to contribute.

The girls were not allowed to watch TV unless the place was empty. It wasn't usually empty until the wee hours of the morning when the local stations signed off. The only outside news the girls got, was from the newspapers brought in by customers.

All of this led the girls to get what was known as the "hooker blues." The girls got drunk at the bar after their shift to kill the blues. They had to get drunk fast because they were only allowed a couple hours at the bar. Then they were off to bed, drunk, and slept until their next shift.

The pimp required each girl to register to vote in Storey County although this is against Nevada law. A brothel is not considered a residence. At election time the girls were given a list of candidates and told who to vote for by the pimp. This was all common knowledge. The Storey County District Attorney did nothing about it. Nor the Attorney General. In Nevada, evil people and institutions are considered cultural institutions. Good people are for prosecuting and humiliating. The worst thing you can do in Nevada, is to bring criminal wrong doing to the attention of the Attorney General. That puts them in the difficult position of having to keep their oaths and do something. Doing something for the People and the State is a lot of trouble.

Girls at the pimp's brothel ranged in age from twenty-one to twenty-four. But there were older women too. Generally as the age increases, the pay decreases. The pimp from time to time brought in underage girls, some as young as fifteen. It was against the law, but who in Storey County would do anything about it? The pimp, of course, denied it.

Each prostitute was allegedly required to apply for a license at the courthouse in Virginia City and was charged a license fee. Storey County didn't require underage girls to be licensed.

Like the prostitute, the pimp is also a victim, though to a lesser degree. Polly Adler, author of *A House Is Not A Home*, explains why:

> *I cannot deny that I mortally hate pimps. Still, in the long run, they are also victims—though not so obviously or so pitifully—along with the girls they exploit. Most of them come from poverty stricken homes, and they acquire their education in the streets and in the pool halls, first out front, then in the back room. Their only talent seems to be that they have a way with women, and they find this out hanging around the dance hall chippies, the drugstore waitress and the high school sweater girls who flaunt their sex and ask for attention.*
>
> *The pimp doesn't feel that he's doing wrong in putting his girls to work. He and the girls are in it together to trim the suckers. He thinks of himself as a smart operator, and sees nothing shameful in exploiting women and living on their earnings...He regards himself as an employer or a property owner, not as a criminal or a parasite...Just as the prostitute never, until the very end, is able to perceive that she is a victim, so the pimp never regards himself as exploited. He would be thunderstruck if it were pointed out to him that he has a miserable life, despised by other men, by madams he meets and deals with, by the underworld and by society. He thinks he is a very clever character, a sharp*

guy, able to make a buck and put up a front...the average pimp becomes an alcoholic and/or a drug addict, and in his last days a panhandler.

The pimp was hounded by the Internal Revenue Service, had wire taps placed on his phones by the Justice Department, convicted of attempted extortion, bribery, perjury and twice for tax evasion, sent to prison and continually entangled in legal battles. All the millions he had made exploiting others, had not made him free nor won him peace of mind. Nor had he truly won society's respect and acceptance which he desperately wanted. And as he grew older, he became tired of the troubles his business caused him. He publicly admitted he wanted to sell his brothel if it would garner enough money to pay his millions in back-taxes and leave him something to live on. It seemed the man who had created a trap for others, was trapped in his own.

The people of Storey County did what they could to get rid of the pimp's corruptive influence on local politicians. They went through voting records and discovered voting registration forms which had been falsified by the pimp's prostitutes under his orders. They brought the information to the U.S. Attorney. A federal Grand Jury was convened but failed to find sufficient evidence to indict the pimp for voting fraud.

They petitioned for a Storey County Grand Jury. The Grand Jury was stacked with the pimp's supporters. It failed to find sufficient evidence to indict the pimp for any crime but concluded he was treated differently from others in Storey County and had unusual influence over county politicians. The Grand Jury did not bring an indictment against anyone for any crime.

The People appealed to Attorney Generals and Governors for help. Nothing was done.

When a Storey County resident questioned the residency of several prostitutes, and filed a legal petition to have their residency verified, the pimp had his prostitutes sue the woman for violation of their civil rights. The woman won her case but it cost her $20,000 in legal fees. The judge ruled she had had every legal right to question the residency of the pimp's prostitutes. But the pimp had made his point: if you cross me you'll pay. Few people in Storey County could afford such large legal fees. Unlike them, the pimp had an unlimited source of money.

And there was fear and intimidation to contend with. Whenever someone spoke against the pimp's corrupting influence in Storey

County they got anonymous phone calls in the night: "You got fire insurance?" or "Do you know where your children are?" Some were afraid Mafia killers would show up in the night and riddle their house with bullets. Or plant a bomb in an opponent's car. These fears were justified. The pimp was Sicilian and authorities had linked him to several Mafia families; the pimp had met with their members at Palm Springs and other places. Some residents feared they would be physically harmed or ostracized if they publicly fought the county corruption. Because of the intimidation and the fear of reprisal, people tended to back-off and did not speak out publicly against it. However, privately they told you how they felt. They wanted the pimp gone. They wanted the crooked politicians gone.

More than once, county employees who voiced opposition to the pimp and the Storey County boys were fired from their county jobs. When anti-prostitution candidates ran against the pimp's politicians, some were threatened and their cars were run off roads in the night. There were rumors of bodies found in shallow desert graves. Perhaps it was paranoia; at least in one instance their fears were justified.

Although the pimp was married, for years he had relationships and affairs with his prostitutes. At least one of these liaisons produced a child. His adultery distressed his wife but she lived with it. Finally there came a day when the wife wanted someone too. She began an affair with a young Argentine boxer, Oscar Bonavena, once the world's fifth ranked heavyweight contender. The boxer's career was not doing well. He liked to gamble and he was not good at it. Bonavena was possibly as self-centered as the pimp. He wanted money, lots of money. He began making brash statements, saying he was going to marry the pimp's wife and take over the brothel. The pimp cherished his whorehouse above all things, including his wife. The boxer could have his wife, but he would be damned if he would rob him of his business that gave him both money and power.

With his vanity and power threatened by his wife's desertion, the pimp vowed to break up the relationship or have Bonavena killed. To his credit, Joe Pastrami encouraged the pimp's bride to go away with her lover until the pimp's anger cooled. But she would not. The pimp put out the word: thousands of dollars would go to the man who killed the boxer. The pimp told confidants the next time the boxer stepped on the brothel's hallowed grounds, he would be killed.

And he was.

On the morning of the killing, Sheriff Dick got the call that the boxer had been shot by a guard in the parking lot outside the brothel. The guard said he shot the boxer in self-defense. The boxer, who never carried a gun, was carrying a gun when he was killed. It was hidden in his boot. Supposedly Bonavena had gone for the gun and the guard popped him with a 30.06 Remington rifle. The guard, an ex-con and an habitual criminal, claimed the boxer had threatened him. Others thought the guard had killed the boxer because he was ordered to and planted the gun in the boxer's boot to make it look like self-defense. The guard was first charged with murder. Charges were afterward dropped to voluntary manslaughter. He was convicted and sentenced to two years in the Nevada State Prison.

There are many strange circumstances about this murder. Willard Ross Brymer, who confessed to the killing, was not seen by an eye-witness at the murder scene. A witness told the cops, "I did not see the one that they booked for shooting [the boxer.] I did not see him any place. I did not see him until at least 30 or 40 minutes after the shooting took place." More importantly, Ross Brymer was legally blind in his right eye. The bullet that killed Bonavena blasted smack through Bonavena's heart—a "clean kill" a paramedic said. It was a very good shot for a man whose brothers always ridiculed for being a very lousy shot.

When the Washoe County sheriff's SWAT team from Reno arrived at the murder scene, the pimp called them "dogs" and ordered them off his property. When a photographer started taking pictures of the victim, guard John Colletti demanded the film—and got it. Lloyd McNulty, Chief guard at the brothel admitted to placing a snubnose .38 under Bonavena's body. No one did anything to McNulty for disturbing a crime scene. And why had McNulty put the gun under the body anyway? By the time the medical examiner showed up, Bonavena's body had been moved. The examiner was unable to accurately determine where the shot had originated from, the angle of gunfire, etc. It all looked real suspicious.

There is sufficient circumstantial evidence that has led many to believe that the murder was a set-up.

The pimp testified during the Brymer trial that he was very, very afraid that Bonavena was going to come to the brothel that night to kill him. Lloyd McNulty and another man, were the usual night guards. But on this particular night, the pimp told McNulty and the second guard to go next door to the old brothel, which was closed and out of business. The pimp brought Brymer and Colletti inside the brothel compound.

The brothel had a lookout tower to oversee the compound and its large parking lot. If the pimp was truly afraid that Bonavena might try to kill him that night, wouldn't it make more sense to keep McNulty and the second guard in the tower, and Brymer and Colletti down below for greater protection? Apparently not. The two guards were told to go to the closed brothel; after Bonavena was killed McNulty was sent for. Lloyd McNulty later told investigators that the pimp had told him, days earlier, to kill Bonavena if he came to the brothel again.

Before the murder, the local Storey County deputy had been informed that the murder was coming down. The deputy drove to Virginia City the evening before the murder, found District Attorney Joe Pastrami and warned him about the murder and asked for help. Joe Pastrami laughed it off. Twelve hours later, Bonavena lay dead in the parking lot of the brothel.

None of this came out during Brymer's trial, nor in the newspapers, nor did the pimp's wife nor McNulty testify at Brymer's trial.

The pimp said Bonavena had come to the brothel to kill him. The guards had only protected him. But Bonavena knew the pimp was protected by armed ex-felons who were usually by his side. He knew the brothel was well protected with a ten foot fence, sound alarm system, that it was full of weapons, a virtual arsenal—two AR-15s semi-automatic rifles, three 12-gauge shotguns, a Mace gun and sidearms in the hands of the pimp's guards—very dangerous men. Only a fool would go to the brothel looking for trouble—or a drunk. And Bonavena wasn't drunk at the time of his death. The autopsy proved that; his blood alcohol level was .07.

The pimp was his usual self at the murder scene that awful morning. He pointed to Bonavena's body as the blood oozed from the wound and coagulated on the pavement, "So we got a dead man here, so what?" Then he ordered his prostitutes to keep his whorehouse open and offered free drinks to his customers while he went inside and chowed down to a home cooked chicken dinner. He acted typically psychopathic. "I just had a nice big meal, the best meal I've had in months," he said. "Now I'm going to get some sleep and a good f—." The pimp was happy. Bonavena was dead and out of the picture; the pimp would keep control of his brothel.

Added to this is the fact Bonavena, several days before his death, stated to the Argentine Consulate in San Francisco, that the pimp had threatened to kill him just days earlier. Bonavena put the statement in writing, signed and dated it. The statement was entered into evidence during the Brymer trial.

Even more incredible, Joe Pastrami, was more or less acting as the pimp's attorney at the time of the murder. Rural Nevada district attorneys are permitted use of their county offices for private practice. During the prosecution of Ross Brymer, District Attorney Joe Pastrami at no time made the court aware that the pimp had told him, just days before the murder, that he was going to have the boxer killed. And there is some question as to why Joe Pastrami dropped the charge against Brymer from murder to manslaughter. And if you read the trial transcript, it is obvious the District Attorney was not aggressive in his prosecution of the alleged killer. If not outright conspiracy to commit murder, Joe Pastrami's prosecution of the alleged murderer was unethical and a conflict of interest. At the very least, he should have disqualified himself from the prosecution. Instead, Joe Pastrami protected the pimp and buried the murder.

Five years later Ovid Demaris in his book *The Last Mafioso*, published a conversation between the pimp and Jimmy Fratiano, a well known Mafia figure. The conversation had taken place less than two weeks before the murder of Oscar Bonavena. The pimp had flown Fratiano to Reno for a chat about the problems he was having with his wife and her lover Bonavena.

The pimp said to Fratiano, "...I've a little piece of work I'd like done. How do you feel about icing a woman? Did you ever ice one before?"

"...don't come up with them questions. What are you, a prosecutor? Are you talking about [your wife.]"

"Let's say it's [my wife.]. Now I'm not saying it is, you understand, I'm just trying to get a ballpark figure. Would ten thousand do it?"

"Let's lay it out in the open...If it's [your wife] it's going to be one hundred grand. Think it over and let me know and I'll let you know."

"I'd like to have it done in South America. She's going on a trip with Bonavena."

"Forget South America. We can do it right here, bury her and nobody'll ever find her."

"Well, let me think about it. A hundred is your rock bottom figure?"

"Yeah, but I wouldn't wait too long if I was you. Somebody else might get the same idea about you, know what I mean?"

Even after this was published, the murder case was not reopened by Attorney General Richard Bryan, afterward Governor of Nevada, and today U.S. Senator.

Possibly most bizarre in all this, was the inaction of Robert List, the Nevada Attorney General at the time of Bonavena's murder and later Governor of Nevada. Attorney General List had sound reasons to enter the case and take over the prosecution of Brymer. But he never did. It was common knowledge amongst law enforcement that the Storey County District Attorney, Sheriff and several Commissioners were receiving payoffs from the pimp. The pimp had said he controlled Storey County officials publicly. He had boasted of it many, many times.

The pimp had publicly stated that he was going to have Oscar Bonavena killed. He told Bonavena to his face that he was a "walking dead man." The pimp had even told District Attorney Joe Pastrami that he was going to have Bonavena killed. There were witnesses present. The authorities had a signed and dated document by Bonavena saying he had been threatened by the pimp. During the investigation a witness came forward and told the cops he heard the pimp offer money to anyone who would kill Bonavena. After the witness went to the cops, the pimp threatened the witness; the witness fled the state. An honest Storey County deputy hunted him down. The witness was scared out of his wits. He didn't want to testify now. He didn't want to get killed.

But perhaps most suspect is what District Attorney Joe Pastrami and Sheriff Del Monte told Storey County Undersheriff Jim Miller, the chief investigator for the case. Miller was honest, diligent, with many years in law enforcement. Pastrami and Del Monte told Miller up front that he was not to bring in outside investigators on the case. They meant specifically he was not to bring in men from the Nevada Department of Investigation, the investigative unit for the Attorney General. Miller told the boys he could not handle the investigation alone. He *needed* outside help. He was going to bring in outside help. And he did. Afterward, Miller received threatening phone calls from the pimp and his psychopathic goons. One evening someone planted marijuana plants in his front yard; the next day he got a call from the Nevada Department of Investigation; they had received an anonymous tip about Miller growing marijuana.

At one point, Miller met the pimp with a federal agent at the pimp's whorehouse. Willard Ross Brymer was in the room. The pimp was angry at Miller. He said to Miller. "I'm really tired of the trouble you've been causing me. I'm gonna have Brymer kill you." Brymer shut the door to the pimp's office, and standing in front of it, drew out a long hunting knife. Miller reached for his gun, pulled it and pointed it at the pimp. "Listen you dumb son-of-a-bitch. You tell Brymer to put that thing away or I'm going to kill him and then I'm going to kill you." The pimp's eyes flamed.

"All right Brymer. Let him go." And the two law officers left the room. The federal agent filed a report. Nothing was done.

For months afterward, Undersheriff Miller and his wife got more threats over the phone. For the next several years Miller's wife carried a gun at all times. The stress eventually caused the marriage to collapse.

Attorney General Robert List had legal right to enter the case and take over the prosecution of Brymer. The Attorney General is the chief law enforcement officer in Nevada. Nevada state law NRS 228.170 stipulates that the Attorney General can take over the prosecution of any crime, in any county, in any court if he believes it is necessary. NRS 228.120 gives the Attorney General supervisory powers over all county district attorneys and can require them to report as to the condition of public business entrusted to their charge.

Furthermore, NRS 228.170 allows the Governor to order the Attorney General to take over a prosecution. Governor Mike O' Callaghan never ordered Attorney General List to take over the prosecution of Ross Brymer. List did not intervene. And though their was substantial evidence to indict and prosecute the pimp, District Attorney Joe Pastrami and Sheriff Del Monte for conspiracy to commit murder, Attorney General List took no action. Diligent Nevada law enforcement officers and criminal attorneys found the inaction of the Attorney General and the Governor incredulous. The author wrote to Governor List and questioned him about the Bonavena case. List never responded.

The murder of Oscar Bonavena and the haphazard investigation and prosecution infuriated many in Storey County. Prostitution maybe all right some said, but the the pimp had to go. He was bringing ridicule to Storey County; he was making the People look like fools.

In spite of the murder of Oscar Bonavena and the increased notoriety, legalized prostitution remained a controversial issue in Storey County which provoked strong feelings on both sides. Some believed prostitution was a hold-over from the wild West that should be left alone. They considered prostitution a fact of life in rural Nevada. They accepted it as if it were horse shoes. Their argument was simple and seemed reasonable:

"Listen, those girls put themselves there. No one forces them. So if they're up for a price, it's their fault."

"It maybe true. But do you know what got them there, and what *really* motivates them?"

"No. It's none of my business. We've had whorehouses in Nevada since the 1860's. Why change it now? It's these new people moving into the state that want to change things. If they don't like the way we do things here, they can leave."

The common consensus seemed to be, if prostitution was going to be around, the realistic thing to do was to license the girls and see that they were regularly inspected by doctors to prevent the spread of venereal disease. Putting them in a legal brothel kept them off the streets and in one place where they could be protected and controlled. Storey County politicians pointed to the money the pimp's license fees and "bed taxes" put in the Storey County treasury, not much, maybe $160,000 a year, but nearly ten percent of the county's operating budget.

In spite of this thinking, while living in Storey County I never heard a proponent of legalized prostitution offer their sister, wife, daughter or mother to work in the pimp's whorehouse. It may have been all right if other men's daughters were whores, but it was not all right for their daughters. These proponents, mostly men, considered the prostitute a useful robot that dispensed sex like a soda machine. A prostitute was not truly human and she did not have the wants and needs of other humans. Proponents of legalized prostitution did not care—or were unaware of what these girls had gone through as children and teenagers, and what they now went through as adult prostitutes: a continued loss of self-esteem; increased emotional pain caused by the social isolation and loneliness of prostitution; the high number of suicides; drug addiction to escape the pain of their lives; the possibility of getting beat up or murdered by customers and pimps; the looming threat of cancer which seemed to afflict prostitutes to a greater degree than other women; acquiring disease or transmitting disease to customers who invariably infected innocent women. Although the pimp said his brothel was perfectly safe, newspaper stories of venereal diseased prostitutes and customers told otherwise.

CHAPTER TWENTY–THREE

My Pal, Sheriff Dick

You cannot make men good by law: and without good men you cannot have a good society. C.S. Lewis

By and by I was overcome with moral conscience. I still had this ridiculous idea that a county Sheriff should be honest and serve the people, rather than serve a pimp, and that a competent District Attorney should root out miscreants and prosecute them rather than shovel whisky down his craw at the local saloon and publicly brag how much he was being paid to not upset the pimp's den of corruption.

No one in Storey County had recently written about the corruption. I thought I should change that. I understood I was headed for trouble with dangerous people. If they had run a woman off the road for running for District Attorney, and if they had been involved with murder, I could imagine what they would do when I wrote that Sheriff Dick, Joe Pastrami and a couple Commissioners were crooks.

But I cared about my friends and Virginia City was our home now. I wanted to do my part to make it a better place. I thought I could do something to change the corruption.

I was an idiot. My wife warned me to stay out of it. Friends warned me to stay out of it. But no. I was a man, and a stubborn one, and I was deep in the throe of a mid-life identity crisis in search of Truth and Meaning. I hopped on my crusade like Don Quixote leaped on his nag. Unlike that dear man I was without the horse; but my eyes were open and my weapon was a pen rather than a lance.

I told the people I was going to war against the Storey County crooks and I asked for their help. The people were all out of juice; they had tried to get rid of the corruption and they had failed. I should have taken notice of that. But no. Instead, I said I was going to recall District Attorney Joe Pastrami. I even went up to the courthouse and learned how to do it.

Then one night I went down to the morgue and vented what I knew would be an unpopular point of view. In *"Something's Rotten In The Courthouse,"* I told the people that the pimp had not paid his "bed taxes" recently, quite a large sum to that poor county, and that Sheriff Dick and Joe Pastrami weren't likely to do anything about it. And if anyone published the truth about what was happening in the county they were likely to get in trouble for it. In part I wrote:

> *"Now George, you know what it says right there in the County Commissioners' chambers, that flag on the wall, 'TRUTH CON-QUERS ALL.'"*
> *"Listen pal, if Truth ever walked into that courthouse, it would be shot in the back of the head or pulverized with a baseball bat."*
> *"That so?"*
> *"Yeah pal, that is so."*

> *Any people who allow their government to be controlled by pimps...ought to have their heads examined.*

This comment made me notorious in some quarters, but in the hind quarters, I was voted most likely to be shoved down the nearest mine shaft.

No. I could not be content with that trouble. I had to go looking for more. I attacked the county Commissioners' favoritism to long time residents and businessmen. Those who had received preferential treatment were furious. And some of them came looking for me at the Union Brewery Saloon.

"Why don't you mind your own business," Bob said to me, the son of a Commissioner. He stood rigid, face flushed, fists tight.

"I made it my business."

"Our family's lived here for generations. We've paid our dues," he said.

"So you should be treated better because you've lived here longer?"

"Well..." he said.

"Well," I asked.

"We've paid our dues up here."

"Everyone pays their dues. That's the way the world is."

"Well," he said.

"Julie, get Bob a beer on me." Julie pulled out the beer, opened it and slid it across the bar. Bob lifted it and started to drink.

I turned to Bob. "I know you're angry. You think I meant to insult your family. I didn't. All I was trying to say, is that everyone up here should be treated equally by the county boys. That's all. I only used your family and other families' names because it does seem to me, you folks are treated differently than some newcomers. Wouldn't you like to be treated fairly if you moved somewhere else and no one knew you?"

"Well, sure."

"Well, that's all I was saying."

Bob drank his beer and I talked and tried to calm him down. His body relaxed. He leaned on the bar easily. Finally he said, "You know what they're afraid of?"

"I have an idea."

"They're afraid you're going to blow it wide open about them and they don't want it. They think you're crazy enough to do it."

"Or I care enough," I said.

The Storey County boys reacted predictably and immediately to all this. They wanted the *Voice* dead. They wanted me dead. They wanted to shut up the troublemaker. But how? They talked about suing for libel. They didn't have a leg to stand on and I knew it. And they knew it. I had told the truth. I would have liked getting those boys in a court under oath—if that would have mattered—and have them explain their various crimes and conspiracies. But I wasn't so lucky. They dropped that idea and came up with others.

It is easier to topple one man than a group of men. There are ways to demoralize a man's efforts. One way is to threaten his life or the lives of his wife and children. That was done. Hate mail and phone calls are useful. We got those. The Darkness wanted to express itself. And it did.

Let me show you how small town politicians subvert freedom of speech: The courthouse politicians and Ol' Al and the School Board organized and came up with an idea: destroy my credibility and the *Voice's* credibility. The communists are good at this and the boys in Virginia City were good at it too. The best way to ruin anyone's credibility in a small town is to begin a rumor. A single rumor is crippling; a second rumor is devastating. The accused has no idea of what is being said and is unable to defend himself before his peers. You are a defendant who is tried for an unknown crime without an attorney. Once credibility is damaged it is hard to restore. The politicians began their guerilla warfare campaign with lies, rumors and innuendo. In all our lives we have never had more untrue things said about our characters. But I will forget that.

The law too, can be a handy tool when infuriated small town souls want to make your life unhappy. We rented our office and we were not responsible for the building complying with county building and fire codes. This now became a problem for us. The local fire marshal, a Virginia City red-neck who was not fond of my opinions, got a phone call from the County Clerk, a friend of his.The County Clerk's husband was the President of the School Board against whom I had filed criminal complaints for falsifying school records and denying access to public records during my Al Ricardo campaign. The President and his board had nothing to worry about. Joe Pastrami wouldn't have prosecuted those guys if they had committed murder. The County Clerk wasn't happy with me for assaulting her husband in print.

Anyway, hell hath no fury like a woman insulted. The County Clerk told the fire marshal that she believed our office was not up to fire code. It was none of her business, but no matter. The fire marshal arrived one morning to inspect our office. We had rented the old morgue for two years. Now the fire marshal had suddenly developed the compulsion to inspect it. It was obvious what his real intentions were. To no surprise he discovered serious fire code violations of which he informed us. Some of these violations he had permitted a neighboring business to get by with. But he would not do so for us. He told us we would have to correct the violations or vacate the office. As renters, it was the landlord's responsibility to bring the office up to code. He wouldn't do it. He was trying to sell the building.

There was little office space in Virginia City, something the County Clerk and the fire marshal were aware of. It looked like the *Virginia City Voice* was dead. But not quite. A local businessman gave us an office rent free. He wanted to help keep the *Voice* afloat. I'd publish his name here except I don't want to see him shot or hanged. We moved into the new office, but by now the wear and tear of putting out a free paper, and embroiling myself in all sorts of controversies had worn me out.

And besides, my pal Sheriff Dick wasn't happy with me. I was nosing around and writing things I shouldn't. Sheriff Dick and a couple of his deputies suddenly took an extreme interest in my well being and my residency in their town. And I suppose here's where I should tell you about Sheriff Dick because he was going to cause us a lot of trouble.

Sheriff Dick Del Monte came from an influential family in Virginia City and was well liked by most. His father had served on the County Commissioners for years and had been as close to the pimp as a brother, "loyal as a German Shepherd," the pimp had said of him. Wonderful comparison. After Sheriff Dick's father died, Sheriff Dick's mother became a Commissioner—with the pimp's help, of course. Sheriff Dick had served three, four year terms and had just been reelected for a fourth. No one wanted to run against Sheriff Dick because everyone knew he would get elected no matter what.

He was fifty-ish, with more weight above his waist than below and had the lop-sided shape middle-aged men sometimes acquire. He had sandy brown hair and mustache. A slightly ruddy complexion warned you he had a temper and when it exploded there would be trouble. He was fanatically vain and chronically over-sensitive. Sheriff Dick didn't wear the khaki uniforms like his deputies. He wore jeans and a plaid shirt with his pistol strapped around his waist. Before becoming Sheriff, Dick was a fry cook. Sheriff Dick's main duty was to drive up and down C Street twice a day, smile and wave at tourists and then jump all over business people for minor infractions.

As far as his public duties went, Sheriff Dick was fairly amiable, direct and firm, and if someone got out of line he tried talking to the offender as a good county sheriff might. And if that didn't do it, Sheriff Dick laid into the offender with thunder.

After his election, he teamed up with the pimp and his voting machinery. There were some who thought Sheriff Dick was never comfortable with himself afterward. And when the pimp bribed Sheriff Dick, it made the pimp feel powerful to have a lawman in his pocket. This was something Sheriff Dick was not proud of and he was highly sensitive about others discovering it. Some in the community were aware of Sheriff Dick's mistake but they did not hold it against him. In fact, many were proud Sheriff Dick was pals with the pimp. The pimp was a celebrity and they liked their Sheriff rubbing shoulders with him. They accepted Sheriff Dick's predicament as naturally as the sunrise.

While Sheriff Dick harangued pitiful business people about their minor infractions—these who earned a fair living in summer and nearly starved in winter, whose collected sales taxes put thousands of dollars in a poor county treasury, local drug dealers did a landslide business but Sheriff Dick did nothing. The pimp was late in paying his "bed" tax, quite a large sum to this poor county; Sheriff Dick and Joe Pastrami did nothing. Sheriff Dick's laxity in these matters didn't bother most, but it bothered me.

After my latest editorial eruption, I had friends who were afraid for our lives. They said I should remember Nancy Ann Leeder and the murdered boxer. A friend had overheard someone say, "There are guys driving around with guns who want to blow Williams' f—king head off for what he's written."

"Suppose his wife and children are with him?"

"That's their problem."

I contemplated this for a long while and concluded it might be a good idea to start wearing a gun. This led to an interesting conversation with Sheriff Dick the day after my latest editorial appeared. I ran into Sheriff Dick at the Delta Saloon parking lot on the main drag.

"Dick," I said, "I'd like to get a concealed weapon permit. I'm sorta worried about protecting my family."

"What?" he barked. His face flamed a beautiful raspberry, "give you a concealed weapon permit? I'll never give you a weapon permit."

"Gee, why's that?" I played stupid.

"Why? I think you're a gah-damn lunatic, that's why. I think you're crazy. I think you should see a psychopath."

"Dick, you mean a *psychiatrist*."

"Wuh, huh, well—yeah. That's what I mean. You should see a gah-damn psychiatrist. You're f—kin' crazy. That's what I think."

"Gee, why do you say that?"

"Why? I'll tell you why. Because of that gah-damn scandal sheet you publish. Who the hell do you think you are? You think you're better than us? I think you're crazy as hell. I'll bet not ten people on this street will speak to you after what you've written." Dick was wrong. I had talked with ten people in the last hour.

"Williams, you're nothing but a gah-damn troublemaker."

"I must be doing something right. Good men are always trouble."

"Horse shit."

"Listen Dick, I have obeyed your laws. I have never been violent. Exercising my First Amendment rights doesn't make me crazy. And I could care less about your opinion of my paper."

"I still think you're crazy and I'll never give you a concealed weapon permit. You can make an application and pay your twenty-five dollars, but I'll never give you a permit."

"Ah, come on Dick. I won't shoot anyone that doesn't need it."

"You're f—kin' crazy."

"All right. Forget the gun. Can I carry a spear?"

"You f—kin' lunatic. You should be locked up."

"I'd bet you'd like that."

"Screw you," Dick said.

Dick turned and started toward his patrol car. I followed him. I reached out my opened arms toward him.

"Don't go away mad, Dick. Let's make up. I thought we were pals?"

Dick got into his patrol car and slammed the door. "F—k you, you asshole." He fired up the engine. I walked over to his car, bent down and leaned toward his face.

"Sure you won't change your mind about that permit Dick?"

"Double f—k you, you lunatic."

"Ah Dick, I love you. You're a nutty, fun guy."

"*F—k you*," Dick sang as his car roared out the parking lot.

Sheriff Dick seemed a little under the weather. Maybe I should ask about the gun permit another day.

Some time later the United States Attorney took an interest in the pimp's effect on Storey County and began an investigation. It is a wonder what happens when the power of the Federal law begins poking its nose around. During the investigation, one Storey County Commissioner resigned, sold his house and left the state. Another Commissioner was beaten at the voting polls. For a time it seemed, there was hope for Storey County. Maybe the People and Democracy might beat the pimp after all.

To live in the Washoe Mountains and stay perfectly sane, you needed to develop a keen sense of humor and an awesome tolerance for human nature. I was good natured enough and tolerant of most anything, except my murder and the murder of my family. I thought a cooling off period was a good idea before I got myself and my family killed.

Besides, I had other things to do. I had a couple new books I was researching and writing. It was as good an excuse as any to get out of Dodge. Let the Storey County boys have the first round. Let them think they had shut up the troublemaker. To hell with them for now. I would be back and finish what I had started. Later.

It was mid-August and hot. I had sent my wife and children to Nebraska for their safety. I closed our office, hitched our camping trailer to the pick-up and pulled out of Virginia City. I drove a hundred miles south to Bridgeport, California below the high, cool peaks of the Eastern Sierra and pitched camp beside a hot spring. And there beside a lovely pool of warm green water, proceeded to relieve myself of my misery by embarking on a three day pity party. I meditated on my foolishness.

"What have you been doing? What did it matter? Where will you live now?"

I was wounded. I was discouraged. I was as lonesome as Noah in his Ark, floating around in an empty sea knowing his former pals were all dead and missing them. I rested and I forgot.

Then on the fourth day, like Lazarus, I rose from the dead and tried to be a Human Being again.

PART FOUR

Into the Wilderness

CHAPTER TWENTY–FOUR

Into the Wilderness

To write a book felicitously a man needs to be delightlyfully circumstanced & entirely free from cares, interruptions & annoyances.
Mark Twain at Hartford to Dan De Quille in Virginia City, March 29, 1875

When I was a boy we lived in a rural neighborhood in Southwestern Massachusetts. Across the street from our house was another row of houses. But beyond the houses there was a thick New England woods of maples and oaks and the slender white bodies of birches. That woods was full of wonders for a curious boy. Blueberries grew in the summer on stout bushes out of the black loam. Grey squirrels lived in the great oaks and made nests of leaves in the crooks of the tall trees. I gasped when the squirrels leaped from one high bough to another. There were nests of yellow-jackets in tree hollows or in the ground and we always troubled the nests and were repeatedly stung as a reward. I remember how my eye swelled shut when a yellow-jacket nailed me for troubling him and his relatives. The bee stings never seemed to deter us and we went back for trouble whenever we needed it.

There was the musty smell of the dry brown leaves we tramped through like drifts of snow and the swishing of feet through the leaves. Bright green moss thick as a chocolate cake grew around the broad bases of gray tree trunks. White toadstools plunged their domed heads out of the black loam; we kicked off their tops for fun. Strange creatures made cocoons on the slender branches of bushes and we broke them open to discover what lived inside.

There was a pond in the woods beneath low tree covered hills that was the home of various slimy, wiggly things. Our gang swam in the pond in summer and collected pollywogs, frogs, salamanders and turtles and carried them home in jars. Wild grapes grew in the white sand around the pond and when we were hungry we picked them and brushed the dust from the grapes on our already dirty T-shirts and ate the sweet, violet-skinned fruit with their jasper-green inner meat, being careful to spit out the bitter seeds.

I loved that woods and when I could not get a few boys to explore it, I went there by myself and climbed the birches to their tips and made them bend me to the ground. There were hidden places in the woods we called forts and they were known to a few boys and were not known to our parents. I spent the best years of my childhood in that woods exploring its mysteries. It was a good place. It was quiet except for the squawking of blue-jays or the cawing of crows or the squeels squirrels made when a human invaded their neighborhoods. I never forgot the peace of the woods. I learned that if you avoided people and stuck close to nature, life was simple and less dangerous.

When I was a young teenager we lived in northern Montana below the great blue skies where slender creeks wound through the gullies of the forever rolling hills, and like the New England woods, there was peace in the hills of Montana. And later I knew the openness of the Southern California desert.

I was tired of people and trouble. I wanted to be in the open spaces and away. I had started two new books. Autumn would be here soon and I wanted some place without distractions and trouble for winter. I called my wife in Nebraska.

"I've come down to Bridgeport. I need a rest. I want to finish the book about the hot springs and the one about Twain on Jackass Hill. There's an apartment for rent. I was thinking about renting it and staying here for the winter. Whataya think?"

"Rent it. I've had it with the aggravation up there. I warned you didn't I," she said.

"Yes. You're always right about this stuff. There's nothing I can do about it now."

"No, I suppose not. Couldn't you see what it would lead to?"

"I was a fool."

"Some things *you* can't change."

"I suppose so," I said.

"Now there are people that want to kill us because of what you've written. I'm worried about the children. I'm worried about us. I don't want anything bad to happen."

"I know," I said.

"You did the right thing. But I knew it would lead to trouble."

"Are you done with your visit," I asked.

"We'll fly into Reno next Tuesday at 3:30 in the afternoon your time. Rent the apartment. I want you to get back to writing your books. You need that now. We'll stay in Bridgeport for winter. I always liked

Bridgeport. But promise me you'll stay out of this small town political stuff."

"I promise," I said. And I always meant to keep my promises, too.

"I love you," I said.

"I love you, too. See you soon," and we hung up.

Things can't possibly be any worse in Bridgeport. Virginia City and the trouble were a hundred miles away. That seemed a safe distance. My stomach felt empty in the hollow below my sternum as it always feels when I'm making the wrong decision and fooling myself. It is unfortunate we cannot tell the future. I would have known how much trouble Sheriff Dick was about to send us down in Mono County.

CHAPTER TWENTY—FIVE

Bridgeport Valley

Bridgeport Valley lays green and peaceful at 6500 feet at the foot of the Sierra Nevada on the extreme eastern edge of California. The wall of the Sierra mountains rises another five thousand feet above the valley some stony peaks snow capped in late summer. The Sierra forms a barrier between eastern and western California. The valley is nearly surrounded by mountains that send down their melted snow in creeks and streams that twist through the valley and make it green in spring and summer. Opposite the western wall of the Sierra are the lower volcanic and pine nut studded Bodie Hills. The steep dark Sweetwater Mountains make a barrier to the northeast. High sagebrush covered foothills are to the south. You enter the valley from the north through a high mountain pass called Devil's Gate and leave it in the south over Conway Pass at 8100 feet. Or you can take a road from Bridgeport that heads east fifteen miles to the Nevada border.

The Paiute Indians migrated to the valley for thousands of years before the white men. In spring and summer they caught wild brown trout in the creeks and lakes. In the autumn they hunted the mule deer. The Paiutes were as familiar with the deer trails as we are with our neighborhood streets. In the spring the mule deer migrate from the desert valleys where they have spent winter and head up to the high country for summer. In the valley and mountains the deer find lush meadow grass and water in streams and lakes. The Paiute hunters hid beside the deer trails in autumn when the mule deer fled from the high country. They killed the deer with their obsidian tipped arrows and spears as the deer passed them.

While their men hunted, the Paiute women and children collected pine nuts in the hills above the valley. They laid blankets of rabbit and deer skins around the stout pine nut trees. They struck the pine cones with long sticks and the pine nuts, about the size of deer droppings, scattered on the blankets and were gathered. The Paiute women stored the valued pine nuts for the long winters in deer and rabbit skins or in willow baskets. Often they used a portion to feed their men when they returned from hunts. Hidden in the sagebrush of the valley near creeks and streams you can still find large, flat granite slabs, with fist-size, circular holes called *metates* where the Paiute women mashed the pine nuts with stone mortars. The women used the mashed nuts to make a meal that is delicious and very rich in protein. These granite slabs are found in the ancient Paiute campgrounds that were used perennially for centuries. The ancient campgrounds contain large "chipping" areas where the Paiute men chipped and hammered obsidian—it looks like very shiny black glass—into arrow heads and spear points. The chipping grounds are sometimes as large as our football fields. The black obsidian flakes left behind by the Paiutes centuries ago shine brightly on the pale sand under the high Sierra sun. If you are lucky sometimes you may find a complete arrow or spear head, and often broken or incomplete heads.

Sagebrush covered Bridgeport Valley before white men came and chopped it down and burned the barn-sized piles of sagebrush and smoked up the valley. The ranchers planted grasses to feed the cattle they imported to the valley. They carved the valley into sections and strung it up with barbed-wire and cut water ditches to irrigate the grasslands. Today the largest portion of the valley is still owned by cattle ranchers whose split wooden posts and barbed-wire fences line the roads across the valley. In spring and summer the valley has more cattle than people.

Bridgeport was born in the early 1860's when gold and silver were discovered at Aurora, Nevada, on the extreme western edge of Nevada about 40 miles from Bridgeport. When it was discovered that Aurora was in Nevada, the Mono County seat was moved from Aurora to Bridgeport. Bridgeport became a tiny trading center when the nearby gold mining town of Bodie boomed in 1878. A wooden two story courthouse was built in 1880 on Main Street, today's Highway 395. It is a typical Victorian public building, two stories high with ornate window and door moldings, a huge double front door and rooms with high ceilings that are a nightmare to heat in winter. The courthouse is painted white with scorching red trim. A green lawn carpets the courthouse grounds and the whole lot is surrounded by a black iron fence. A black cannon sits on the front lawn. The courthouse is the center of town and the pride of the community. Nearly every visitor wants its photograph.

When the last of the Bodie gold mines shut down during World War I, Bridgeport felt the loss of business. By the 1930's Bodie had become a ghost town. In 1962 California made Bodie a California State Park and National Historic Site. Ironically, these many years later, Bridgeport still profits from Bodie; the Park attracts hundreds of thousands of visitors each year. Many stop in Bridgeport for food, lodging, camping and fishing supplies. The Sierra streams and lakes around Bridgeport are popular fishing and boating spots and there are several federal and private camp grounds.

The high country above the valley is wild with black bears, mountain lions and big horn sheep; and the foothills have deer, coyotes, foxes, jack rabbits, rattle and gopher snakes, field mice, beaver and ground squirrels. Brown hawks sit on telephone poles along the highway. Vultures, black against the blue sky with their jaggedly cut wings, circle above the valley. In the spring, men haul sheep and cattle into the high meadows where the grass is long, moist and green. The cattle are allowed to roam the mountains unattended. But the sheep have to be looked after. Poor Spanish speaking shepherds live in small camping trailers in the high country from spring to early autumn. The shepherds spend hour upon solitary hour watching over the rich men's sheep with a dog or two. To amuse themselves they carve their names with jackknives into the soft grey skins of aspens that darken the high canyons. As the years pass and the aspens fatten, the carvings widen into thick black marks on the trees. Some carvings go back a century.

From time to time the shepherd's blood rushes when he must shoot a coyote that has killed a lamb and there is always the danger of black bears and mountain lions that come down from the higher country to feed on the sheep. Sometimes the sheep ranchers hire a professional hunter to track down and kill the renegades. And sometimes at night the shepherds use a tool the rancher leaves him, a sort of automatic cannon that booms each minute and scares the mountain lions and bears away from the sheep.

Toward the first of October, the cowboys ride into the mountains and roundup the cattle and steer them toward the lower country. The cattle and sheep are stuffed into double-decked trucks and hauled to Nevada valleys for winter.

The summers in the high country are wonderfully bright and the sky is very blue. In late summer black thunderheads hover above the mountains and storm the valley in the afternoons and the valley is alive and fresh with the pungent wet smell of the sagebrush. The September frosts kill the summer grass and the green meadows become dead and brown. The aspens in the high canyons first turn to gold, then to red, then brown as the autumn deepens. And with the first good snow fall everything is made white and cold.

CHAPTER TWENTY-SIX

The Town

The village of Bridgeport is six blocks long and four blocks wide. Along Main Street, which is a highway there are several motels, four gas stations, two grocery stores, a part-time bakery, one bank, a gift shop, three sporting goods stores, one county museum, four restaurants and a volunteer fire department. It is a wooden town of steep pitched frame cottages and narrow two stories. The Mono County courthouse is in the center of town. Bridgeport is the seat of Mono County and several County buildings are located on a back street, the Sheriff's Department and the jail. The post office is on another back street where people pick up their mail from locked boxes. There is an elementary school, but the junior high and high school are thirty-five miles north at Coleville. Mono General Hospital is on the north side of town and provides limited services. Once it was a full service hospital where operations were performed and women had babies. That is all gone now.

Maybe four hundred people live in town. Most are employed by various government agencies. Being the county seat, a large number work for the Mono County in the courthouse. Cal-Trans employs a number of men to repair highways. The Forest Service has a station where about fifty are employed. What these folks do in winter is a mystery; some say they hibernate like the bears. The California Highway Patrol has an office on Main Street. Once a month the California Department of Motor Vehicles sets up shop to meet the needs of locals.

The Paiute Indian reservation is east of town where about twenty families live in modular housing built by the Government.

The rest of the people either run small businesses or are employed by one. There is one plumber; and one heavy equipment operator digs footings for new houses and trenches for septic systems. The economy is based on tourism and various government payrolls. The tourist season begins in late April with the opening of fishing season and ends in October after deer hunting.

Thirty miles away the Marines have a Mountain Warfare Training Center at Pickle Meadows at the foot of the Sonora Pass. The burr headed Marines used to be a familiar sight in town and brought in a lot of money for the local businesses. That was before a few town fathers decided they didn't like the Marines in town. The Marines were going to build family housing in Bridgeport on land donated by the Bureau of Land Management. A few town fathers didn't like the idea of their daughters dating Marines. It never occurred to them that the Marines would be married. The patriotic town fathers complained to a local county Supervisor who wrote a letter to the Marines and told them they should build their family housing elsewhere.

The Marines did as they were asked and built their family housing forty-five miles north near Topaz Lake. And they took 14 million good American dollars with them. The local businesses could have used those 14 million Marine dollars in the dead of winter. Because for six months the local businesses make a fair living from tourists; and the other six months they nearly starve. Apparently, the larger souls in the community would rather starve than have the Marines around.

Being situated in the isolated wilderness, you must have a good reason to live in Bridgeport. If you don't work for a government agency, or run a business or work for one, then you are retired, disabled or unemployed and soon to leave town. The locals like the wilderness and they like living away from cities and people. They are quiet people who keep to themselves and are highly selective of whom they share their lives and secrets. They are highly independent, clannish, self-reliant, and hence their marriages drop like flies. The isolation, severe winters, poor economy and lack of social activities have a disastrous effect on families.

Men seem to handle the isolation better than women. The men have things to amuse themselves, like fishing and killing defenseless animals with high powered canons big enough to bring down King Kong with a single round. But the women have nowhere to shop and grow tired of the ninety mile drive back and forth to Bishop or Carson City for food shopping and K-Mart. Groceries were high because the food was hauled in a long distance and the local stores could not buy large quantities to lower the unit price. Rather than support the local stores, the townspeople made a hundred and eighty mile round trip each week to do their shopping and get a break from the small town.

We rented an upstairs apartment in Bridgeport across from the courthouse. I hauled in my word processor and got ready to write for the winter. I had started writing about Mark Twain when he was up in Jackass Hill across the Sonora Pass. I planned trips across the Pass until it closed with the first snowfall. I was also exploring Mono County for recreational hot springs and writing a guide book. Mono County is full of geothermal activity.

A large window faced southwest and the bright mountain sun was warm on fall and winter mornings and the living room was a bright and cheerful place to write. In October the tourists went away and the traffic through town dropped off. We lay in our bed at night next to the wall that faced Main Street and listened to the drunks argue as they left the bar next door. The diesels roared past on the highway and their big engines rattled the windows. It had been a long time since we lived in an apartment, not since we were first married. It would only be for the winter we said. Next summer we would camp in the mountains and go back to Virginia City in the autumn. And there I would finish the crusade I had unwisely begun.

CHAPTER TWENTY–SEVEN

Morning Walk

It was winter now and when we looked out our windows the valley floor was all white and the mountains were white except for the darkening of the pine nut trees. The town trees were stripped of leaves; the water had frozen to the limbs and now the trees glistened like crystal pieces in a glass blower's shop. This morning the sky was clear and blue and I knew it would be colder without the low lying clouds that seemed to warm the wide open valley. While my wife and children slept I pulled a sock cap over my ears and put on my long winter overcoat with the fur lined hood. I zipped the front and tied the cord around my neck that tightened the hood around my head and pulled on my gloves. I walked down the stairs of our second floor apartment feeling the cold in the stairway come through my pants and I knew it would be very cold in the early morning outside. My breath became white puffs when I made the sidewalk. The highway was white with snow and reflected brightly like a mirror where the snow plow had cut the snow slick. The town was quiet. No one was on the street; not a car moved. White streams of smoke puffed gently from stove pipes atop the wintered cottages and houses and the streams of smoke slanted slightly in the direction of the air current. My shoes crunched in the snow; it was the only sound.

All the windows on our vehicles parked on the street were opaque with frost as if they had been sand blasted. I crossed Main Street to the General Store. I looked in the window to see if Scott was there. The store was still closed and I knew Scott would not open until eight. I turned left at Center Street and walked toward the grasslands at the edge of town, turned right and walked down the back road along the barbed-wire fence toward the East Walker River. The tip of my nose burned in the cold morning air. I stood on the bridge above the river and looked down into the cold dark water. A single, big brown trout, maybe four pounds, held himself in the middle of the river near the bridge. His head faced up stream and his tail barely weaved back and forth as he held himself steady against the strong current. He was no more than ten feet from my hand. I watched him for a long while and when he became aware he was being watched, he darted under the bridge into the black waters and I lost him. Tomorrow morning I would come again and find him in the same spot beneath the bridge.

I walked to the far side of the bridge and crossed the river, and stepped down the embankment to the east side of the river and walked along the river's edge through the withered grass, each blade coated with crystals of frost and snow. I followed the river as it twisted through the meadow toward the lake. My heavy leather boots swished through the frosty grass. Stands of thick brown brush grew in places beside the river. I circled around the brush and followed the river. I walked fast to keep warm. Brown mounds of cattle manure lay in the meadowlands but the cattle were gone to the lower desert for winter.

Geese were gathered in small groups along the river to feed on their way south. The big birds waddled awkwardly across the meadow, bending their long dark necks down to the ground as they pecked with their black beaks at the seeds in the grassland where the wind had blown the snow away. I quietly worked myself nearer to the geese until they erupted in a swoop, their great gray-brown wings stretched and flapped, they lifted into the air and quickly flew a safe distance and tumbled in a pile farther down the river.

I walked along the river to where it entered Bridgeport Lake. There were more geese down by the lake shore and great white birds floating on the water with long necks and long golden bills. Occasionally they took flight and soared a short distance and plunged into the lake, what little water was left in the lake. The reservoir had been drained last summer by Nevada ranchers who owned the water rights. All of the fish in the reservoir had been killed and the silt from the draining had killed the wild trout in the Walker River beyond the dam. It had caused hatred amongst the local fishermen and business people. Not only had the ranchers killed the trout, but they had badly hurt local business. Fishermen fished Bridgeport Lake and the Walker River beyond the dam for the big brown trout. Even after the spring plantings, it would take several years for the trout to reach the size the sports fisherman liked. It was bad. Mono County and the California Department of Fish and Game were about to sue the Nevada farmers and ranchers for damages.

I cut south through the meadow, skipped over the shallow water ditches that watered the meadow in the summer but now were dry and empty. I climbed over the barbed-wire fence and up the embankment to the little airport runway and walked down the runway toward town. There were several small metal hangars at the end of the runway. Only two prop planes were tied to the tarmac. In the summer there might be a dozen planes. The summer planes had flown away for winter.

I made south Main Street and walked up the sidewalk past the motels and gas stations and the one bank to the bakery and on to the General Store. It was open now. I went in and the wood burning stove in the back of the store made it warm. Scott Etheridge, who had just taken over the store with his wife Kathy, was there. Scott had the coffee on and the coffee smelled good and he asked if I wanted a cup. We each had one and we talked the morning talk about what was going on in town. I grabbed some milk and bread for breakfast and Scott wrote it down on our tab that we would pay with one check at the end of the month. It felt good to be trusted and good not to need your wallet when you wanted something at the store. I looked at the headline in the Reno newspaper, saw it was more bad news and left it. Scott had things to do and I had work, too. We said good morning and I left and crossed the street and climbed the stairs to our apartment. I kissed my wife and kids good morning, got something to eat, sat down and began writing.

I was writing about Mark Twain when he was up at Jackass Hill on the western slope of the Sierra. That was where Twain had stumbled on the Jumping Frog story that had won him his first national recognition. I was having trouble making the sentences clear and simple. But I knew it would get better with time and rewriting and rewriting. I hoped to finish the book by spring and publish it for the summer season. We would see.

CHAPTER TWENTY–EIGHT

Hot Springs

When I finished writing we had lunch and I asked my wife, "How about a soak in the hot springs."

"Oh, but it's so cold outside."

"Once we get in the water it will be fine."

"Oh, stop it."

"No, really. I was up there last night and the snow was falling on my head and melting in the springs. It was wonderful. Come on. The kids won't be home for a couple hours."

"Oh, all right. But if it's too cold, I'm not going in."

"It'll be fine. You'll see. I'll get some wine at Scott's. You get the towels. Meet you at the truck."

I walked across the street to the General Store and bought a liter of Chablis and joked with Scott, crossed back and got in the pick-up truck. After several false starts in the cold, the truck roared and the oil pressure gauge's red needle climbed and after five minutes the engine purred. My wife came down from the apartment, opened the door and threw in the towels and we headed south down Main Street. About a mile out, a dirt road heads east into the pine nut hills. I turned left onto the dirt road that was now white with snow and climbed the road into the hills for a mile and came to the long ridge of travertine that looks like a tan whale where the hot springs are. We drove down the narrow entrance between the walls of travertine and came to the springs. The hot white vapor rose in the cold air.

Travertine Hot Spring has several pools of hot water filled by a good stream of water that emerges at the top of the travertine ridge, and winds down a cut in the stone and drops into the pools. The pools are small and made of rock and sand. They are sitting pools and the hot water comes up to the middle of your chest. The water flows from one pool into the next, so that each of the pools has a different temperature. The hottest pool is the one the hot water first enters and each pool away from that one is progressively cooler. We always got in the second pool that was next to the hottest. An ethereal white mist rose from the hot water in the cold winter air making the hot spring look hotter than it really was.

There was no one at the hot spring, so we took off our clothes and laid them on the big white boulders and eased into the hot mineral water. The pools had sandy, clay-like bottoms and many women used the sulphurous smelling clay as a skin cleanser. They said the clay made their faces feel clean. The sandy bottoms of the pools could be hard on your bottom so we sat on pieces of carpet. We soaked with our bodies stretched out in the water with only our heads sticking out. You could only take the hot water for maybe ten minutes and then you had to get out, sit on the pool's edge to cool off, and when you got cold, slide back into the water.

I grabbed the wine and put the cups on the pool's edge and filled the cups and we drank the sharp acid wine in the hot pool, holding a cup in one hand out of the water, sipping now and then and looking across Bridgeport Valley that was all white now to the beautiful and grand Sierra. The sky was clear and blue, the sun so fiercely bright, it could still burn the skin. We were each with the one we loved and the children were in school and my work was done. We could soak and talk and relax and just be a man and a woman rather than husband and wife and a mom and a dad. We soaked and the hot mineral water blushed our skin a bright pink and washed away all the troubles we had had far away and there was nothing now but blue sky and peace of mind.

When the hot water's heat had pierced the flesh and warmed us deeply, we got out, dried quickly in the cold air and dressed. Then we walked hand and hand around the hot springs to the other pools and smelled the crisp, clean mountain air that was fresh in winter and fresher with the close, clean smell of the pine nut trees.

When the warmth from the hot springs wore off, we climbed into the pick-up truck and drove back to town. The children would be home soon from school. Edie walked across the street to the General Store, bought a good cut of steak and put the bill on our tab and walked back and started things for dinner. I read over the morning's writing and made corrections and worried, as all writers worry, and wondered when I would get the book finished.

CHAPTER TWENTY–NINE

Saving a Hospital

That winter a bitter controversy arose over the Mono County Board of Supervisors' efforts to close Mono General Hospital at Bridgeport. Mono General was the only hospital for a distance of 90 miles north to Carson City, and 60 miles south to Mammoth Lakes. A tour bus carrying a load of senior citizens had recently crashed into the Walker River. The wounded were hauled to Mono General and stabilized; critically injured were air lifted to hospitals in Reno. Mono General Hospital had helped save many lives.

Like many rural hospitals, Mono General had been plagued for years. It was hard getting doctors and nurses to stick it out in the wilderness. The hospital was always in the red and strained the slender county budget. The Supervisors had repeatedly interfered with hospital administrators and fired doctors and staff. The current Board was determined to either close the hospital or turn it into an emergency room. But by law, an emergency room had to be attached to a hospital. If the Board closed the hospital, there would be no medical services for a distance of one hundred and fifty miles in the Sierra wilderness.

Led by president Bent Bently, the current Board of Supervisors was determined to seize the hospital issue by the jugular and subdue it. Naturally, residents of northern Mono County were terrified. What would happen to heart attack victims or pregnant women or children who suddenly became seriously ill in the middle of a winter night when snow and ice covered the mountain highways? The community rose up to stop the Supervisors from closing the hospital which in turn might save their lives.

Unlike our stay in Virginia City, I had promised my wife I would stay out of small town squabbles. But when friends in Bridgeport asked me to help them save their hospital, I forgot my promise. Our friends worried about their families and they worried about visitors whose business they depended on. My wife warned me to stay out of the controversy. And others warned me. But of course, I knew better.

"How can helping people hurt anyone," I asked like a happy puppy wagging his tail.

"Stay out of it. You'll regret it," my wife warned. But, no. I would not listen.

I began meeting with a small group who were determined to save the hospital. It would be tough. Three of the five member Board of Supervisors were from the southern end of the county where most county residents lived. The southern county had a privately owned hospital at Mammoth Lakes. The southern county Supervisors had made it clear they were unsympathetic to the concerns of northern county residents. The southern Supervisors seemed to believe, northern county residents could use the private hospital located at Mammoth Lakes, sixty miles from Bridgeport. A portion of the highway between Bridgeport and Mammoth Lakes is very dangerous in winter when white-outs cause accidents. The difficulty of traversing this highway in winter could determine whether an emergency victim lived or died.

Because of my work as a researcher and writer, I knew how to collect information. The right information might help stop the Supervisors from closing the hospital. I began collecting information. I telephoned county, state and federal officials. I contacted local and regional media for publicity. The Reno *Gazette-Journal* sent down a reporter and the hospital controversy received attention in a series of articles. A Sacramento television station sent reporters and the story of a small, isolated town trying to save its hospital was aired to thousands.

I appeared at Board of Supervisors' meetings, and along with other concerned citizens, spoke in favor of keeping the hospital open. It took only one Board meeting to realize what we were up against.

Mono County government was controlled by a five member Board of Supervisors. You could tell what this Board thought of itself by the way the Board room was laid out. The Board sat up front on a high pedestal behind a dark wooden console that made a solid barrier between the People and the Board. The Board sat up there as if it were the Supreme Court. A citizen who wished to express his opinion at a Board meeting, had to stand before the Board and speak into a microphone while the Board looked down on him as if he were a bug. To eliminate difficulties with citizens as the Board bulldozed its way toward autocracy, the Board scheduled its meetings during the day when most citizens worked and were unable to attend public meetings. The Board had less trouble that way.

It was a horrifying experience for a citizen who was used to Democracy to watch this Board in action. And it became obvious why it had won the disgust and hatred of the people it allegedly served.

It is strange what happens to an ordinary citizen once he or she has been elected to political office, the metamorphosis of an ordinary-joe who would talk with you about the weather, to a pompous know-it-all who overnight has developed the wisdom to remedy the world's woes, and now hasn't the time to listen to his fellows' pleas or suggestions. Who was once a friend or an acquaintance is now someone you'd have murdered. Such was Supervisor Bent Bently. He was the sort of public servant none of us should grow up to be.

Bently presided over the Board of Supervisors. He had run for office after running his business into the ground. Unemployed, he had managed to convince a majority he could do a good job for the county. Mono County voters as a whole are a trusting lot and they took Bently at his word.

Bently reminded you of the cartoon character Porky Pig. Except Bently was without Porky's good nature and humor. Bently, usually attired in his one black suit, a plain white shirt and black tie, looked as grim as an undertaker. The bulge of his pregnant stomach pushed so hard at his lapels that the buttons were nearly torn from the fabric. Bently's chubby crimson face was his emotional thermometer and you could observe the intensity of his trigger-temper by the varying degrees of redness in his face. Bently tried hard to appear controlled but he was easy to rattle. The presence of citizens in the Board room invariably caused his face to flush fifty points; and when he was asked a question, even in the most polite manner, his face burned fifty percent redder.

Bently, like some of the other Board's members, had peculiar ideas about public service. He seemed to believe that the public were a pack of fools that must be endured. Whenever he was questioned and didn't feel like answering, he refused to answer the question or answered in a cutting, obnoxious manner that infuriated the intelligent and intimidated the timid. "I will not be interrogated," was a common reply. This response came out of Bently's background as a cop. Like some men who have served too long in law enforcement, Bently had wrongly come to believe that every citizen is a potential criminal who cannot be trusted. Therefore, a question was an "interrogation." Bently would tell people to, "shut up" at public meetings and threaten to throw them out if they didn't. He refused to allow some citizens to speak at public meetings violating both the citizens' First Amendment rights and rights protected by the California Brown Act. Bently had picked up some bad manners as a cop. If not for the civilized behavior of Mono County citizens, he would have been beaten to a pulp frequently or hanged from the nearest telephone pole.

Bently had migrated to Mono County from Southern California into which he carried the arrogance and selfishness that had been bred there and spread them around Mono County as if he were Johnny Apple Seed. Bently still held affectionate feelings for Southern California, particularly Los Angeles. This was astonishing for anyone representing the people of Mono County. The people despised the City of Los Angeles for having stolen water rights from Mono and Inyo counties and for having destroyed the Owens Valley farms in the 1920's. I sat stunned at one Board meeting when Bently confessed that he would do, "anything in his power" to help the City of Los Angeles gather further water rights in Mono County. If there had been anyone in the Board room that day besides myself, Bently would likely have been mauled. The people of Mono County had fiercely fought the City of Los Angeles for decades on many water issues, particularly the Mono Lake controversy.

Mono Lake is a great saline sea twenty-five miles south of Bridgeport. It is a haven for thousands of birds that flock each year, mate and raise their chicks on its several islands. The millions of brine shrimp that thrive in Mono Lake are an abundant source of food for the birds. Mono Lake and its bird sanctuary were nearly destroyed by the City of Los Angeles when it diverted streams from entering Mono Lake and into its aqueduct. Mono Lake's plight caused many to come to her aid, including David Gaines and the Mono Lake Committee, the Sierra Club, the Audobon Society and people and institutions all over the world.

There was one good thing about Supervisor Bently. He gave you greater appreciation for the men who created the Constitution of the United States. Bently, on the other hand, thought the Constitution was a ship in the U.S. Navy.

The remainder of the Board was as nearly as dispiteous as Bently, not because they were as obnoxious or as rude—that was impossible, but because they permitted Bently to behave in such an insulting manner and never castigated him. It was the stupidest, meanest public body I have ever witnessed. When the Attorney General ruled on a legal matter, they ignored his ruling although by doing so they broke the law. They ignored the advice of their legal counsel. They insulted the California Legislature after the Legislature gave Mono County nearly $300,000 to help save Mono General. Bently wrote the Legislature and thanked those boys by telling them they had missed a "golden opportunity" to help out Mono County in a bigger and better way!

Armed by Bently, the Board tormented hard working employees who did not entirely agree with their Gestapo tactics. One of those they particularly took pleasure in tormenting was Marguerite Ivey, a dear, saintly woman and Mono General's Administrator. Marguerite Ivey literally worked day and night, day after day, trying to save the hospital while the Board frustrated and ridiculed her.

In contrast to the Board of Supervisors, Marguerite Ivey was an example. She was one of those rare human beings who are willing to work hard, sacrifice and endure pain and loneliness to help others. When the Board got Marguerite behind closed doors away from the public's eyes and ears, they yelled at her and made her life miserable. But Marguerite was a wonder to behold. She restrained her anger, held her tongue and gave back soft answers for the meanness the Board dumped on her. She understood she could not save the hospital for the People without the consent of the Board by whom she was daily tortured. Marguerite struggled quietly, privately, with severe patience to enlighten a pack fools anyone but her would have told to go straight to hell.

Though the Board eventually drove Marguerite into a hospital with the return of a deadly cancer she had whipped once, and was to whip again, she nearly single-handedly saved the hospital. Yet I doubt if more than a handful were aware of her great efforts, and doubt she got so much as a thank you from those who believed democracy would somehow run itself.

During the controversy, Supervisor Bently wrote a report on the hospital situation. It was supposed to present the facts so that the Board could reach an intelligent conclusion. Instead, the report was full of lies and misinformation.

These were two of the most glaring errors: 1) Nearly $300,000 sat in the California treasury and would be given to Mono County as soon as the Board quit fooling around and came up with a reasonable plan to save the hospital. And 2) it would be inexpensive to close the hospital. The truth is, the hospital had been built with Federal funds appropriated by the Hill-Burton Act which appropriated money for rural hospitals. If Mono General was closed, the county would have to pay back nearly a half-million dollars to the Federal Government.

The report also made it stunningly clear, that Supervisor Bently was more interested in helping the private hospital located in his district. Public hearings indicated Bently may have had a personal or business interest in helping the private hospital. When asked whether he had received money or other benefits from that private hospital, Bently gave his usual reply, "I will not be interrogated," etc..

On the morning of Mono General's final hearing, a group of townspeople had hanged the Board in effigy; their scarecrow-like figures swung gayly from a tree in front of the big white and red courthouse. So many had gathered for the meeting, that it was moved across the street to the Community Center. It was an open meeting and everyone had an opportunity to speak for or against closing the hospital.

When it was my turn, I said that if Mono General was closed it would be the first time in over a hundred years that the county was without a public hospital. I said Bently's report was full of lies and misinformation and it was clearly meant to mislead the public and the Board, and I pointed out its errors.

If a Supervisor voted to close the hospital based on the report, their decision would violate the public trust. Furthermore, I had contacted federal health officials and questioned them about Mono General. They had informed me that they were never contacted by Bently about closing the Federally subsidized hospital.

Finally, there was substantial evidence that board members had colluded with the private hospital in efforts to close Mono General. (Not surprisingly, the administrator of the private hospital was fired afterward and Bently did not run for reelection.)

By the overwhelming turnout of citizens in favor of keeping the hospital open, media publicity and fact finding, the people got what they wanted. Bently and the Board backed down and Mono General was saved. Democracy won in spite of the Board.

In retaliation, the Board voted to hire the out-going Bently as the county General Accounting Officer. Bently, who had failed at business and his ability to govern finances was questionable, was now in charge of Mono County's money! This action solidified in stone that the Board were fools. At least the people thought so, and they got rid of the worst at the next election.

Though I had merely helped the town save its hospital, I had acquired several new political enemies, who, as I had been warned, were going to do their best to make our lives hell.

PART FIVE

---•⊷⊰⊙⊱⊷•⊷⊶---

And the trouble follows

CHAPTER THIRTY

Commie Bill

Sometimes after I finished writing in winter, I visited with the locals. Over sodas and coffee we talked about the local problems: the destruction of the wild trout habitation caused by the Nevada ranchers; the low count of the deer; the stupidity of the Supervisors on certain issues. It was during these bull sessions that Commie Bill showed up. Bill was an entertaining character and his views to some extent were typical of some of the men who had come to live in the Sierra.

In the warm months Commie Bill lived with his wife in a small travel trailer amongst the bushes and trees beside a lovely mountain stream. Before he met his wife he was known as Grizzly Bill because he lived by himself in a tent in the forest and bathed infrequently, although there was plenty of water to clean up. The townspeople could smell Bill a half-mile away and prepared themselves for his arrival by leaving town.

In time, Bill had the luck of meeting Ann, a good strong woman, kind and tender hearted who loved Bill like she would have loved a lost puppy. Ann watched over Bill and kept him out of trouble and it was difficult. For Bill had one serious delusion: he believed every problem in our world could be traced to a communist. He thought all senators and congressman were communists. He thought the FBI were communists. He thought I was a communist. He thought the local butcher was a communist. Bill would get fired up about the commies until Ann caught him and barked, "Bill!" and Bill shut up until Ann was a safe distance away. And then Bill started in on the commies again. As long as Ann was around, the community was safe from Bill's harangues. Ann knew how to keep Bill on a leash like a trained animal. Another good thing Ann did for Bill was to make him take baths regularly. Afterward Grizzly Bill didn't seem like a proper name. So it was changed to Commie Bill which seemed to fit Bill's new image.

Commie Bill earned a portion of his living trapping defenseless animals in the mountains, coyotes, foxes, beavers, rats, squirrels, cats, dogs, anything with fur that he could sell legally for a dollar. I felt sorry for the animals because they died in misery to keep Bill in beans and bacon. Bill thought he was a Mountain Man. But unlike the true mountain men of old who lived and trapped alone and footed it up and down the mountains, Bill drove a 4X4 truck or one of his three-wheeled motorcycles. These noisy contraptions woke up every thing in the forest from the hibernating bears to the spirits of the dead Paiutes and warned them that Bill was on the loose again, away from his keeper, with his traps and high-powered rifles and looking to trouble the wild beasts of the forest who didn't trouble anyone. But they had been forewarned. The bears went back to sleep; the deer laid back down under the trees, and the blue jays and woodpeckers curiously watched Commie Bill tear up the dirt roads, making a hell of a racket, troubling their previously peaceful homes.

Commie Bill was raised in Los Angeles. After high school, Bill wanted to live in the wilderness and be a mountain man and trap animals and get away from the city. It wasn't a bad dream and I admire Bill for his ability to live in the wilderness and be comfortable far from the comforts of Los Angeles.

Everything may have gone all right for Bill if the Federal Government did not have certain laws. Bill liked to live in the forest but the Forest Service said you couldn't so Bill had trouble there. Then there were certain animals you couldn't trap, like cats and dogs, and that made life hard. One day it dawned on Bill he couldn't kill all God's creatures which meant he had to make money in other ways. So Bill painted houses and emptied trash cans and did whatever he could to earn a living. And all the while, Bill felt badly that he had compromised his career as a mountain trapper.

Ann tolerated Bill's need to live in the wilderness by agreeing to live in a small trailer beside a mountain stream. Finally Ann wanted, like any normal woman, to have a regular home. Ann found a place in town and she made Bill against his will go and live there with her. I sort of felt sorry for Bill after that because he liked living in the woods and I didn't think he'd do well in a house. But I was wrong. Ann house broke Bill and after a while even Bill liked taking showers and having a home and Ann was happy to have her own nest.

Although Bill believed our governments, both federal and local, were controlled by the communists, he was not registered to vote and he did not participate in the democratic process. When we tried to explain the seriousness of the Supervisors closing the hospital, Bill thought by God the hospital should be closed. It was a waste of his money and he'd save on his taxes. It didn't occur to Bill that he didn't own property and didn't pay property taxes anyway.

I asked Bill, "What will happen if Ann gets pregnant and needs a hospital to have your baby?"

"We don't need no hospital," he said.

"But Bill, how will Ann feel about having her baby out here in the sticks with no doctor and no hospital?"

"Oh, we'll manage."

Bill had never had a child and he didn't understand the complexities of bearing children or the sensitive and anxious feelings a pregnant woman gets. We had wives and children and had been through it. We were patient and tried to explain it to Bill but it was wasted effort. We didn't worry about Bill too badly though. Ann would know what to do. And if that meant moving to the city to have her baby, by God, she would see that Bill got her there.

The wilderness seemed to attract others like Bill who saw the world as an extraordinarily hostile place and moved to the Sierra to escape it. Living in the wilderness didn't calm their fears but actually seemed to worsen them. They had come up here with their guns and their pick-up trucks and their beards and beer to get away from all they feared. They didn't like people much, and they certainly didn't like you. You tried to reason with them but it was useless. Being far, far away from normal society freed them to cling to their delusions. There wasn't much you could do about it.

CHAPTER THIRTY—ONE

The Resurrection of Big Ugly #1

Despite Commie Bill's delusions about the communists, he became my inspiration. He had lived in the forest freely for as long as Ann had tolerated it. I admired Bill's carefree life and I wanted to have it. We had holed up in our little apartment all winter and we wanted to be on our own again. We wanted to camp in the mountains for the spring and summer. But how to do it comfortably? Our camping trailer had grown smaller since we had lived in the apartment. A tent was too small for a long stay. We needed something bigger and more luxurious. I looked around for temporary housing for our camping adventure.

I found Big Ugly #1 sitting by itself and lonesome. It was a thirty-seven foot travel trailer built in 1952. It was a homely looking thing, two toned and the paint was faded but the body was perfect. Two windows were broken. The door was unlocked; I opened it and went inside. The odor of wet mildew hit me as I entered. The trailer was full of the left behinds of the previous tenant, Bob somebody. It was an absolute mess. Bob's newspapers and magazines were all over the floor along with clothing, empty booze bottles, and all sorts of miscellaneous junk. In the middle of the trailer there was a bad leak and melting snow dripped from the ceiling. The water had damaged the ceiling and the kitchen floor below the leak. I walked through the trailer. Except for the water damage in the kitchen, the inside was in good shape.

It would need a good cleaning, the rich but dirty maple paneling washed down and varnished, the kitchen floor and ceiling replaced, and linoleum and carpet laid in the front room and bedroom. The roof was the only serious problem. The old roof sealant had cracked and pealed and caused the leak. The old sealant would have to be removed and new sealant applied. It wouldn't cost much, a little work and a gallon of sealant.

The trailer had a front and back door. The front door led into the living room. There was a couch that opened into a double bed. The children could sleep there. There was a gas stove with an oven in the kitchen and an old refrigerator from the 1950's. Ole Bob had left a couple of trout in the freezer section and the trout were dried and stuck to the freezer. There was lots of storage space and several closets. The bathroom had a toilet, wash sink and a good size bath tub and shower. My wife and I could use the back bedroom. Sliding wood doors closed off the bedroom and bathroom.

The old trailer wasn't the ideal recreation vehicle because it was big and heavy. But with a little remodeling it would do for spring and summer camping. It was better than a tent. I would have to install holding tanks for water and sewage, change some plumbing but that wouldn't be difficult.

That evening after dinner I broke the news to Edie.

"You know how we've always wanted a big trailer to camp in?"

"Uh-huh."

"I've found one."

"Really?"

"And I've already paid for it."

"Already paid for it?"

"It was too good a deal to pass up."

"How much?"

"You won't believe it. The trailer is thirty-seven feet long and I got it for $300."

"Three hundred dollars! Oh, yeah. What's it look like?"

"Well, it's an older trailer. It will need cleaning and fixing. But we can do it for less than a thousand dollars. Then we can camp in it this spring and summer," I said, never suspecting what the Mono County Sheriff had in store for us.

So I showed my wife the trailer. She saw the mess and was obviously stunned.

"I know, I know. It looks bad," I said. "But we can clean it up and make it into a nice little summer cabin."

"This thing looks awful," she said and smiled, "but we can make it something special." That afternoon we went to work and cleaned out Bob's junk and hauled it to the dump.

We parked Big Ugly #1 in the parking lot near the post office in the center of town. That monster looked like a beached whale. The townspeople looked it over on their way to the post office, scratched their heads, "What's that fool gonna do with *that* ?" They had no respect for Big Ugly #1. They could not imagine Big Ugly #1 handsome and useful again.

Toward the first of March the days began to warm. I hauled out our kerosene heater to Big Ugly and lit it up and kept it going and dried out the trailer. With the heater on, the trailer was warm and cozy; the walls and floor were thick and insulated. Dried out it began to smell better.

We hauled out buckets of warm water and cleaner. Nearly four decades of smoke and grime smudged the maple paneling. But the blackness washed off and the warm, golden wood reappeared. After several days the wood was all bright and the trailer smelled still better. We varnished the paneling, and when that wonderful stuff hit the maple wood, it covered the scrapes and mars like magic. The paneling became bright, warm and golden.

We cleaned the oven and washed out the refrigerator and threw Ole Bob's crusted trout in the trash. We tore out the old linoleum in the kitchen, removed the damaged plywood and laid down new flooring. I climbed up to the roof, scraped off the old sealant and replaced it. Then I hosed down the roof to make certain it didn't leak. The roof was as snug as a bottle.

We painted the cabinets, laid new linoleum in the kitchen, new carpet in the front room and bedroom. I removed the old gas water heater and converted the empty space into a closet for the kids. I would install a small RV water heater under the kitchen sink.

I crawled under the trailer, installed a large plastic holding tank for the toilet, put in a new RV toilet, installed a holding tank for our drinking water, built a bed for our bedroom, fixed the two broken windows and put a new lock on the front door. I ripped out the old busted copper water pipe and put in new pipe for the water and propane stove and refrigerator. Edie made new curtains for the trailer.

I installed a 12 volt electrical system for lights and the RV water pump. Then I bought a 500 watt gas generator to run the television and the video recorder when we wanted entertainment.

As spring warmed the mountains the townspeople came outdoors and the activity around Big Ugly #1 drew attention. The curious stopped by and we invited them in. Those who had seen the insides of the trailer before, marveled at the difference cleaning and work had made. Rex Neil, a local businessman who had loaned me tools, stopped in to see how the renovation was going.

"So what ya gonna do when ya get it all fixed up," Rex asked.

"We're gonna haul it into the hills and camp for spring and summer."

"Gee, that sounds nice. I'd like to camp out all summer too."

"Ya could ya know."

"Oh, hell, I got the house in town. Don't think the wife would leave it to camp out all summer. But it sure sounds like fun. "

"It's something we've always wanted to do, Rex. Just camp out for the summer and enjoy the Sierra in peace. A little trailer or a tent with the two kids would be hard. This seems the best way. Most comfortable way, anyway. Come out when we get settled."

"Sounds good. We'll have a little party. Whataya say?"

"Let's do it."

When finished, Big Ugly #1 was entirely self-contained. It had its own fuel and heat system, drinking water and sewage holding tanks, a propane refrigerator and stove. Everything we needed to live comfortably, including television and my computer system, was stored inside it. It was a home on wheels and it had cost us less than a thousand dollars.

On the last day of March, we moved out of our apartment. We hitched Big Ugly to a 4x4 pick-up, connected the towing lights and pulled out of town. The townspeople gave the big beast a double take. "Now what the hell they gonna do with that?" We were going camping. We had found a lovely spot in the boonies beside a mountain stream. It was on private land and we had asked permission to camp. It was a lovely park of grey skinned aspens and green grass. It was beside a main dirt road and easy to get to. The mountain stream purred day and night and there seemed no place more peaceful on Earth. We did not drink the stream water because of the fear of giardia which can turn your large intestine into a sewer and put a victim in the hospital for a vacation. We hauled in our water from town in five gallon jugs and poured it into the holding tank. I emptied the sewage tank into containers every week and put back into the earth what came out of it. We burned our paper trash in camp fires and hauled out bottles and tin cans to the dump. We respected the wilderness and kept our camp clean and orderly.

Weekend campers showed up occasionally. But mostly we had the camp to ourselves. Farther up the road, the shepherds were already camped for the season in a high mountain meadow. Sometimes they drove the sheep through our camp to water the sheep in the stream. Their mules were packed with food and bedrolls and a big copper bell hung around the leader's neck and clanged and could be heard for some distance in the quiet of the mountains. As I wrote in the morning, big double-decked trucks roared past with sheep or cattle and the dust flew up from the road in a cloud and drifted in the spring breeze.

There were trout in the stream but it was not fishing season, so we did not fish the stream. The fishing season would open at the end of April.

We reveled in the independence and self-reliance of Big Ugly #1. In the mornings I fired-up the generator that powered the electric lights and television. We could receive two TV stations from Reno on the amplified television antenna. The morning television shows were on while my wife fried eggs and bacon and the kids got ready for school. We were as comfortable and cozy in Big Ugly #1 as if we were in a house in the city but we were high in the Sierra. We had the best of both worlds, all the wildness and peace of nature and we could plug into the outside world by turning on the television.

Shortly before eight, Edie and the kids piled into the pick-up truck, and my wife went down the dirt road to the highway and drove to town and dropped the kids off at school and opened her hair cutting business which she ran for the summer. I made coffee on the propane stove and went to work. I was still writing about Twain up on Jackass Hill and it looked like I would finish the book soon. I had recently completed and published *Hot Springs of the Eastern Sierra*.

When I finished writing, I made lunch and sat in the sun and listened to the stream. The blue jays cackled in the aspens and a red-headed woodpecker drilled the soft skin for bugs. I had the rest of the day to walk beside the stream and explore the mountains or go to the hot springs and meet visitors.

It was fiercely black in the mountains at night. When you took walks and the moon was not in the sky you could not see your feet. The sky was very black so that the stars stood out clearly and seemed so near so high in the mountains. We were alone in the wilderness beside the creek. It felt good to be away from the city and be at peace in nature. We were happy and everything was fine. But you could trust people to ruin it.

CHAPTER THIRTY–TWO

The Psycho Cops from Hell

It seemed a sad thing to Sheriff Dick in Virginia City that we had escaped him. And worse that we were living peacefully in the wilderness near Bridgeport. Our leaving town had denied him the opportunity to make us suffer. Anyone who crossed Sheriff Dick and the Storey County boys should suffer. Sheriff Dick leaned back in his swivel chair in his office across from Joe Pastrami's office—Joe was absent that morning, drunk as usual, and Dick thought of ways to make us suffer. He twiddled his brown mustache between his right thumb and index finger. He cranked-up his twisted brain and tried to find a way to make me pay for punching a hole in his elephant vanity. Sheriff Dick thought and thought and plotted methods of torture.

Except for the hospital controversy, I had lived quietly at Bridgeport, wrote my books, minded my own business and hadn't made any new enemies. So I thought. Unknown to me I had committed several unpardonable sins:

I had embarrassed Supervisor Bently at public meetings while trying to save Mono General hospital. That was sin number one. I was happily married and didn't bother anyone. That was sin number two. And third, I had just published *Hot Springs of the Eastern Sierra* which publicized three hot springs in the Bridgeport area. Two of these are on public lands and belong to every American. Some of Bridgeport's dear souls thought the hot springs were their personal property. Bridgeport's Psycho Cops from Hell agreed. The Psycho Cops went to the hot springs for parties and they didn't like outsiders showing up. My new book publicized the hot springs. Sounds like such a petty thing doesn't it? It was. The Psycho Cops and Sheriff Dick thought a lot alike. And the two of them, a hundred miles apart, were about to teach us a lesson about exercising your civil rights in small towns.

Bridgeport's Psycho Cops from Hell were several men in their thirties who weren't qualified to wash dishes at the local restaurants and were made deputies by a community whose compassion was moved to mercy. They were raised in Bridgeport or had lived there a long time. The Psycho Cops were a sort of neurotic Boy Scout troop. In between annoying decent people in the community, they gathered at a local bar, got drunk and went around town threatening people who were minding their own business. You felt sorry for their parents. You worried about these guys and wondered who would take care of them when they grew up. A previous member had sexually molested a female inmate. He was fired but never prosecuted. That's the way things were in Bridgeport. Public servants who did awful stuff were let off while citizens who committed minor crimes were crucified. It was sort of like Storey County.

You probably met guys like the Psycho Cops back in junior high school when the blood vessels of adolescent boys were suddenly given an overdose of testosterone and former good boys became pushy young men looking for a fight to prove themselves. The Psycho Cops were mental adolescents wired for trouble with no place to go. They tooled around Bridgeport in their white sheriff cars with the gold stars on the doors, eating candy bars that got them further wired, bored to death and hoping someone would show the slightest sign of getting out of line so that they could be their usual nasty selves. Their greatest thrill was picking up some hitch-hiker who had the misfortune of passing through Bridgeport, discover he had an unpaid parking ticket a thousand miles away, arrest that sorry soul and haul him to jail. This gave their lives meaning. They wouldn't have lasted a day on a city police force. But out there in the sticks where competent law officers were hard to find because of the low pay, the Psycho Cops found jobs.

The current Psycho Cops consisted of four bad officers, Meanness, Ignorance, Stupidity and their troop leader, Captain Moron. They were four sorry officers amongst a number of good officers who didn't bother anyone and did a good job for the community. The Psycho Cops gave the sheriff's department and Bridgeport a bad name. A previous undersheriff had tried to get rid of them but had failed. Visitors who had had run-ins with these guys said they would never vacation in Bridgeport again. Though complaints were filed against the officers, Sheriff Stricknine did nothing to change the situation.

After our difficulties in Virginia City, I wasn't looking for trouble. If I was in a public place and the Psycho Cops came in, I left. But it is a peculiar irony that the man who most wants Peace in this world, is the man Trouble comes looking for.

After two months camping in Big Ugly #1 beside the creek, we moved to a meadow closer to town. The meadow was posted with three Bureau of Land Management (BLM) signs. BLM land is public land and camping is permitted by the federal government. The BLM establishes limitations on stays depending upon the area. I assumed by the posted BLM signs that our new campsite was public land and camping was permitted. We had camped in the meadow before and never had a problem.

A blue pick-up drove up one morning and a tall, slender cowboy complete with Levi's and a cowboy hat got out and approached. He told us his name. Let's call him Flintstone. They were known as the Friendly Flintstones because the only things they seemed to care about were cattle and sheep, and they made trouble for anyone who stepped on their property. They owned hundreds of acres around Bridgeport, and leased hundreds more from the BLM. Their ranch was across the border in Nevada. The Flintstones brought their cattle and sheep up to the high country for the summer. In the fall they stuffed the animals into double-decked trailers and hauled them back to Nevada.

The cowboy introduced himself as so-and-so Flintstone. He then informed me that we were camped on his land and asked us to leave. I asked about the BLM signs. He said he had posted them to tell people to close the gates. I had never heard of a private citizen posting Federal signs, but no matter. I said sure, we would move off his property.

To make certain we would not make the same mistake again, I purchased a Forest Service map to locate public lands for camping. A half mile away there was BLM land on the top of a hill in the pine nut trees. It was in the sticks.

"Well," I said to myself, "this camp will be even better." A couple friends helped us tow Big Ugly #1 up the hill to the BLM land. But as we drove back down the hill we met Deputy Meanness. My friend said, "Let me do the talking. I know these guys."

"Whatdaya up to," he asked. The deputy looked sternly at me.

"I'm trying to find out where he's put his trailer," he said coldly and I knew there was going to be trouble.

"We're camped on BLM land," I said.

"Why don't you ask people before you park your trailer on their property," Meanness asked.

"What do you mean?"

"We had a complaint about you trespassing out here."

"The meadow is posted with BLM signs," I explained.

"Everyone around here *knows* this is private land," he fired back.

"I'm sorry. We didn't know. The BLM signs threw us. I told the owner we would move the trailer as he asked."

"He says you've refused to leave."

"You can see we're not camped on his property."

"So you say you're parked on BLM land, huh," Meanness asked.

"Yes."

"Well, I'll tell you what I'm gonna do: I'm gonna call BLM and tell them where you're camped and make sure you have to move that trailer every two weeks." The deputy believed camping on public lands was limited to two weeks. By notifying BLM of our campsite, he apparently hoped BLM would make us move. This would be inconvenient and troublesome.

I didn't know what the man's problem was. Obviously it didn't have much to do with us.

"Well, call BLM if that's what you want," I said. Meanness drove up the hill and inspected our camp.

I wasn't overjoyed with Meanness and went to the Sheriff and the District Attorney and explained what had happened. We had never refused to leave the Flintstone's property and had done as they had asked. What was going on? Then we filed a written complaint for harassment.

We weren't the only ones who had had trouble with the deputy. Within six months, two local businessmen had filed complaints for harassment. We had filed the third.

A couple days later the Sheriff ruled on our complaint. He said I had caused the officer trouble, and not the other way around.

And so began a nightmare with Bridgeport's Psycho Cops that lasted almost a year and caused hard feelings for everyone involved to this day. All of it could have easily been avoided with the slightest good will. Good will was out of the question. The Psycho Cops became pawns in plot to punish us. For what? Who knows.

The next day Ignorance and Stupidity stopped me on the highway and ticketed me for not having our truck registered in California. The truck had been on California highways less than two weeks.

The next day they came to our campsite on BLM land. They said we were not camped on BLM land. We were camped on *private* property. They brought maps and showed me where they believed we were camped.

"Has the owner filed a complaint," I asked.

"Well, no."

"Can you show me the boundaries of the property staked by a surveyor?"

"Well, no." They shuffled their boots in the dirt; their eyes wiggled
back and forth. My patience was wearing thin.

"Would you like some coffee and doughnuts," I asked.

They looked at each other. "Uh, no," they said.

"Listen fellas, a Forest Ranger was here yesterday and he said we
are camped on federal land. What's the problem?"

"Well, that can't be. Uh...the map shows you're camped here on
this private property."

"Private property, huh," I asked. "Well, why are you here if the
owner hasn't filed a complaint?"

"Well, uh..."

"Why are you here if the owner hasn't filed a complaint?"

"Well, you just can't camp here," they said.

"Why not? We're not bothering anyone. And what's more, I don't
believe we're camped on private land. And even if we were, no one's
complained. You've got no reason to be here."

The two looked at each other, shuffled their feet and wiggled their
eyes. "Well, none of that matters. This is private property. You can't
camp here."

"Who says we can't?"

"Well..."

"Well," I asked.

So here's what Ignorance and Stupidity did. They went back to
Bridgeport and telephoned the alleged property owner three hundred
and fifty miles away in Los Angeles. They told him we were camped on
his land and asked him if he wanted to file a complaint. No, he did not.
He told the officers he had leased his land to the Flintstones.

So they called the Flintstones. Did they want to file a complaint?
No, they did not. Nor did they ever file a written complaint against our
family.

It got more irrational.

About this time, the Psycho Cops learned from Supervisor Bently,
that we had lived in Virginia City and that Sheriff Dick had run us out
of town. Apparently what was happening, was that Bently, who was
still nursing his political wounds, had encouraged the Sheriff and the
Psycho Cops to enlighten us.

The Psycho Cops called Sheriff Dick in Virginia City. Why? You figure it out. Sheriff Dick's opportunity for vengeance dropped into his lap. He told the Psycho Cops what they wanted to hear: I was a troublemaker, I was crazy, I was a liar, I was dangerous, and I had done him great harm. Sheriff Dick *didn't tell* the Psycho Cops that he was a crook and took bribes from a pimp and was an embarrassment to every honest lawman. And that he was still furious about what I had written about the corruption in Storey County.

When the Psycho Cops heard all this, their lives suddenly acquired a reason for existence. I had sinned against them. I had sinned against Sheriff Dick. I should be taught a lesson. And they were just the guys to do it. What Sheriff Dick didn't finish back in Virginia City, they would.

Then a few days later while I was eating lunch at the Sportsman's Restaurant across from the courthouse and minding my own business here come the Undersheriff, deputies Ignorance, Stupidity and the Assistant District Attorney, the Phantom of the Court. They asked me to step outside. The Undersheriff did the talking.

"We've received a written complaint from the Flintstones that you are trespassing on their property. I am notifying you that you are trespassing. You are to vacate the property in three days."

The Flintstones had not filed a written complaint. The Psycho Cops didn't have a complaint nor evidence we had committed any crime. It was obvious we weren't dealing with rational people.

So here was the situation: We were camped on BLM land. But if we didn't move our camp, the Psycho Cops would arrest my wife and I, impound our trailer and all my research materials. We would be forced to post bail. And the way things looked, we would be convicted and fined. We had no alternative but to move our camp.

The night before the Psycho Cops came to arrest us, we moved the trailer off BLM land. When the boys showed up the next morning, all set for the arrest, we had disappeared to their grief.

That should have settled it, right? No. A few days later the Psycho Cops arrested me on the truck registration ticket and hauled me to jail in the back of a patrol car. I posted bail and got out.

I had had it.

I went to the Undersheriff. "We've done nothing to harm you nor your officers. We have broken no laws. I have repeatedly asked you and your officers to leave us alone. Yet in spite of my requests, your officers have continued to deliberately harass us while camped on public lands, given us unwarranted registration citations, accused me of causing an officer trouble, illegally forced our family from federal lands and now you have arrested me.

"I am filing complaints with the Attorney General at the United States Department of Justice against your department, each offending officer and the District Attorney, for conspiring to deprive us of our Constitutional and civil rights while camped on Federal lands. I'm filing complaints with the California Attorney General, with the Board of Supervisors and with the Mono County grand jury. And then I'm filing a *ten million dollar civil suit for damages* against this department and your officers!" The Undersheriff looked at me glassy eyed and somewhat stunned. I meant what I said.

To think that a few lines written in an obscure publication a hundred miles and a state away was partly responsible for all this, was incredible. Dear Sheriff Dick had found a way to make our lives unhappy. It wasn't a very intelligent move. But then, what could I expect.

CHAPTER THIRTY–THREE

Getting Their Attention

When you are a stranger in an isolated town in the wilderness far from civilized help, and your enemies wear badges and guns and they have a vindictive district attorney behind them, you are in trouble. The simplest thing would have been to pack up and get out of Bridgeport. But my work wasn't finished. Besides, we said we were going to camp in the Sierra and nothing was going to change that. Talking and reasoning had proved futile. It seemed our only option was to file a civil suit and ask a judge to order the Psycho Cops to leave us alone. We were reluctant to do this; we had never sued anyone; we had never needed to sue anyone. After serious consideration we realized we had done all we could to make peace. Some men have difficulty respecting the rights of others and must be restrained. The law and the courts are recourses.

It is usually necessary to make a claim against the public entity before the plaintiff files suit. It then has time to respond to the claim. Once the response time has elapsed the plaintiff may begin litigation. We filed our claim for damages against Mono County, the sheriff's department and District Attorney Style Elver. Mono County did not respond.

Writing and filing a suit is not as difficult as some would like us to believe. The suit document has a basic form; if you do a little research in a law library and seek advice, you can learn how to write a complaint and save thousands of dollars. I was fortunate to have a friend who had filed suits on his own and won cases. He helped me. I made copies of our suit and went to the County Clerk's office with our filing fee and filed suit. Papers were served on the defendant, Mono County.

The harassment immediately ended.

Once a suit is filed and the defendant served, if the defendant does not respond within the prescribed time, the plaintiff wins by default. Simply by filing the suit we had put the Sheriff, the Psycho Cops and the District Attorney on the defensive.

I was in the law library the morning the Mono County counsel walked in to work on our case. The man did not know me. I watched him as he hurriedly yanked books from shelves and researched our complaint. He wrote frantically on a yellow legal pad on the long wooden table. There was some satisfaction knowing that a layman unskilled in the law could create a document that caused such excitement.

When I was forced to appear in court on alleged vehicle registration violations, I pled innocent. When the cases came to trial I disqualified county judges and forced the county to haul in judges from a 125 miles away. I subpoenaed the Sheriff and each officer involved, put them on the stand and grilled them. Their testimonies were full of lies and they backed up each other with lies. I spent two and a half hours trying simple registration cases.

During these trials the Psycho Cops testified they had telephoned Sheriff Dick in Virginia City who had given them misinformation about our character and reputations.

When sued and confronted in court, attitudes changed. The Psycho Cops felt victimized. They accepted no responsibility for their troubles. They scurried around town looking for others to trouble although their legal counsel advised them against it. It didn't matter. They couldn't help themselves.

We had illegally been forced from our first camp on public lands. That would not happen again and we would make sure of it. We bought a BLM map and located an ideal campsite in a meadow beside a creek seven miles from town and moved there.

Now word spread amongst some of the larger souls that we were "squatting" on Federal lands. To "squat" is a term formerly used to describe persons who deliberately take possession of private or federal lands. All we wanted to do was camp and be left alone. We were not squatting and we did not intend to take title of private or public land.

Occasionally the boys drove by our camp. One day, Ignorance, drove up in his pick-up with a rifle hanging across his back window. He glared at us with a hateful expression while witnesses watched. None of us knew if he was going to pull the rifle. He made his point, swallowed his beer and high-tailed it to town.

I followed him and found the Sheriff. "Listen," I said, "we have nothing personally against you nor your officers. And we've done nothing to cause this animosity toward us. If that deputy comes to our camp again with a weapon, I will assume he means to harm us and I will take the appropriate action. PLEASE *leave us alone!* "

The Sheriff finally got the message and we were allowed to camp in peace.

CHAPTER THIRTY–FOUR

Francisco the Mountain Shepherd

At the far south end of the high meadow where we camped that summer, where the meadow broadened and the aspens lined the creek, a lonely shepherd, Francisco, lived. He kept watch over a flock of about three hundred sheep. In the morning he moved the sheep to the creek for water. Then he led the sheep into the meadow, or up the sagebrush covered hillsides where the sheep grazed for the day. In the evening he moved the sheep to the creek before bedding them down.

Francisco wore a straw cowboy hat when he worked the sheep in the meadow. The hat shaded his eyes and kept the bright Sierra sun away. The hat had holes in it you could stick a finger through. The bright sun poured in through the holes and warmed his head in places. But the holes let in the air, too. He wore a white T-shirt and the edges were frayed around the collar. Tennis shoes covered his feet as he walked the meadow. He carried a long stick in the meadow. There were rattlesnakes. Francisco killed them with the stick. He moved with a quick, eager pace as if there was always something important to do. He was lonely and poor and the two made him eager to share himself and his food.

Francisco was forty-two, slender, bronze skinned, his black hair cut short and combed back neatly. He had dark friendly eyes. Several of his front teeth were capped in silver and they flashed like fishing lures when he smiled.

His home was a beat-up camping trailer parked beside the road at the edge of the meadow. The trailer was blue and white, but the blue paint had oxidized and chipped. Each of the wheels was snug in dug holes that kept the trailer in place. A silver, twenty-five gallon propane tank stood at the front of the trailer and supplied fuel for cooking and heat. A fifty gallon drum held Francisco's supply of drinking water. He bathed in the creek and relieved himself in the bushes.

Two black dogs kept him company. They had clipped stubs for tails. One, an Australian Shepherd, had one black eye and one baby-blue eye. The dogs bounced around visiting trucks and barked happily and wagged their tails. The dogs took their commands in Spanish and looked confused when they were given orders in English.

One morning I drove down the dirt road at the edge of the meadow to visit the shepherd. He was our only neighbor and his camp was about a mile from ours. His lone trailer light burned like a friendly beacon at night in the darkness of the meadow.

The shepherd came out of his trailer as I drove up. "Hola, buenas dias," I said, as I got out of the truck.

"Buenas dias," he said back. This will be interesting. I had studied Spanish in high school and college but had forgotten most of it. I remembered a few verbs and a sad collection of nouns. I stumbled in my broken Spanish and Francisco stumbled in his broken English. We amplified our ineptness with hand gestures and managed to communicate like prehistoric cave creatures.

In the weeks that followed I brushed up on my Spanish by using a Spanish-English dictionary. It was frustrating to try to speak a language I had learned but mostly forgotten by not practicing. Francisco patiently waited while I stopped in mid-conversation and searched the dictionary for a word. He helped me by reteaching me words I had forgotten. I taught him some English. After a time we communicated all right.

Francisco was from a village outside Santiago, Chile. He had earned a meager living as a baker before his marriage broke apart. He was earning very little when he read an ad in the newspaper about a job in America. He went to see about the job and to his surprise got it. He was going to be a shepherd in the mountains and deserts of California. He would earn six hundred dollars a month. He contracted to work in America three years. Now he regretted signing-on for so long. He had five children back in Chile and some were very young. He had agonized over leaving them. He did not have a choice. He was poor. America offered Francisco the opportunity to earn what in his country would be a small fortune. If he saved his money he could go back to Chile moderately wealthy. His children would not be poor any more.

When he signed-on he wasn't told that a third of his earnings was deducted for food. The foreman delivered the food to Francisco once a week in the meadow. It was always more food than he could eat.

Francisco's dream was to earn enough in America to buy a small herd of cattle. Each month Francisco divided up his pay check. He kept a hundred dollars for himself and sent the balance to a friend in Chile who looked after his children. His wife had deserted the family. His friend paid for the children's food and clothing, and each month purchased one cow. Francisco hoped to have thirty-six cows when he returned to Chile, and whatever calves that had been born while he was away. The cattle would mate and the herd would increase. He would be a rancher and sell his beef. He would make a good living for himself and his family. But now he was very lonely away from his children. He had been in America for a year. He wrote many letters to his children and looked forward to their letters. The foreman dropped them off once a week and picked up letters to be mailed. Francisco asked me into his trailer. From under his pillow he pulled a packet of letters from his children. He smiled sadly and tenderly rubbed the letters.

I was the only American that had stopped to speak to him. He said the others drove by or waved.

One day Francisco said, "You must come to dinner. Please bring your wife and children. Will you come Thursday evening?"

"Yes. Thursday is good. We will bring food."

"No, no. It is not necessary. I have what we need. Come after I have put down the sheep."

Thursday evening came and my wife and children piled into the pick-up. The dust rose in clouds behind the truck as we drove down the dirt road to Francisco's trailer. It was cold and the night was black and the silver stars stood out clearly. We aimed our truck toward the tiny light at the far end of the meadow.

Francisco saw our head lights and opened the trailer door to welcome us. The warm, yellow light spread out into the blackness. "Hola, Jorge. Buenas noches. Y tu familia," he said.

"Hola Francisco. Estamos bien," I said.

"Hola Francisco," my wife and children echoed. They were practicing their new language.

We piled into Francisco's trailer. It was about sixteen feet. The kitchen table was on the right and seats were alongside as in a cafe. A single propane lantern above the table lighted the trailer. We took off our coats and laid them on Francisco's bed to the left. We slid into our places on each side of the table.

He had set the table neatly with plates, forks and knives. He had folded toilet paper for napkins and each place setting had a toilet paper napkin. The trailer was filled with the warm smell of unfamiliar food and spices.

"Smells good, " I said, as Francisco nervously made us welcome.

"Empenadas," he said, and pointed to fist size, half-moons frying in the bubbling oil.

He was still preparing dinner. A thin dusting of white flour was spread across the top of his propane refrigerator. He rolled an empty, green, liter-size wine bottle over the tawny dough. He rolled the bottle back and forth to flatten the dough. He worked rapidly with skill.

When the dough was flattened, he cut the dough into rectangular strips six inches wide. He cut fast and with precision. He said that he was making meat pies. In Chile Francisco had baked the empenadas in his home and sold them in the streets.

"What is the dough made of," I asked. Flour with a table spoon of salt, two table spoons of baking powder, a little butter and water, he said. You must boil the water before you mix it with the flour. The hot water makes it easier to mix the dough.

He plopped handfuls of meat on the dough strips. The mixture was beef and chicken with lots of chopped onions, cumin, salt, black pepper and paprika. He had cooked the meat earlier and chilled it. "It is always best to chill the meat," Francisco said. "Tastes much better that way."

He placed slices of hard boiled egg on each of the meat mounds, black olives and several raisins. "The raisins make it very good," Francisco said, "you must have raisins." Then he cut the dough strip in six inch sections and folded the dough over the meat. He quickly trimmed the outside corners of each section and made the squares into half-moons. He sealed the edge of the half-moon pies with the flat end of a spoon and the edges were equally spaced along the semi-circles like the lips of little valleys.

He carefully slid the empenadas into the golden oil; the oil bubbled and spit, then settled into a steady boil. He fried the empenadas for five minutes, lifted them out and laid them on a dish towel where the oil collected. He piled the empenadas into a large plate and put the plate in the center of the kitchen table.

"What are these," our daughter asked.

"They are empenadas," I said, "a meat pie of beef and chicken and spices. You'll like them."

Alongside the empenadas were doughnuts Francisco baked earlier and plums and apricots for desert. There was a bowl of finger sized white things in tomato sauce. They looked like small, white carrots. I don't remember what Francisco called these. They were a mixture of potatoes, egg and flour. Francisco said you mix mashed potatoes, flour, water and egg into a dough. Then you roll the dough into a long, half-inch wide roll. Then you cut the roll into finger size sections. The fingers were boiled for several minutes and served. They tasted like a firm pasta.

Francisco motioned for us to eat. He said he would wait to eat. He stood aside while we ate.

The empenadas were very good. After we settled into dinner, Francisco sat down and made his plate.

We finished dinner and Francisco motioned to the children to have a doughnut or fruit. Our daughter had a plum and our boy helped himself to a doughnut. We complimented Francisco on the empenadas. My wife asked for the recipe.

Francisco made us an after dinner drink. He poured red wine into half a glass of milk. He smiled as he set it before us. It tasted bitter and strange but we smiled and drank it. When we had finished the drinks I went out to the truck and brought in Scotch and club soda and showed the Scotch to Francisco. His eyes smiled.

"Scotch," I asked.

"Scotcha? Si. Muy bueno." It was very expensive in his country, he said. I poured shots into three glasses and added club soda and the golden liquid bubbled. I handed the drinks to my wife and Francisco. I raised my glass, my wife hers and Francisco's his. "To Francisco. Gracias for the dinner," I said. We drank the Scotch and I made more drinks.

The food and the Scotch warmed us and we began to talk. It was still difficult to communicate complex thoughts in Spanish. I often stopped to consult the Spanish-English dictionary. It was like being in Spanish class again. We asked Francisco about his life in Chile. As he answered in Spanish, I told my wife and children what he was saying.

He had grown up in a large family. His father deserted the family when he was a boy. Francisco quit school in the third grade and went to work in a bakery where he learned his trade. His life had always been troubled. He married but it was bad. His wife was lazy and began to sleep with other men. Finally she ran off with another man. His wife was "loco" he said. He was glad and sorry she was gone. He was still having trouble with her. She had stolen several of his cows and sold them. He worried about her stealing more cows.

We talked until near mid-night. The propane trailer light hissed and drew white moths that collided against the outside window. The children had fallen asleep on Francisco's bed. All of us were tired. It was time to go home.

As we got our coats on and woke the children, Francisco brought out large sections of meat from his refrigerator. It was fresh lamb, pounds of it. He said it was more lamb than he could eat and he didn't want it to spoil. He wrapped the lamb and handed it to my wife. Then he pulled a box from the corner. It was crammed with canned vegetables, condensed milk, white and brown sugar, beans, packages of dry soup. "Take this. It is more than I need," he said. We accepted the food and thanked him. Edie gave him a hug. Francisco bowed his head sheepishly.

He helped us carry the food to the truck and we laid it into the back of the pick-up. "Muchas gracias, " I said and reached for his hand and shook it hard.

"De nada," he said. We piled into the truck, the children half asleep. We said goodnight, and I started the truck. We waved good-bye as Francisco shadowed his doorway.

"He's a nice man," Edie said. I turned the truck and started down the road to our trailer.

"Yes. And the meal was wonderful, " I said.

"And the lamb. Do you know how expensive it is in the market? He must have given us sixty dollars worth," Edie said.

"I don't think we've ever had lamb, have we," I asked.

"No. We couldn't afford it. How should we prepare the lamb for dinner? We could bake it."

"Or make lamb stew," I said.

"That sounds good."

"Tomorrow I'll make stew while you're at work and it will be ready when you get home," I said.

"We should invite Francisco," she said.

"All right. I'll ask him over."

"Isn't it strange," Edie said, "this poor foreign shepherd who can't speak English was so kind."

I put my hand on her shoulder. "I'm sorry about the trouble we've had this summer."

"It's not your fault. It's not our fault. It had nothing to do with us. We both wanted to camp. We wanted the experience. Let's make the rest of it something to remember. I'm sorry for the trouble, too."

"We could leave, you know. Just pack up and leave here," I said.

"They would like that wouldn't they? No. We said we would camp the summer. That's what we'll do."

"Right," I said. "I love you."

"I love you, too," she answered. The children lay against her like a feather pillow and slept. A grey jack rabbit, big as a dog, pole vaulted across the dirt road in front of the head lights.

The next day after I finished writing I pulled the lamb from our propane refrigerator and laid it on the cutting board. The lamb smelled new and strange, stronger and more wild than beef. I cut the lamb into strips and then cut the strips into bite size chunks for the stew. When the meat was all cut I dropped it into the frying pan and browned the lamb in butter with salt and pepper. I peeled the potatoes and cut up carrots and onions and plopped them in a big pot of water and mixed in the lamb. I sprinkled salt and pepper and threw in a couple bay leaves, set the gas flame on medium-low and let the pot simmer for two hours. Then I mixed the corn starch with warm water separately and poured the corn starch into the pot and the soup thickened into stew. Dinner was nearly ready.

I had invited Francisco and he was to come after he put the sheep down. As I got the biscuits ready for dinner, I heard my daughter shout excitedly, "Daddy, Francisco's coming in the meadow with his dogs."

"OK." I went outside and saw Francisco marching through the meadow carrying the stick he used to kill the rattlesnakes in the meadow. Our folding table was set up outside the trailer. Edie had thrown the table cloth over it and the kids had set the table and the folding chairs were circled around it.

"Hola Francisco," our daughter said when Francisco made our camp.

"Hola," Francisco said and hugged her with his right arm. I shook his hand and welcomed him and asked him inside. Our thirty-seven foot trailer was a mansion compared to his little trailer. He looked around and his eyes widened. It was warm and cozy, a large television was turned on in the front room. The kitchen was large with a long counter, a big refrigerator, a large stove and two sinks.

"Please sit down," I said and motioned to the couch. Francisco sat down.

"Want a Scotch," I asked.

"Si. Muy bueno." Edie got the ice from the freezer, clinked the ice into glasses for the three of us, poured Scotch into each glass and added club soda. Edie handed Francisco his drink.

"Muchas Gracias," he said.

Francisco sat on the sofa and watched the television. He looked puzzled. It was all in English. He was watching Wheel of Fortune and Vanna White was changing the letters.

"Muy bonita mujer," Francisco said.

"Yes, very pretty," I said. "America loves her."

We had purchased a portable satellite dish and we were able to watch stations thousands of miles away. On one of the satellites there was a Spanish network. I went over to the TV and tuned the receiver to the Spanish network. The evening news was on. When Francisco heard his language, he sat up and leaned forward. He listened intently. The newscaster was talking about Chile and showed pictures of Chilean politicians.

"Un mal hombre," Francisco said and pointed to the TV.

"What he say," my daughter asked.

"He said he is a bad man. This is news from Chile."

Francisco watched the news and sipped his drink. I watched his eyes. They were the eyes of a man lonely for his country and his people and his children thousands of miles away.

When the news was over, Francisco told me what he had learned. He had liked hearing about his country and seeing pictures of it on the television.

My wife put the biscuits in the oven and when they were ready I poured servings of the lamb stew into bowls and we ate outside around the folding table beside the stream that wound through the meadow. The lamb meat tasted different, stronger than beef but very good.

When night came we went inside the trailer. The generator was on and I turned the television to various American programs. As we watched the shows I told Francisco in Spanish what was happening. After another Scotch he leaned back on the couch and relaxed. He had lived in his little trailer for months. Now he was in our little mansion watching the news from his country and seeing these peculiar American shows and he was with a family and children the ages of his children.

The high mountain meadow was our neighborhood, Francisco and ours. No one else but the sheep shared it. There were a few visitors each day who sped down the dirt road. You could hear the hollow, rumble in the ground long before you saw their cars that sped down the dirt roads and made clouds of dust that floated casually in the air. The visitors did not trouble us, nor we them, nor did they stop to speak to Francisco. We lived at one end of the meadow, Francisco at the other end. He could see us when we came home to Big Ugly #1 and if it was evening and the sheep had been put down, he walked through the high meadow grass to our camp, occasionally killing a rattlesnake with his stick.

We invited Francisco inside, had dinner and wine. Francisco talked about his life in Chile, we about our lives in America and my Spanish began coming back to me.

CHAPTER THIRTY–FIVE

Into the Desert

At the end of September, Francisco walked through the meadow one evening with his stick and the two black dogs. He had news. They were moving him down to Smith Valley, Nevada for the autumn. From there they would ship him and the sheep down to the Mojave Desert in California for winter. Next summer he would return to the meadow. If he stayed in America. Being around our children had only made him more lonesome for his children. He wanted to go home. He wanted to go back where people spoke his language. He was tired of sheep.

The night before they moved Francisco from the meadow, he came to us again. He was leaving in the morning he said. He was sad to leave us. We had helped him get through the summer. And he had helped us. We had all learned something. We said we were sad to see him go. Francisco hugged my wife and children and we hugged and I wished him well. That night the big double-decked truck came in the darkness and the men loaded the sheep. In the morning I went outside and looked toward Francisco's camp and saw that it was gone.

Then it was October and the sun did not burn as brightly. The frosty night air had turned the dark stands of aspens in the high canyons and gullies first to a blaze of yellow, then to an orange-red glow. The green meadow grass had dried and the individual blades had fallen to the freezing nights and the gush of autumn winds down the mountain canyons. Leaves on the brush beside the creek curled and dried and fell from the branches and the naked stems of the brush were already turning the red-purple color of winter. The creek spun through the meadow like liquid ice, nearly frozen. The first snows were not far off.

The summer season was over. Trouble with the local cops had interfered with writing and research but I had managed to finish one book and most of a second manuscript. I was looking forward to the quiet time of autumn to finish the book.

Edie and I talked it over. Before going back to Nevada we decided to spend a couple months in Bishop, California in the Owens Valley. I wanted to research the Owens Valley water wars with the City of Los

Angeles in preparation for another book. Research would take a couple months and then we would go home to Nevada.

We broke camp that evening. We hitched Big Ugly #1 to the four-wheel drive and pulled it forward. We cleaned up the mess the dogs had made under the trailer, bits of chewed paper and lamb bones. We left our camp clean. I disassembled the portable satellite dish and wrapped up the wiring and stored it in the pick-up. The folding chairs, the table and the generator went into the truck. I checked the trailer lights to see if they were operating and checked the trailer's brakes. I didn't want the Psycho Cops to ticket us for anything. I would drive the 4x4 and tow the trailer; Edie would drive the pick-up with the children. I could not haul the trailer faster than thirty miles an hour because it swayed. The 90 miles trip to Bishop would take three hours. If we left before sunrise, Highway 395 would be nearly deserted and we would miss the rush of autumn travelers on their way to Los Angeles and Reno.

At 4:00 A.M. the following morning the alarm clock rang. We forced ourselves out of bed, woke the children, grabbed a quick breakfast and piled out of Big Ugly # 1 into the trucks. I led the way and pulled Big Ugly #1 up a steep dirt road out of the mountain valley to the highway. We turned south and began the long climb up Conway Summit. We reached the Summit at 8100 feet and I pulled over. Again I checked the trailer lights and brakes before we started down the steep Conway Grade into the Mono Basin. This and the Sherwin Grade north of Bishop were the two most dangerous places in the trip. If I lost Big Ugly #1 here I was dead. I put the truck into low gear and took my time down the grade. The trailer occasionally swayed when I went too fast. I slowed down and Big Ugly #1 tucked its tail in and followed behind obediently.

We made Bishop by eight in the morning. We had located an RV space at a trailer park north of Bishop at Rovanna. It had once been the housing area for miners who worked the tungsten mine up Pine Creek Canyon. Foreign competition had driven tungsten prices down; now only a skeleton crew worked the great mine.

We climbed up Pine Creek Canyon through pastoral Round Valley where cattle grazed and deer watched us as if we were creatures from another world. It was a clear autumn morning and we all felt good to be away from our difficulties in Bridgeport. We turned into the trailer park, found our RV space and tucked in Big Ugly #1. I leveled the trailer, plugged in the electricity, hooked up the water and connected the black water tank to the septic system and we were settled.

For seven months we had hauled water to our camp. Now it was astonishing to turn on the faucets and let the unlimited water flow inside the trailer. The children played with the water in the afternoon, washed down the trucks and watered the plants and themselves.

Our new camp was a good quiet place to spend autumn and a good place to write. The weather was warmer in the desert and the sun seemed brighter. There was a lush green meadow behind our camp and stands of aspens along Pine Creek. It was a good trout stream. Scores of deer lived in the meadow beside the creek and clustered in groups of six or seven; one antlered male and his harem. The deer seemed perfectly at ease as we stood and marveled at them. They bent their long necks toward the earth and nibbled, raised their heads to watch us, and lowered their necks to feed. On some mornings the children found a family of deer laying comfortably together, unafraid. Sometimes I heard a rustling in the bushes outside the trailer at night and, opening the trailer door, discovered deer munching the tender leaves on the bushes we had watered.

Our camp was at the eastern foot of the Sierra. Steep grey rock walls rose from the foothills like skyscrapers. In the distance there was a canyon with a darkening of trees and I knew there was a spring or a stream there and looked longingly toward that canyon. One Sunday morning we followed the dirt road up the steep switch-backs to discover this new and secret place. It had been a dry year and the stream bed was dry. I dug my hand into the white sand and felt the cold dampness of the underground stream.

From our new camp we had a glorious view of the Owens Valley and the high wall of the White Mountains that made a wall on its eastern border.

PART SIX

Endings and Beginnings

CHAPTER THIRTY—SIX

Back To Nevada

If a prosecutor has... a significant personal interest in a civil matter which may impair his obligation in a criminal matter...then, he is ...disqualified from initiating or participating in the prosecution of that criminal case.
Sinclair vs. Maryland, 1976

It is axiomatic that a prosecutor should never try a defendant with whom he is embroiled in civil litigation.
Blanton vs. Barrick, Iowa Supreme Court, 1977

Our three month stay in Bishop had been pleasant except for the Psycho Cops and Mono County's dear District Attorney, Style Elver. Elver was a fair haired California boy-man who appeared in court in jeans and tennis shoes, usually adorned in a green sports coat that looked like it had been picked up at a thrift store. Elver became District Attorney because no one else wanted the job. To justify his life and office, Style Elver prosecuted people who shouldn't have been prosecuted for crimes they hadn't committed. And he *didn't* prosecute Mono County public servants who should have been prosecuted for crimes they *had* committed. After Elver had destroyed lives and reputations and the accused was found innocent or charges dropped, Elver didn't give the former defendant so much as an apology. Elver didn't have to apologize; he was a public servant; he was immune. District Attorney Style Elver wasn't a very pleasant person. But then, he was a lawyer. I should be sympathetic. Still, Style Elver brought out the worst in a person. The latest lawyer joke gave grim satisfaction:
Question: *What's black and brown and looks good on a lawyer?*
Answer: *A Doberman pinscher.*
Our suit against Mono County was wearily working its way through Mono County courts. The various vehicle registration tickets were *causes of action* in our suit. The Psycho Cops went to District Attorney Style Elver and cried on his shoulder. They were sad we had sued them. They said we were mean; they said we made them cry. Style Elver

should punish us if he wanted to win their respect. Style should use the *law* and the *courts* to do it.

While in Bishop, it was necessary from time to time to drive to Bridgeport to file court papers and appear for our suit. On one of these trips I was ticketed in Bridgeport again for not having our truck registered in California. Seems a petty thing now. But it caused us a good deal if aggravation. I had to drive about a thousand miles back and forth to Bridgeport to resolve the difficulty—or be arrested—again. It did not matter how many times we had told District Attorney Elver we had no wish to become California residents and register our vehicles in California. The Psycho Cops needed to prove they had legitimately given us those citations. If I were convicted it would make their harassment look better in court. It didn't matter how Style convicted me. And they would lie on the witness stand to help Elver. Style Elver didn't need encouragement. *He was furious that he had been named in our suit.* Style Elver became the Psycho Cops' new instrument of torture.

What misery the Psycho Cops hadn't accomplished, Elver did. In order to make his point in court, he obtained our children's school records without our consent in violation of our rights to privacy. He sent off duty cops ninety miles to Bishop to discover where we were living. He subpoenaed the innocent person from whom we rented our RV space and made her drive a hundred and eighty miles to and from Bridgeport to appear in court. He put me on the stand and asked me personal questions about my wife and our marital relationship. I told Elver if he wanted to know about my wife, he could subpoena her. Besides, what did my wife or our children's school records have to do with my traffic citations?

He put the Psycho Cops on the stand and used their perjured testimonies to convict me of crimes I had not committed. Style Elver and his boys gave me a lesson in bad justice and bad cops I have not forgotten. And I don't want you to forget either.

Despite all the aggravation, I continued writing about Twain on Jackass Hill and by Christmas I had finished the manuscript. I would have finished it six months earlier if not for the Psycho Cops and Elver. No matter. The book was finished and it would do well.

Our stay in Bishop had been restful and productive and the people had treated us well. I was finished with my research in California. Now we were rested and ready to settle things back in Storey County. Before we left Bishop I wrote a claim for damages against Storey County officials for conspiring to shut down the *Virginia City Voice*. And for transferring misinformation to the Mono County Sheriff's Department. I mailed the claim to the Storey County Board of Commissioners.

It was a clear, cold winter morning in Bishop; the sky was very blue. My neighbor saw me outside our trailer looking at the sky, grinning like a fool.

"What are you so happy about?"

"We're going home today."

"Where's home?"

"Nevada."

I pointed northeast to Boundary Peak the highest point in Nevada at 13,140 feet. Below Boundary Peak, Montgomery Pass makes a way over the White Mountains to Nevada.

"I'm taking this big ugly trailer over Montgomery Pass. We're going back where we belong," I said.

I unhooked the water, sewer and electrical lines from Big Ugly #1 and packed them in the trailer. We hitched the trailer to the truck and pulled out of the Owens Valley, climbed Montgomery Pass and crossed the White Mountains.

Our truck and trailer crawled in the night through a snowstorm as we rolled into Hawthorne, a tiny military town near the southern shore of Walker Lake. The Army manufactures ammunition in Hawthorne and stores gobs of it in hundreds of half-buried bunkers that line the valley like barns. It was too dark to see the bunkers but I knew they were there and I told the children about them.

As we pulled out of Hawthorne the red lights flashed behind us. I pulled over, got out and walked back toward the patrol car. It was snowing and my fingers numbed in the cold. I shoved my hands in my coat pockets and tucked my head into my chest. The officer walked up to me.

"Say, your trailer lights are out," he said. I looked at the tail end of the truck where the light wires connect to the trailer. The wires were disconnected.

"Hell. I can fix them if you let me."

"Be a good idea. The road's real dark between here and Yerington. With the snow, visibility will be bad. You don't want someone plowing into ya with your lights out. Pull into the parking lot over there and fix your tail lights. I'd hate to see ya get rear-ended."

"All right. We've had enough trouble. We've been over in California for a while, and I'll tell ya..." He put his hands up and stopped me.

"I saw your Nevada plates," he said. "No need to tell me. I've been over there. I love it here."

"We felt relieved as soon as we crossed the state line," I said.

"Isn't that the truth. Well hell, it's cold out here. I gotta go. And welcome back."

"Thanks. Really mean that."

"Nothing," he said.

I hopped into the warm truck. "Jesus," I said to my wife and kids, "I love Nevada."

Back in Nevada we settled down. After two and a half years of wandering around like Abraham and his tribe, we felt good and safe.

I stopped into the Silver Queen Saloon in Virginia City to see Gordon Lane. "Well," Gordon said, "you back to stay?"

"Yeah, Gordon."

"Then let's have a welcome home drink. It's on me." Gordon made me a Scotch and soda and made himself a screw driver. Doug Kick and the Bad Crew showed up that afternoon, of course. Louie Beaupre laid out his latest jokes. Balderdash laid out his; we all groaned. God, how I had missed them. It was good to be home.

We showed up in Virginia City one evening for the Senior Citizens' St. Patrick's Day corned beef and cabbage dinner at the high school gym. A lot of our friends were there. And most of our enemies. It was beautiful.

I went to the bar and found that black bearded Canadian woodsman Louie Beaupre bartending, astonishingly happy.

"Louie give me a couple of cokes for the kids, a Scotch and soda and a Chablis."

I turned and looked for Sheriff Dick's table and found it. I corralled my wife and kids. "I've found the perfect table for us." We struck out for Dick's table and when he saw us coming his face flushed that beautiful raspberry color. We put our drinks down and pulled up chairs.

"Hello Dick," I said. "I've really missed you."

Sheriff Dick turned his head without saying a word and didn't look back the rest of the evening. Our claim was filed against Storey County. The last thing he wanted was to get hauled into federal court and get fried by a diligent attorney. The whole corrupt mess would unravel.

Joe Pastrami was there, sober for a change. It was still early in the evening. My pal the County Clerk was there, the dear woman who had attempted to shut down the *Voice* because I had pointed out unpleasant things about her husband, the President of the School Board. Ol' Pat was there, too, and Ol' Al, Superintendent of Storey County schools. They seemed remarkably subdued. A million dollar claim really improves attitudes.

I was tempted to start up the *Virginia City Voice* again, but my wife's wisdom prevailed. So I didn't. The claim was filed; we had time to file suit in Federal court. But I wasn't content with that.

I wasn't very happy that the Storey County boys had shut down my newspaper and made our lives miserable both in Virginia City and Mono County. For nearly twenty years Nevada Attorney Generals had allowed the Storey County boys to operate as corruptly as they wanted. The pimp, Sheriff Dick, Joe Pastrami and the Commissioners felt impervious to the power of the law. The Nevada Attorney General had the power to begin an investigation, indict and prosecute. But no Attorney General had. Why?

Perhaps the people of Storey County could not stop the corruption legally. And maybe no public officer would help them. But the corruption could be publicized and the publicity might encourage the Attorney General to do something. And if the Attorney General did nothing, the inaction would speak for itself.

I began a thorough investigation of the county corruption spanning thirty-five years. I interviewed Storey County residents, county, state and federal officials. I went through newspapers, books, articles and county and state records. Everything I learned was going into a book, a permanent record that would detail and expose the corruption. It was far worse than I had suspected.

Bribery of Storey County public officials was the least of it. Willard Ross Brymer, the man who had confessed to shooting Oscar Bonavena, confessed to two Federal agents that he had murdered four prostitutes for the pimp. He had taken one girl down to the Truckee River and held her head in the water until she stopped struggling. The agents confronted the pimp about Brymer's confession. The pimp played innocent as always. "That Brymer, Christ he's crazy," he said. "I told him I had this problem with one of my girls. The next thing I knew he took her down to the River and drowned her. That Brymer's nuts." Later, when narcotics charges against Brymer were dropped, Brymer recanted. But why had Brymer confessed to killing *four* prostitutes? Why not one or two? Why *four*?

A prostitute who worked at the pimp's brothel alleges that a fellow prostitute while working at the brothel got out of line and was murdered. Her murder was common talk among the girls. And there was this strange thing about Dr. Death who inspected the pimp's girls. Three girls were alleged to have died from his mysterious injections.

Nothing was done about the alleged seven murders. It was out of the Feds' jurisdiction. The Storey County Sheriff and District Attorney of course did nothing. The Attorney General didn't budge. No one did anything about the murdered women. They were just dumb prostitutes.

Around this time of my investigation, the Internal Revenue Sersvice and a judge did something I agreed with. The pimp owed the IRS 13 million dollars in back taxes. For eight years he had fought the Internal Revenue Service over the bill. To prevent the confiscation of his whorehouse, he had gone into Chapter Eleven bankruptcy. This gave him time to reorganize and come up with the money to pay his income tax. But after eight years, the bankruptcy judge had grown weary of the pimp's and his attorney's ploys and changed the Chapter Eleven to Chapter Seven bankruptcy. That put the pimp's whorehouse into the hands of his creditors. The chief creditor was the IRS.

The Government seized the pimp's whorehouse, his restaurant and his trailer park. And then they went after his houses in Reno. For a week there was talk of the Government running the brothel. But Sheriff Dick, Joe Pastrami and a county Commissioner blocked the take-over. They said the brothel didn't meet building codes. The new owner would have to rebuild the place. Then there was the brothel license. It couldn't be transferred. The Government would have to wait ninety days for a new license. The Storey County boys were playing hard ball. They were making it tough for the Government to take over the pimp's whorehouse. Losing that beauty was like losing a gold mine. They wanted the Government to back-off and let the pimp run his whorehouse in peace.

There seemed something very wrong with the United States Government running a whorehouse. At least the People thought so. The Government decided it would not go into the whorehouse business after all.

Temporarily blocked by the Storey County boys, the bankruptcy judge got fed up with the mess and turned over the pimp's properties to the IRS. The IRS auctioned off the brothel for a million and a half dollars. Everything inside the brothel was sold, from boxes of condoms to cheap paintings, some of these Tijuana treasures going for several thousand dollars.

The pimp's well wishers were there. They thought it a sad day that his "institution" was being shut down. The pimp was at the auction signing autographs for fans; many were women. The local TV crews were there, too. The pimp never missed a hair of publicity.

The tax sale did not earn enough to pay the pimp's liabilities. He was still in debt to the IRS for about eleven and a half million dollars. The debt would accrue interest daily. It looked like the pimp's Storey County kingdom had been demolished.

CHAPTER THIRTY–SEVEN

The pimp's return

The devil...the prowde spirite...cannot endure to be mocked. Thomas More

Wrong. Three months later he was back in Storey County. He had side-stepped the IRS by having his attorney create a new corporation and having the corporation buy back the brothel at the IRS' tax sale. In Nevada a corporation does not have to divulge the names of the share holders. By creating a new corporation, the pimp had escaped paying the remaining eleven and a half million dollars in back taxes. And he got his brothel back. The pimp had made fools out of every honest American taxpayer. And he had made the Feds look like idiots.

During the IRS seizure of the brothel, the Storey County Commissioners—by this time they were two new guys and one new girl—voted to remove the pimp's brothel from the brothel district. This was publicized in the papers. It seemed to anyone who could read, that the pimp and his brothel were permanently out of business in Storey County.

Wrong. After the new corporation bought back the pimp's brothel, he claimed his previous Storey County business license was still valid. This seemed ludicrous to every sensible person. But not to the pimp. The IRS may have seized his property and business and sold them, but they had never taken his business license away. Only Storey County could do that and it hadn't. According to Nevada State law the Storey County Commissioners had to give the pimp a hearing before they revoked his license. The pimp's argument seemed to have a leg to stand on. The Commissioners were confused.

At a public Board of Commissioners meeting, the pimp showed up. Here was the man I had heard so much about. His face had a flat, dull expression and his eyes were often down instead of looking into the faces and eyes of others. He looked like he had the weight of mankind on his shoulders. But he was no Christ. He wore a black overcoat that came down to his knees, gray expensive slacks, shoes shiny and black and coat and tie of which he seemed very proud. He walked with his hands in his coat pockets, head tucked into his shoulders like a mole. It made him seem humble and human; this was the part of his charm that people liked and were fooled by. He looked like a bad actor in a cheap gangster film. Underneath the expensive clothes was a boy in an old man's body and he was damn angry he hadn't gotten what he wanted.

The pimp began his assault on the Storey County Commissioners that morning by quoting Shakespeare, although he had likely never read a word of that writer and wouldn't have understood it if he had. He told the Commissioners he was going back in business, that in fact, he had never been *out* of business. This was a lie, of course, but then when the pimp lied he was only being true to his nature. He had lied for so long and gotten so good at it, he didn't know he was lying.

One Commissioner bravely said the pimp's business license became invalid when the IRS seized and sold his brothel. Storey County laws substantiated this; a business license could not be transferred.

Still, the pimp went forward. He represented himself pretty good for a guy with a grade school education. Then the female member of the Board, Sally Salami, who had managed the pimp's whorehouse and run for county Commissioner and won thanks to the pimp's votes, piped up. You might have thought Sally Salami was the pimp's attorney. Everyone in the room did. Sally Salami said the pimp's business license was valid. Then Joe Pastrami got on the band wagon, and then Sheriff Dick. They all said the pimp's business license was valid. It was nonsense and everyone knew it.

Two Commissioners agreed the pimp's business license was in question. That didn't matter much, though. The bunch of them argued for a long while and then the pimp piped up and threatened the boys. He was always threatening someone. The FBI had a file cabinet full of people the pimp had threatened to kill or beat up. The pimp became furious when he didn't get his way. Or when he felt insulted. He *always* felt insulted.

"Either you give me my business license and let me go back into business or I'm out of this county," he yelled at the Commissioners. "I'll take my money and go to Brazil," or something like that. This got the Board's attention and they quieted down. The Board let the pimp go back in business—against their own laws. After all, if the pimp was kept out of business, Sheriff Dick and Joe Pastrami wouldn't get their money. They would have to work for a living. Everyone in the Board room that day knew who was being paid off and who wasn't. It was as plain as ice and fire.

It seemed like a good time to resurrect the *Virginia City Voice* and finish what I had started. My wife didn't resist me this time.

"What do you think they'll do when you publish this," she asked after she read over the newest edition of the *Voice*. "Think they'll try to kill you?"

"No." I lied.

The pimp and the Storey County boys might try to kill me or consider it. They hated the truth and anyone who told the truth about their criminal activities. Nothing I wrote would end the corruption in Storey County. I knew that now. I just wanted to make a point. The last time I had written about the corruption they had run me out of town. I wasn't running anywhere anymore. I was an American writer granted rights and privileges by the Constitution. I would exercise those rights and be damned with their threats and their guns and their evil. I would have my say.

For the last edition of the *Voice* there was a new play, *Blessed are the Crooked for they shall inherit St. Joe's Money,* a satire on the last Commissioners' meeting. Some called the pimp "Joe" and thought him a saint. All right. Then I would canonize him. This is how it went:

The players:
Sheriff Dick Del Monte: Crook
District Attorney Joe Pastrami: Crook
Commissioner Sally Salami: Crook
Commissioner Karl Larson: Baffled and embarrassed
Commissioner Larry Prater: The only one in the Board room that gave a damn about the People of Storey County and doomed in Storey County for his courage and honesty.
St. Joe: The pimp.

Setting: Storey County Courthouse, home of the Big Top.
Scene: Storey County Board of Commissioners meeting

Act 1, Scene 1

Commissioner Prater: Let's see if I understand you St. Joseph. Your brothel was seized by the IRS who took ownership and sold it to an unknown party. Correct?

St. Joe: Yes, that's right.

Prater: This was your place of business, correct?

St. Joe: Yes.

Prater: And it was seized and sold by the IRS?

St. Joe: Yes.

Prater: And now you're telling us you think you have a valid Storey County business license although your business and the property were seized and sold. And you're telling us you're going to open for business tomorrow at the same place that was sold?

St. Joe: No, we've already been open for business. We've never been out of business. And I don't think my license is valid. I know it is.

Prater: You've never been out of business although county records show that the IRS owned your former property and sold it. You say you've been open for business already?

St. Joe: Yes. That's right. The IRS got my business and my property but I still have my business license and I'm going to run it.

Prater: Where are you going to run it?

St Joe: Well, right where I've been running it the last 35 years.

Prater: But St. Joe, your property and your former business have been sold to someone else?

St. Joe: Doesn't matter. I'm still going to run it.

Prater: St. Joe, I really question whether your license is valid. After all, your business was sold and the property where it was operated was sold. You do remember that don't you, St. Joe?

St. Joe: Well, of course I remember it. I was signing autographs that day. The people of Storey County love me. I've done so much for them. Why, I'm a God to them.

Sheriff Del Monte: Well, I've got no problems with St. Joe's business license being valid Mr. Prater.

Commissioner Sally Salami: That's absolutely right. St. Joe's business license is perfectly valid.

District Attorney Pastrami: Absolutely correct. I see nothing wrong with St. Joe doing business as usual.

Commissioner Larson: Uh...

Prater, flushed and somewhat stunned by the proceedings, at this point shut his eyes, opened them, hoping he had been having a nightmare. Wrong. It was the same place with the same faces and the same unbelievable words coming out of the same unbelievable mouths. Prater was considering vomiting on the Board's table to better express himself. Instead, he grit his teeth, held his breath and it all went back down the same pipe it had come up. But Prater was rendered speechless.

Prater: Uh...

At this point Commissioner Sally Salami got on her band wagon. Apparently she had forgotten she no longer works for St. Joe—or maybe she does, who knows. She was elected by the People of Storey County to represent ALL the People of Storey County. However, citizens present at the Board of Commissioners meeting were convinced Salami was St. Joe's attorney and just happened to be on the Board of Commissioners by mistake.

Salami: Sheriff Del Monte, you're the head of the licensing board. What are you going to do about this license problem?

Sheriff Del Monte: What license problem?

Prater: The one we've been discussing.

Del Monte: St. Joe doesn't have a license problem. There's no need for the licensing board to vote on his license. Why, he's even paid it up to date.

Prater: Fellas, and Mrs. Salami, I just don't see how a man can have a valid business license and not own the property and not own the business. Why it just...

Commissioner Larson: Uh...

Commissioner Salami: Oh, Prater give us break. Technicalities. Technicalities. Whadaya think this is, a perfect world?

Prater: Well, uh...

Sheriff Del Monte: Jesus Christ, Prater, give St. Joe a break.

Pastrami: Yeah, Prater. What the hell's wrong with you? Don't you know how we run things up here? That ain't just anybody out there. Why, that's St. Joe. You should be out there on your knees kissing his butt. Don't you know how much St. Joe loves us and all the good things he's done for us? Damn it, Prater. Whata we gotta do, draw ya a picture?

Del Monte: This is the way it works up here: We love St. Joe and St. Joe loves us. We do for St. Joe what he can't do for himself. And he does for us what we can't do for ourselves.

Pastrami: Yeah, like getting off our lazy, corrupt butts and working for a living.

Del Monte: Yeah, Joe, you tell him.

Salami: Yeah, Prater. What's wrong with you? Why, St. Joe gives the young girls of Storey County a place to work with a roof over their heads and he lets them eat regular. Why, St. Joe, he's right up there next to God Almighty for Chris-sake. St. Joe runs a clean place and he makes certain those neurotic girls don't get AIDS and give it to their customers to go home and give it to their wives. Wives? Jesus Christ, what a way for a woman to live. A good woman is a good whore, by God.

Citizen in the audience: Uh, Ms. Salami, is it true what I heard about you being in Hawaii and, you know, earning your living as a prost...

Salami: What the hell you trying to say? Just because I worked for St. Joe and I love him with all my soul and if he asked me to cut out my heart and eat it for him I'd do it, doesn't mean I was any whore down there.

Prater: Well...

Commissioner Larson: Uh...

Sheriff Del Monte: St. Joe, forgive Mr. Prater for he knows not what he does. Just ignore him. He ain't got no manners. Pray for us St. Joe and give us your blessing.

St. Joe: Blessed are the crooked, for they shall inherit my money. Go my children, and may hell be not far from you.

And so it went and so it goes. The People of Storey County never had it so good.

No. That wasn't enough. I went on.

Williams to Open Competing Whorehouse

George Williams III, former author and publisher, this week announced he is leaving his career as a writer and turning to prostitution as a new career. Asked why, Williams said, "After observing this week's Board of Commissioners meeting, and seeing St. Joe in action, how he yelled at the Commissioners, DA and Sheriff and made them shake in their shoes, I saw how powerful pimping and money is in Storey County. And by God, I was damned envious.

"You know, each of us have had the same opportunity as St. Joe, to start our own whorehouse and get rich and famous. But none of us have taken advantage of it. When I heard St. Joe yelling and demanding at the Board of Commissioners meeting, it was like hearing God himself...

"It came upon me like a revelation. For the first time I clearly understood that I've been wasting my life trying to write books and tell the truth and be an honest good person. St. Joe and the politicians on his payroll—you know Del Monte, Salami, Pastrami, made it damn clear, that I, well hell, that all of us,

have had it all wrong. We have wasted our lives working hard and being honest and paying our taxes like good Americans.

"Just look at the example of St. Joe. He doesn't work. His girls work on their backs and knees for him. He doesn't have to pay his IRS back taxes of 13 million dollars. Why, it seems he doesn't have to pay the IRS any taxes at all. Look at the benefits of his career. He makes lots of money. Millions. His girls do the whoring for him and he just collects the cash. He gets to wear expensive clothes, drive beautiful cars and he gets to have sex with any of his girls any time he wants. Now that's what I call the good life. What an example St. Joe and his boys have been to us. They have all taught us something we should be grateful for. And this is it: What is good, is really bad. And what is bad, is really good. They understood it all along. And now they've helped me understand it.

"So I'm going in the whorehouse business, too. Right here in Storey County. And you know where I'm going to build my whorehouse? In the county parking lot right next to the courthouse on B Street, next to Piper's Opera House. It's gonna be a really beautiful whorehouse, too. Why, it's going to be the biggest and best damn whorehouse in the world. It will make St. Joe's chicken ranch look like a peanut farm...

"Here's how I imagine it. It's gonna be a big ole Victorian mansion three stories high—about as high as the courthouse. I'm going to paint it red, just as red as blood. That's right, just as red as blood to symbolize that killing your enemies is good. And I'm going to have a big, long shute going from my top window right down to Sheriff Del Monte's office so I can just throw my payoffs down that shute and I won't have to go down there and face him every time he wants his money.

"And if the people of this county have been impressed with St. Joe's alleged generosity, just let me tell you what I'm going to do....I'm going to give every female Storey County resident, regardless of age, race or color, first chance at working in my whorehouse...I don't care if a woman's so ugly she could peel the paint off a fire hydrant. I'll let her work in my whorehouse for free. I won't charge her a damn dime. That's how generous I'm gonna be.

"And if Sheriff Del Monte and those boys and girls thought they were getting paid well by St. Joe, wait till they get a load of me. Why, St. Joe will be spitting nails when he learns how much more he'll have to pay after I'm done with them. Why, I'll bet my whorehouse will drive St. Joe's peanut farm right back to Oakland where that dear man came from.I have seen the light. I have seen the Truth. I understand. Being a pimp and running a whorehouse is the best damned proof of the American Dream...

No. It still wasn't enough. I went on.

County To Offer New Classes

In an effort to encourage our high school girls and boys toward the lucrative profession of prostitution in Storey County, this county's chief and most profitable industry, and to instill in their young heads the values Storey County holds most dear, Storey County voted this week to offer these new classes to begin after Christmas vacation.

For high school girls:

Whoring For Fun and Profit: This class, taught by Sheriff Del Monte, will teach the teenager the benefits of prostitution, the opportunity to meet rich and successful young men—and old married ones too, how to make lots of money to buy bright, sleazy clothes to tempt the most moral church goer. Girls will learn how to handle their first customer, how to lie to their parents and boy friends about their new occupation, how to relieve the pain of prostitution with drugs and suicide, and how to give back to Storey County what the county has given to them: the wonderful opportunity of whoring. Why complete your high school education, when you can be down there in St. Joe's whorehouse and making thousands of dollars a week and meeting new and exciting men and living the good life?

Whorehouse Management: This class, taught by Commissioner Sally Salami, will teach those girls not particularly interested in whoring, the proper way to run a whorehouse. Salami, an expert in the field, will cover such things as: keeping your girls in line with drugs, how to wash down your customers with Lysol, how to collect money from customers and prostitutes, how to inspire and encourage girls to keep up the good work as good whores. Mrs. Salami's encouraging motto: "A good girl is a good whore."

For high school boys:

Pimping: The Way to Fame and Fortune: Taught by the famous St. Joe himself, high school boys will learn how to "turn out" high school girls into the exciting and profitable world of prostitution. St. Joe will provide examples of seductions from his personal life. Boys will learn how to convince a young girl you love her and have her best interests at heart by turning her into a good whore, how to avoid paying federal taxes, how to pay off Storey County politicians, how to defraud county elections, how to buy votes with whisky and turkeys, how to intimidate county politicians by yelling at them at Commissioner meetings, how to betray friends by testifying at their trials, how to go to prison for committing felonies and making the most out of your prison vacation, and much, much more. No high school boy should miss this exciting, inspiring "hands on," class with St. Joe himself. Why, getting his autograph alone is worth it.

Law and Prostitution: Taught by our own highly esteemed District Attorney Joe Pastrami, who personally wrote Ordinance 39 which made prostitution legal in Storey County and made this county world famous. Pastrami will begin by teaching boys and girls how prostitution has always been an important part of Storey County's social structure and how it must continue for the benefit of county politicians. Also covered: how to side-step county laws, how to be a district attorney and yet still have a profitable career as a pimp's attorney and much more. However, Mr. Pastrami said some early morning classes may be cancelled if he has been on a bender and can't remember in which saloon he left his underwear hanging. He encourages all boys and girls to just show up and hope he shows up, too.

I wasn't convinced I had gotten my point over. So just to be certain, I thought Sheriff Dick should post signs at Storey County's borders. Just so visitors would know what they were getting into:

County To Post New Signs

Sheriff Del Monte will be posting new signs at the borders of Storey County. These signs will be placed on the Geiger Grade, Highway 341 and on Interstate 80 near Lovelock. Del Monte informs us the new signs will read:

Welcome to Storey County
Home of the Biggest Whorehouse in America.
The Constitution of the United States
does not exist beyond this point.
You have no voting or civil rights.
Some politicians are bribed crooks.
We pamper pimps and punish the good and honest.
Wrong is right; right is wrong.
Illegal drugs are legal.

There. That should do it.

CHAPTER THIRTY–EIGHT

Making A Point

I_____do solemnly swear (or affirm) that I will support, protect and defend the Constitution and Government of the United States, and the constitution and government of the State of Nevada, against all enemies, whether domestic or foreign, and that I will bear true faith, allegiance and loyalty to the same, any ordinance, resolution of any state notwithstanding, and that I will well and faithfully perform all duties of the office of_____ [name of office] on which I am about to enter...so help me God...under the pains and penalties of perjury.

The official oath of office as sworn by the Governor and the Attorney General of Nevada

When the Storey County boys and girls read the latest *Voice* , they were livid. They wanted my head. I wasn't surprised.

There was one more thing to do to drive home my point. Some of the boys and girls had just been reelected. They were to be sworn in at the next Commissioners' meeting. Good. We would be there.

When my wife and I showed up for the Commissioners' meeting you could have cut the tension in that room with a chain saw. In behind us came the pimp with one of his prostitutes. Immediately Sheriff Del Monte pointed me out to the pimp by motioning with his head. The pimp misconstrued his directions and turned to a harmless soul behind me.

"You Williams?"

"No, I'm not Williams."

"Oh yes you are."

"No. I'm not."

"Yeah, you're Williams," the pimp said. "I'm going to get you arrested this week on a gross misdemeanor. We're going to get you..." and other threats that made the poor man shake in his shoes.

"Listen, I'm really not Williams." He turned to the man in front of him. "Would you tell this guy I'm not Williams?"

"He's not Williams."

I turned to the pimp. "I'm Williams."

The pimp shut up, looked away and didn't say a word. Then he sat down with his girl behind my wife and I.

The Storey County boys and girls stood up and smiled as they took their oaths of office and sat down. Sheriff Del Monte's expression grew into that raspberry shade I had grown fond of. His eyes darkened and narrowed as he glared at us. I smiled pleasantly at Dick.

As we left the Commissioners' room, the pimp and his girl went out in front of us. Outside the room the pimp turned to me, angry, losing composure.

"You Williams?"

"That's right."

"You got an attorney."

"What's it to you?"

"You're gonna need one. I'm gonna get you arrested for a gross misdemeanor." The pimp was throwing around his threats again. I didn't know what "gross misdemeanor" he was talking about. I had done nothing illegal. But if I were convicted of this mysterious charge it could put me in jail for a year.

Here was the little man who had made himself rich off of busted-up troubled women. Here was the man who some alleged was responsible for the murders of young women. Here was the man who had seduced, bribed and ruined many good men who had trusted him or accepted his money or his whores or his help. Clever and absolutely amoral, unafraid to tempt or threaten any man as long as he could get away with it, the pimp had survived while his victims were destroyed.

I wasn't impressed with his money. I wasn't intimidated by his his threats. I clicked my tape recorder on and reached it toward his mouth.

"You threatening me," I asked.

The pimp shut up and took his prostitute back into the Commissioners' meeting.

A couple nights later I got a phone call. It was from a friend of District Attorney Joe Pastrami. It was a warning. Joe was all shook up. The caller said the latest *Voice* had irritated the pimp to such a degree that he was considering having one of his psychopathic gorillas rearrange my cerebellum with a .45. Joe quoted the pimp as saying, "We've got to shut this guy up," meaning me. Joe didn't want anything to do with murder. He had been down that road before. The last time the pimp had someone murdered in Storey County, he had to clean up the mess. Joe said I better layoff the pimp. If I didn't write any more about him in my paper I wouldn't be killed and I wouldn't be arrested. The pimp would guarantee it. I thought the pimp was awfully considerate not to kill me for telling the truth.

With this threat on my life, I went to the Nevada Attorney General. We had a new one, Frankie Sue Del Papa. I told Frankie Sue's secretary I was worried about our earthly welfare and wanted to speak to the Attorney General about it. The secretary said leave my name and number. So I did.

Here's what we got from Frankie Sue Del Papa four days later: diddly squat.

I thought it peculiar that a citizen and his family who might shortly have their heads blown off was of such little interest to the chief law enforcement officer for the state of Nevada. But then, this is Nevada where Attorney Generals can have strange friends.

But I am a persistent soul. I called Bob Pike, Chief Investigator for the Attorney General. I thought Bob might be interested in my troubles. I was told to leave a message. So I did. It only took ten calls to get one of Bob's. No matter, I had him. My wife and I met Bob Pike alone at the Attorney General's offices in a private, confidential meeting. We laid out our long sad story, how the pimp and officials in Storey County were harassing me for writing the truth, the threat on our lives, etc.. Bob sympathized, and that made us feel good.

And then I asked Bob, "What are you going to do about it?"

This was Bob's answer: diddly squat.

It didn't seem to bother the Chief Investigator too greatly that a journalist had been threatened by the pimp and county politicians who were notoriously corrupt. It was out of the Attorney General's jurisdiction, Bob said. Like hell it was, I said. [See Nevada Revised Statute 228.120 (3) The attorney general may "*Appear in, take exclusive charge of and conduct any prosecution in any court of this state for a violation of any law of this state, when in his opinion it is necessary, or when requested to do so by the governor.*" See also Nevada cases *List v. County of Douglas, Junior v. State,* and Justice Mowbray's dissenting opinion in *Ryan v. Eighth Judicial District Court.*] Bob said I should file my complaint in the county where I lived. He was wrong, of course. But I was ignorant of the law. And so was Bob.

It seemed all right to Bob Pike that Storey County District Attorney Joe Pastrami shot his mouth off about how much the pimp paid him.

Felony bribery of county officials didn't trouble the Chief Investigator. Worse, it didn't bother him to learn that Joe Pastrami was fully aware that the pimp had had the unfortunate boxer murdered, and yet, had not indicted and prosecuted the pimp, nor relieved himself from trying the case due to prejudice, but instead, had gone on and prosecuted the accused murderer! Bob had lived in Nevada longer than us; he was used to this stuff.

Then Bob Pike left me with these comforting words: I should be careful. The pimp was "capable of anything."

I thought it curious that the Chief Investigator for the Attorney General was aware of the pimp's potential to cause others great bodily harm and had such little concern for our predicament. But then, I was probably expecting too much of him.

Within two hours of our private, confidential meeting with the Attorney General's Chief Investigator, Joe Pastrami was notified that we had met with Pike and was made aware of the details of our meeting. It's a real lonesome feeling when you learn you can't share your deepest fears with the chief law enforcement officer for the state of Nevada.

When I examined the voting tallies of District 3 in Storey County— the pimp's district, things got clearer. Frankie Sue Del Papa had done well in District 3 in two elections. She had received two thirds of the brothel district's vote in her bid for Attorney General. I doubted Frankie Sue would investigate any wrong doing by Storey County officials. Nor our complaint. Maybe if the pimp was murdered in Storey County she might investigate that.

About this time my investigation led me to the Nevada Criminal Files Repository. These files allegedly contain information about Nevada's most notorious criminals. The files are supposed to be open to members of the print and electronic media. Nevada state law says so. [See Nevada Revised Statute 179.] Two times while attempting to access the pimp's criminal records I was escorted out of public offices by Nevada Highway Patrolmen, who made it clear to me, that if I did not leave I would be arrested. This seemed very strange, that a journalist and historian should be denied access to public records by police officers who had nothing to do with the records.

So I called Attorney General Frankie Sue Del Papa and told her what was going on. I asked Ms. Del Papa to inform the Nevada Highway Patrol, and others, that Nevada law permits journalists to access public criminal records and that those who were preventing me from doing so were breaking the law. Frankie Sue Del Papa said to me, "You know Mr. Williams, you've got an attitude problem," and promptly hung up. Never heard from Frankie Sue again.

Well. Who else can help? Nevada Governor Bob Miller seemed like the answer. So I called Governor Miller. He didn't call back. I called his aid, Brian Harris. Harris said he would do what he could to help me access criminal records that were being hidden by Wayne Teglia and Jan Capaldi of the Criminal Files Repository.

My wife and I finally met with Colonel Bill Yukish, Chief of the Highway Patrol to find out why his officers were taking me out of public offices every time I showed up. Besides my wife, there were three other officers present in the room, one scribbling notes. I asked if I could tape record the meeting. Yukish said I could not. I explained my investigation to Yukish, and showed him my published books, their published reviews and showed him an eight page print-out of my books that were currently on the shelves of Nevada libraries. Yukish said there was some question as to my being a member of the media. Not only was I a writer, I explained, but I was a journalist and a publisher. I then attempted to read the definition of "media" and "medium" to Yukish from Webster's Dictionary. Yukish said he didn't want to hear it. I read Yukish the definitions anyway.

Colonel Bill Yukish turned to his three men and said, "Well, boys, what do you think? Should we get an Attorney General's opinion whether Mr. Williams is a member of the media?" This was something that would take three or four months.

Then I asked Yukish why his officers had escorted me out of public offices. Yukish handed me a sheet of paper, an obscure Nevada law. He had high-lighted the section about persons interfering with the "peaceful conduct" of activities in public offices. I had always behaved professionally I said. Well, he said, people had felt threatened by me. I had never threatened anyone I said. "Well, Mr. Williams, you just wouldn't take 'no' for an answer," Yukish said.

"Why should I?" Apparently my crime was that I was diligent and persistent in my research.

I knew what Yukish was really saying. People in high places didn't like me nosing around about this corruption stuff. If I caused them more trouble trying to access public criminal records they were going to arrest me. They were looking for any excuse. It's an eerie feeling when men in law enforcement become your enemies for no good reason.

I spent the rest of the meeting yelling at Yukish about my rights to access public records as a citizen and journalist. "What have you got to hide here," I asked.

Yukish smiled. "Nothing," he said.

Like hell. I gathered my books and papers and walked out. Yukish and his boys followed us and made certain we left the offices. They had a good laugh over that. "That crazy Williams," they said. And they laughed about it. "Really showed him, didn't we?" And they laughed about it.

I did receive a letter from the administrator of the Nevada Criminal Files Repository which stated the Repository contained no criminal information on the pimp.

I filed a criminal complaint at the Attorney General's office against Wayne Teglia, the person in charge of the Repository's criminal records and his assistant Jan Capaldi for concealing public criminal records. The Attorney General took no action.

Finally, I went to Governor Bob Miller's personal secretary, Marva Johnson. I told her I would like to make an appointment to meet with the Governor to discuss his helping me access criminal records which I felt I was being denied. I asked Marva for an appointment several times and left my phone number.

I never heard from Marva Johnson. Nor from Governor Miller. Nor from his aid, Brian Harris. Subsequent phone calls to Harris were not returned. Strange, because Governor Miller had run on a law and order platform. So much for law and order in Nevada.

From my dealings with the Attorney General, the Governor's office, the Highway Patrol and the Criminal Repository folks, I got the strong impression that Nevada state officials would not help my investigation. But they would do what they could to frustrate it.

The FBI were helpful, too. They said they couldn't do anything to protect my family unless the pimp blew my head off. I should bring them my corpse. They needed evidence.

About this time I met a guy who had been in the maximum security part of the Nevada State Prison. He had vacationed there for shooting a guy in the head. Surprisingly his victim lived.

This former inmate had been roommates with some of the pimp's former hired guns. He told me a tale about these guys that would make you hang yourself. The pimp's thugs weren't human. They were subcreatures who not only did not know the difference between right and wrong, the concept of right and wrong never entered their brains. They would just as soon kill me and my whole tribe as step on a cockroach. They would kill anyone for a bag of marijuana or a tube of tooth paste or a can of beans. They were dangerous people and I didn't want anything to do with them. And then the former inmate left me with those reassuring words Bob Pike had left me with: the pimp was "capable of anything."

"Well," I said to myself, "I've had my say about the pimp and the Storey County boys, anyway. I don't need to elaborate on it."

With this encouragement from the Attorney General, the Governor, the Chief of the Highway Patrol, the FBI and the former prison inmate, I sent a message to the pimp: I will not write about you *in my paper* as long as you spare my life and the lives of my family. It was a difficult compromise for a man who considers compromise a form of punishment. But I had a family to consider.

But I never promised the pimp I wouldn't write a book. And he never asked me not to. So instead of a few words about him in an underground newspaper, I wrote a book that will outlast his *damned impenitent soul!*

With the last issue of the *Voice,* I was done with it. If Attorney General Frankie Sue Del Papa thought it was good for the People of Storey County to live under the power of the pimp, to be threatened with death whenever a citizen stood up and spoke the truth, and if the Attorney General thought a corrupt county government run by thugs and murderers was an ideal form of democracy, who was I to question this woman's wisdom?

I cannot change some things. But I can write about them.

CHAPTER THIRTY–NINE

In the Long Run

I do not know why one man chooses to do good, and another chooses to do evil. Nor do I know why one man is made more naturally good than another. Some men have to work harder than others at being good. I am one of these. It does seem to me that each of us is given an area of choice, a space of free will, where we are allowed to choose what we will serve, good or evil, God or the devil.

John Steinbeck had something to say about this. In his novel *East of Eden*, he wrote, "In uncertainty I am certain that underneath their topmost layers of frailty men want to be good and want to be loved. Indeed, most of their vices are attempted short cuts to love. When a man comes to die, no matter what his talents and influence and genius, if he dies unloved his life must be a failure to him and his dying a cold horror. It seems to me that if you or I must choose between two courses of thought or action, we would remember our dying and try so to live that our death brings no pleasure to the world.

"We have only one story. All novels, all poetry, are built on the never-ending contest in ourselves of good and evil. And it occurs to me that evil must constantly respawn, while good, while virtue, is immortal."

C.S. Lewis shared a similar thought: "...pleasure, money, power, and safety are all, as far as they go, good things. The badness consists in pursuing them by the wrong method, or in the wrong way, or too much. I do not mean, of course, that the people who do this are not desperately wicked. I do mean that wickedness, when you examine it, turns out to be the pursuit of some good in the wrong way...Goodness is, so to speak, itself: badness is only spoiled goodness. And there must be something good first before it can be spoiled."

Sometimes a man makes one naive or stupid decision and pays for it the rest of his life. And sometimes if a man is unwise or vain or prideful or blind, he refuses to admit his mistake and it becomes a perverted seed that grows inside him and the man goes bad. He becomes an enemy of good men. What am I to do when I am confronted by such an enemy?

I am told I should pray for my enemies. Nothing could seem more unrealistic and foolish. *Me? Pray for my enemies? Those who have done their best to harm me?*

Give me a break.

But if I should come to believe that when I pray for those who have harmed me, I pray for myself—for the part of me that meant good but missed the mark, then praying for my enemies makes sense and is practical. For in praying for my enemies I admit my failures and release my enemies from theirs.

So it is never easy to judge another man's life. So much of what we have done, both for good and for evil, is hidden from others. Maybe if we knew others as well as we believe we know ourselves, we would be surprised at the good and the evil we would find. Perhaps there is a time to come, a world to come, when we will discover that those we judged harshly had more good in them than we ever imagined. And those we considered good were a far darker breed.

But for now, and for our world, it seems the truest way to judge a man is by the sum total of his actions. For they are the fruit of our lives. In my life I must ask myself: Have I done more good than evil? And for the wrong I have done, have I gone to those I harmed and tried to make it right? And I must give myself honest answers if I am to find peace with myself.

While completing this book, one of the Storey County boys involved in the corruption and other crimes, an insider, found me one evening. I was his priest and he was the confessor. Everything I had written was true, he said. The bribery, the cover-up of the Bonavena murder, the murders of the prostitutes, it was all true. He was afraid he said. He didn't want to go to jail. It was all falling apart in Storey County. And me, of all people, to tell this to. Maybe he knew I would understand.

I did for him what I'd like someone to do for me. I told him he had to get free of the pimp. He had to do it or the pimp would destroy him as he had destroyed others. When it all fell apart the pimp would let him swing by his lonesome like he did to ole Harry Claiborne. I told him I believed God cared about him—in spite of his sins—and that he could find help in Him if he gave Him a chance. He looked at me curiously. And that was the end of it.

Sheriff Dick Del Monte is still Sheriff of Storey County, Nevada. He was recently reelected for a fifth, four year term. He is still well liked by most, despite his crimes, which I suppose is good for him and says something about the tolerant and forgiving natures of the People of Storey County. I've heard he will be retiring after this term, which is good, and I'll have to root around for someone new to carve up.

Joe Pastrami was reelected Storey County District Attorney for a fourth term. He is still drunk much of the time but he has cut down on his nightly parties. He doesn't hang his underwear on Virginia City's crystal chandeliers so often. I sort of miss that.

The pimp recently retired from the whorehouse business. So he says. I don't believe it. He still battles the IRS which refuses to leave him alone. There is not a man for whom I have greater sympathy. Hell is a heartbeat away.

Willard Ross Brymer, who confessed to killing Oscar Bonavena and four prostitutes, spent two years in the Nevada State Prison for the Bonavena murder. When he was released from prison he fooled with drugs again, got busted and was sent back to prison. This time for life as an habitual criminal. However, through a legal loophole he was paroled in 1991 and now lives in California.

The pimp's personal body guard, who some allege was involved in the Oscar Bonavena murder, is said to be legally blind.

Some say the blood of murdered prostitutes cries out from their hidden desert graves. And no one has done anything to quiet the crying.

A Storey County Commissioner, formerly on the pimp's payroll, escaped from Storey County during a federal investigation and fled to Phoenix, Arizona.

Wayne Teglia, Director of the Nevada Department of Motor Vehicles, who ordered police officers to remove me from public offices in my attempt to access public criminal records, was asked to step down by Governor Bob Miller and resigned.

To the best of my knowledge, to this date no Nevada Attorney General has *thoroughly* investigated the corruption in Storey County nor the allegations of murder and conspiracy to commit murder by county officials.

Former Storey County District Attorney Bill Wrong recently ran for District Attorney in Reno and lost. Not once did he mention he had been

Storey County District Attorney. I ran into Bill a while back and apologized for giving him such a hard time in my paper. Bill said he forgave me, which he should. And then I asked Bill for the money he and Judge Yahoo robbed from me.

Ol' Al Ricardo, the former Superintendent of Storey County Schools is gone from Storey County and gone from Nevada. He was hired for other jobs from which he was fired, and other jobs from which he was fired and other jobs— oh, you get the picture. Al finally ended up deep in the heart of a Federal bureaucracy. Just where I said he belonged. Al may not have believed it or understood it, but I was probably his best friend when he was in Virginia City. I even sent Moses to warn him. What more could I do? Al didn't trust my advice. I'm sorry about that, and I'm sorry for Al.

Down in Bridgeport, California, for his part in tormenting us, a former Assistant District Attorney known as the Phantom of the Court, was awarded a better county job and bought a new house. Supervisor Bent Bently no longer works for Mono County but has gone on to bigger and more disastrous ventures. Deputy Ignorance was suspended from the Mono County Sheriff's department for threatening the life of a citizen. According to some, Mono County District Attorney Style Elver still prosecutes people for crimes they haven't committed. The Mono County Psycho Cops from Hell still torture innocent Americans who have the misfortune of stumbling into Bridgeport. That may change after this. But I won't hold my breath.

Our suit against Mono County was thrown out of court. The judge said we had failed to file a proper claim against the County before filing suit.

Francisco the Mountain Shepherd went back to Chile after our summer together. We hope he is happy with his family.

Marguerite Ivey, who nearly single handedly saved Mono General Hospital for the People of Mono County, finally got tired of being yelled at by backwoods politicians and left Mono County and was immediately hired somewhere else. Recently Mono General Hospital became an emergency clinic.

We have prayed for all of them. It is the least we can do. After all, they gave me this book.

There is a moral in all this I suppose: If you ever feel cooped up in the city and long to leave the noise and trouble for some peaceful little town because you believe life will be simpler there, here are my suggestions:

First, douse yourself with gasoline and light a match. Then point a loaded .38 toward your right inner ear and pull the trigger. Then fill your bath tub, plug in an electric heater, drop it in the tub and step in. And if you've survived all this, find a busy railroad track, lay your head on one rail, your feet on the other and wait for the next locomotive. And if after all this you still want to move to a small town, then take my prayers and an automatic weapon. *For you will need both!*

CHAPTER FORTY

Endings and Beginnings

When Gordon Lane, that dear terrible man whose central purpose in life is to make people happy, retired as keeper of the Union Brewery Saloon in Virginia City, those who loved Gordon and the Union Brewery were saddened. For forty years Gordon Lane welcomed strangers as if each were a friend. Many became friends.

There was a party for Gordon's retirement. A good crowd showed up and the Reno *Gazette-Journal* sent a reporter to witness the funeral. Gordon was his usual good natured self; he drank, sang songs and was obliviously happy. The world could go on its same miserable course. Interfering with it wouldn't do much good. Let it be. Some of us said Gordon's retirement was an end of an era and may have understood it in our heads, but not down in the deep part of us where joy and sorrow live. No one truly believed Gordon Lane wouldn't be behind the bar any longer. He was a fixture in Virginia City; his Union Brewery Saloon was a Nevadan institution.

Gordon and his wife had plans. They wanted to move to the desert and build a house. Everyone protested. They didn't belong in the desert; they belonged in Virginia City. But times and Virginia City were changing. Gordon couldn't run the Union Brewery forever. Though fit and healthy as a young man, his legs were tired from standing behind the bar for four decades. Gordon needed a break; he wanted to build a house in the wide open desert he loved.

But as if to please those of us who would miss him, he consented to bartend two days a week at the Silver Queen Saloon across the street from the Union Brewery. The old crowd went over there the days Gordon worked. He was still the same old Gordon, still had that slippery grin. And behind the grin was the serious intent to get you tipsy if he could. Gordon meant no harm; he just wanted to see you happy. Still, it seemed wrong he wasn't behind the bar at the Brewery. We could do nothing about that. Times were changing.

A younger couple took over the Union Brewery Saloon. They had been customers of Gordon's and loved the Brewery too. They promised Gordon they would run the saloon as he ran it. That would be impossible, of course. It was nothing personal and this is nothing against them. There was only one Gordon Lane and without him the Brewery would be different. It couldn't be helped. The new owners did their best. But you felt bad when Gordon's old customers from out of state showed up and asked, "Where's Gordon?"

"He's not here anymore."

"You're kidding?"

"No."

"I've been coming here for twenty-five years. Come here every year from Seattle. Not here, huh?"

"No. He's retired. He works a couple days at the Silver Queen."

"What days?"

"Thursday and Friday."

If the old customer was lucky it was Thursday or Friday and they went across the street. Gordon was still the same old Gordon, as consistent as the moon.

"I can't believe you're not at the Brewery, Gordon," they said.

Gordon smiled and didn't say much about that. He talked about the house he was building. He invited his old customers to come out and visit.

After a while, Gordon stopped bartending at the Silver Queen, too. Doug Kick, Joe Pastrami, Edie and I and a few others were there the last night. It was quiet and sad. We toasted Gordon. He said, "Happy days," and lifted his glass to those of us witnessing the genuine death of an era.

When Gordon Lane left the Union Brewery Saloon, a lovely human oasis slowly dried up and blew into history. No one could believe that dear ramshackle place was gone. Not gone physically. Just gone. For a while the old crowd came in and there were good times. Forest Catlett, Gary Greenlund, Wally White Shoes, Roller Skatin' Murray and other pianists played the piano after their shifts and Jack Curran strummed his banjo. And the music was good. But it was like having a surprise party and the honored guest doesn't show up.

Eventually big speakers were installed in the back corners of the Brewery and another generation's music began blasting from them. The wonderful conversations that had filled the legendary Union Brewery Saloon, died. Little by little the Human Beings drifted away and a new generation drifted in. Gordon's well worn piano top was closed over the old keys; the piano bench was tucked under and dust grew on its head. The piano players didn't play the piano anymore. They couldn't hear themselves over the loudspeakers. A sadness grew inside the Brewery.

Along with Gordon Lane's retirement, there were other changes in Virginia City. Harold "Chief" Frankhauser, who had bartended in Virginia City for thirty years and was a popular character, got cancer. He had an operation and couldn't talk after that. The town gave a benefit to raise money for Chief. We all missed hearing him tell us "Oh, go to hell." That was Chief's way of saying hello. Chief's cancer spread. He recently died.

Merle Koch, who played piano every Sunday evening with his Dixieland band across the street at The Stope, died. He was a friendly man and a terrific pianist and his band drew a loyal crowd. The town gave Merle a funeral at the old Presbyterian Church on South C Street. Clyde Amsler played "Do You Know What It Means To Miss New Orleans," on his clarinet while an acoustic guitarist accompanied him. It was a nice song to say good-bye to Merle. After Merle's death things changed and the old Sunday night jazz crowd dropped off.

To save money, other saloons stopped hiring the old piano players whose honky tonk music made Virginia City an entertaining and musical place. With no work, the piano players left town and tried to find work elsewhere. Forest Catlett and Roller Skatin' Murray were two of many.

The new drunk driving laws with stiff penalties were making an effect on the town. The Highway Patrol kept watch over the steep, dangerous mountain roads going to and from Virginia City. And people were drinking less and showing more concern for their health. The night business dropped off. Saloons that had stayed open late began closing early.

Many of the local business people had grown weary of dealing with the Chamber of Commerce. They dropped their membership and wouldn't go to Chamber meetings. There were many new business people in town. The old timers that had given the town charm and character were dying off or retiring.

Technology even reached Virginia City and brought the twentieth century with it. Gordon Lane's simple three channel cable television system was upgraded with a satellite dish that pulled in a bunch of channels. Instead of people talking at the bar and sharing their lives and telling jokes, now the eyes stared at the television and a station beamed down from a satellite twenty-three thousand miles above the earth.

Many of the characters who made Virginia City a strange and entertaining place died or left town. No Ears Harry escaped to Reno. Patrick Hanley, who bartended in Virginia City, got Harry to an alcohol recovery ward. Patrick said to Harry, "If I ever see you drunk in Virginia City again I'll kill you." That persuaded Harry to stay in Reno where he's pulled himself together with the help of those loving souls at Alcoholics Anonymous.

Mexican Richard, No Ears Harry's roommate, died alone in their room. It was winter and the landlord had turned the heat off. Richard came down with pneumonia which killed him. That and the drinking.

George the Meat Man was recently found sitting on top of his car on the road to Reno. He was acting very strange. He couldn't remember how he got on top of his car or what he was doing. He had had a stroke. They put him in the hospital and he died shortly after his release. Out in the desert, Gordon Lane hadn't heard about George. I went out and told Gordon the news. Gordon smiled as I began to talk about George, and his eyes welled up when I told him George had died.

Jerry Parsons, a bartender, shot himself in the head down at the old freight depot. He had been drinking heavily. Cowboy, another local bartender, who dressed sharply in tight jeans, broad cowboy hat and flaming Western shirts, shot himself in the head. He had girl troubles and he had been drinking. Both suicides stunned the community.

Tiny Carlson recently bought the Silver Queen Saloon and intends to refurbish the upstair floors and turn it into a hotel again. He still advises people how to run their businesses. Not long ago, Doug Kick and I were in the Silver Queen Saloon visiting Tiny. One of the town's casino owners was across the street sweeping the boardwalk. Tiny saw him and bolted out the door and zipped across the street. Tiny took the broom out of the casino owner's hands and instructed him how to sweep a boardwalk. Then he gave the broom to the owner who went back sweeping while Tiny coached him.

Crazy Bob is still crazy and his groceries, once retrieved at the dump, have become leaner since Storey County closed the Virginia City dump. I don't know how Bob makes it now.

Talking Helen is as tough as ever. Helen still makes food for parties and pays for it herself. But she has held off roasting another pig. The fire marshal has advised Helen to hire a new crew next time she roasts a pig, which of course, I understand. We have adopted Helen and she us. We help her when she needs her car fixed or needs something hauled up to Virginia City. We have lunch occasionally and

Helen keeps me humble by pointing out my character defects, which I suppose is necessary and good for me.

Gordon Lane has finished building his house in the desert. It took him five years. It's a huge fortress. A few of us went out there from time to time and slugged some nails and shoveled dirt. But Gordon built most of it himself. The house is on a sandy hilltop beside a dry lake that becomes an ocean after summer cloud bursts. Then the dry white bed fills up and milky waves lap at the hill where Gordon has built his and Anne's home. This bit of natural science has caused Bill Avansino to name the place "Lane's Landing." Funny, because it's out there in the middle of the desert.

Doug Kick and I often get together for lunch in Virginia City. We are known as the Odd Couple. We mourn the absence of Gordon Lane behind the bar, "that terrible, terrible man," as Doug still calls him. "You know, we should have taken Gordon to the veterinarian and had him put to sleep. It would have saved us a lot of trouble."

Virginia City was the best place and the worst place. When it was good, it was very good. And when it was bad, it was horribly bad. I have never met people who could make a soul laugh as deeply as those folks did, and do still. Nowhere have I found people more human and more vulnerable. I want to remember the good parts. The bad parts will roll away with time. They always do.

After nearly three years of roaming around like Abraham and his tribe, and getting chased by two sheriff departments in two states, we settled in rural Nevada near Carson City. Carson City is a comfortable town of about forty thousand and I hope it stays that way. Of course, it won't. Change comes to every place and to every one. People are what make a place good or bad. The town is friendly because of the people. They have come from everywhere and the mixture makes the difference. I cannot fully express how grateful I feel when hunting for an item at the grocery store and the clerk leads me, nearly by the hand, to the hidden item. Or to be recognized and spoken to by name at our bank. Little acts of kindness make us feel welcome. The town is small enough to be comfortable and big enough for the things we need. It is clean and easy going. Best of all, it's not in California. We have space and clean air and blue skies most of the time. Whenever we forget why we left Southern California, we drive to Reno. Two hours of smog and traffic brings it all back.

I have worked through most of my mid-life mess. Our adventure and the writing of this book helped. Sometimes when you care too much you try too hard and you lose yourself. Each of us has only so much to give, and when we give beyond that point our giving eats us up. We get tired and discouraged and resentful. Then we must go back to the place where we felt safe and rest. That does not mean we have lost courage or have given up. We need to know when we need a rest and take it.

I am more or less back in my right mind, as right as it will get I suppose. I am going to stay a writer. If nothing else, the experience of the past four years has shown me that writing can make a difference. Writing may not change the world. But writing can make people think and feel and encourage and sometimes it can make people act. Not always, but sometimes. Now I am trying to use my writing to do the little good I can before I leave this planet. Writing is still the most challenging and most difficult craft I am learning. And the learning process never ends. That makes writing fun and aggravating.

When I finish writing in the spring and summer I sit with my wife in the back yard of our new house and look across the valley to the dark and high mountains and the wide blue sky. Flocks of Mountain Bluebirds cackle as they fly over us. Sometimes a lone hawk circles in the sky. At dusk the black and white nighthawks come out and flip crazily as they hunt bugs in the evening air.

We can see the gray rock dome of Mt. Davidson above Virginia City. It is good to go up to Virginia City and visit friends. And it is just as good to live outside Storey County and not have to deal with the corruption. The sky here is nearly always blue, often cloudless and the air smells clean. In Southern California the Hill was taken away from us. Here in Nevada we have thousands of hills and little smog to kill the hundred mile views.

Thunderheads, gray-black with rain, swarm the mountains on summer afternoons. The lightning flashes silver and the thunder booms seconds afterward. The thunderheads favor the mountains and make the high peaks the depository for their precious water to this dry land. Sometimes the thunderheads mistakenly drop their loads on our neighborhood; in minutes the gutters run full and just as quickly dry up when the rain quits.

In autumn the weather is nearly perfect. As the days grow chilly, the wild horses come down from the mountains and invade our neighborhood. Six or seven horses gather on a single lawn; in little time the lawn is cut as clean and low as if clipped by a lawn mower.

Sometimes in the late afternoons when I finish writing and I am lonesome for the joys and difficulties of other men's lives, I stop by a local saloon. It is the last of the old time neighborhood saloons, a friendly after-work bar of men who work with concrete and steel, timber and hammers, wrenches and oil. The controversial topics are fishing, hunting and throwing dice. The men who frequent this place could care less what I do for a living and their ordinary lives are a pleasure to hear about.

The walls of the saloon are covered with old black and white photographs of Carson City when it was a thriving supply center for the Virginia City mines. There are pictures of the miners, the old railroad and the mines and mills that helped create Carson City. Hanging high above the back bar is a photo of an unfortunate man, naked to the waist, hands tied behind his back, and hung by the neck from a telephone pole. A hand-written sign above the photo, stabbed to the wall by an ice pick, warns customers: *"He didn't pay his bar tab!"*

Occasionally amongst these men, I have a Coke, sometimes a Scotch and puff on a filthy cigar and talk about the ball game on TV and laugh when I hear the saloon keeper tell the crew, "The first time you guys ask me the score, *the game goes off!"*

When I first went into this mid-life crisis thing, I was warned running to diversions would only prolong the crisis. A man sometimes goes out too far for his own good; he turns away from what is true out of fear or anger or hunger. He loses himself as he tries to find himself. If he is willing, and fortunate, God finds him and brings him back.

Coda

I was in a deep sleep when He came again.

"I ben' watchin' ya with dat book ya ben' writin'. Preedy good stuff."

"Well..."

"Did ya do like ah told ya?"

"Well, I tried."

"Did ya tell de truth, boy?"

"I tried to."

"An' wha' did ya get for it?"

"I made some very good friends and a lot of enemies."

"Ain't dat duh truth. Woo boy, ya gots yaself in a mess of trouble with ya writin'. Lonesome, wadn't it?"

"At times."

"Hurt didn't it?"

"Yes," I said. "Did you mind me making you out as a black slave?"

"Haw, haw," he laughed. "Naw, dat was my idea, bud."

"I thought it was mine?"

"Ya fool writers, always a thinkin' my ideas is yo ideas."

"Oh, well, I see."

"Was it worth it, boy," the Lord asked.

"I don't know. What do you think?"

"It's always worth it, boy," He said, "always worth it."

"Caring is a hard business. That's what I've learned," I said. "Show me someone who wants to do right with all their heart, and I'll show you someone whose future is full of enemies."

"Ain't dat duh truth. But a good man has lotsa friends, too. Don' forget dat."

"Plenty of both I guess. I'm getting cynical, Lord."

"Yeah. I ben a watchin' dat. Ya gots to work on dat, boy."

"Staying human is hard. I get angry and intolerant and I'm no good to anyone. Sometimes I'd like to tell the whole world to go straight to hell."

"Ah know and ah understand."

I was quiet and He was quiet, too. Then I asked, "How do you do it?"

"Do wha' boy?"

"Put up with us?"

"It's mah nature to jus' loves ya all."

"I don't know how you do it," I said.

"Das ahright. Ya be knowin' in time."

"The problem with pain Lord, is that it changes us."

"Das right. It'll make ya bettuh o' worse. Das right enuff, son."

"I like that."

"Ya like wha'?"

"I like you calling me *son*."

"Ah son, das ahright."

"Lord, what do we do with the pain?"

"Ya use it tuh grow wid. Pain is food for ya spirit."

"Yes, I can see that. But what about the bad pain, the pain that makes us crazy and cynical and mean?"

"Well, dat ya gots tuh give tuh me. Das de only way tuh beat it. Ya gots to give *all* a dat tuh me."

"All the bad pain and anger and our inability to forgive?"

"Yeah. All a dat. Ah take dat away and make it clean an' right for ya. It'll take a while. But don' ya worry, it be ahright in time."

"It's hard to believe I'll ever be better. I want to be better with all my heart, but it's so hard."

"Ya will boy, ya will. Ya gots to trus' me on dis. *Trus' me* on dis."

"All right. I'll try. But it's hard."

"Das ahright. We's gots lotsa time, lotsa time."

Thanks

Though a writer does his work alone and is ultimately responsible for it, many people can and do help him in his endeavors. In my life, my wife Edie has always been supportive of my research and writing and has been a fair and reasonable critic, often helping me to edit comments which seem clever to me, but in reality would injure the feelings of the person I am writing about. If this book has seemed overly harsh on some, trust me it would have been worse if not for the advice of my wife. I thank my wife for her help and for the hundreds of hours she patiently listened to me discussing this book.

My thanks to Gordon and Anne Lane who permitted me to write about their personal lives in this book.

To the Bad Crew—Gordon Lane, Doug Kick, John "Jack" Curran, "Tiny" Charles Carlson, Louie Beaupre and "Balderdash," your views on the world, your encouragement, your reprimands and humor were like an oasis in a world gone dry.

I thank Bill and Carol Fain and Earl and Annmarie Markham of Virginia City who financially supported the *Virginia City Voice* when it was not in their best interest to do so. You were more than fair to me.

To the people of Virginia City, some of whom at times may have felt insulted by what I wrote in the *Voice*, I give you my apology. I meant well but sometimes missed the mark. Some would say I *always* missed the mark. That's all right too.

During the course of living, researching and writing this book, I was led to many good men and women in law enforcement, and former law enforcement officers, of county, city, state and Federal Government. I owe them a huge thanks for their candor and information regarding the criminal activity of various individuals. I would like to acknowledge them by name. However, as requested by them and in order to protect both the officers and their families from possible harm, I will not publish their names. I have thanked them personally and I have made them aware of their contributions to this book.

Steve Volek, of the Reno City Attorney's office served this writer promptly and professionally in my attempt to access a Reno Police Department investigative report. Officers of the Reno Police Department were marvelously helpful and encouraged me in my research and writing.

Harold Parrish provided me with photographs of Gordon Lane at the Union Brewery Saloon.

Kevin Lamb, John Quinn, Doug Kick, Malcolm Childers, Jack Curran and Gordon and Anne Lane read over parts of the manuscript and made useful suggestions, many of which were used.

Jeffrey M. Kintop, State Archives Manager of the Nevada Division of Archives and Records helped the author by researching the correspondence files of former governors of Nevada.

Ann Pinzl of the Nevada State Museum helped the author to identify plants and flowers of the Washoe Mountains (Virginia Range.) Thanks for your time and trouble.

I thank God for Lee Hanson, Al VanCapelle and John Milataru who showed up at the moment I was about to give up my investigations, who stood by me, encouraged me, prayed for me and my family and put their faith where they live. You guys probably saved my life. There is no doubt you helped save my neck. May God's great Mercy and Grace keep you.

Doug McQuide, Greg "Chief" Striver, Debbie Carnett, Maggie Long, Bob Lewallen and Estella Foster of the Gold Hill Hotel, Gold Hill, Nevada, showed the author hospitality and kindness that was much appreciated during the "come down" from this book. Thanks.

Robert Pierce was a tremendous help in preparing the manuscript for publication.

To those good men in Nevada law enforcement and their families who were threatened by the pimp for doing their jobs, you have my thanks and this State's thanks. There is an ultimate justice.

And to those dead but good men who had the sense to create and implement the First Amendment of the Constitution of the United States, the world owes you.

Order these great books by mail today
Autographed and insribed by George Williams III

NEW! In the Last of the Wild West. The true story of the author's attempt to expose the murders of prostitutes and corruption in Virginia City, Storey County, Nevada, home of the largest legal brothel in the United States. 272 pages. AUTOGRAPHED. $12.95 quality paperback; $24.95 hard cover.

ROSA MAY: THE SEARCH FOR A MINING CAMP LEGEND Virginia city, Carson City and Bodie, California were towns Rosa May worked as a prostitute and madam 1873-1912. Read her remarkable true story based on 3 1/2 years of research. Praised by the *Los Angeles Times* and *Las Vegas Review Journal*. Includes 30 rare photos, 26 personal letters. 240 pages. AUTOGRAPHED. $10.95 quality paperback; hard cover, $16.95. Soon to be a television movie.

THE REDLIGHT LADIES OF VIRGINIA CITY, NEVADA Virginia City was the richest mining camp in the American West. The silver from its mines built San Francisco and helped the Union win the Civil War. From 1860-95, Virginia City had three of the largest redlight districts in America. Here women from around the world worked the world's oldest profession. Author Williams tells the stories of the strange lives of the redlight girls, their legends and violent deaths. Based on newspaper accounts, county records and U.S. Census information. Perhaps the best and most informative book on prostitution in the old West. Plenty of historic photos, illustrations, map and letters. 48 pages. AUTOGRAPHED. $5.95 quality paperback; hard cover, $10.95.

HOT SPRINGS OF THE EASTERN SIERRA Here are more than 40 natural hot spring pools author George Williams III has located from the Owens Valley, through the Eastern Sierra recreation corridor to Gerlach, Nevada. George has tracked down every hot spring worth "soaking" in. Included are many secret springs only known to locals. George gives easy to follow road directions, and his "2 cents" about each spring are informative and entertaining. Maps by the author help you find these secret springs easily. 72 pages. AUTOGRAPHED. $6.95 quality paperback; hard cover, $12.95.

THE GUIDE TO BODIE AND EASTERN SIERRA HISTORIC SITES True story of the rise and fall of Bodie, California's most famous mining camp, today a ghost town, National Historic Site and California State Park. Known as the toughest gold mining town in the West where millions were made in a few years, murders were a daily occurrence. Has a beautiful full color cover with 100 photos on an 8 1/2 X 11 format. 88 pages. AUTOGRAPHED. $10.95 quality paperback; hard cover, $16.95.

THE MURDERS AT CONVICT LAKE True story of the infamous 1871 Nevada State Penitentiary break in which 29 outlaws escaped and fled more than 250 miles into Mono and Inyo counties, California. They vowed to kill anyone who got in their way. In a terrible shootout at Monte Diablo, today known as Convict Lake just south of Mammoth Lakes ski resort, the convicts killed two men. They fled to nearby Bishop where they were captured and hanged. Includes 18 rare photographs and pen and ink drawings by Dave Comstock. 32 pages. AUTOGRAPHED. $4.95 quality paperback; hard cover, $12.95.

MARK TWAIN: HIS ADVENTURES AT AURORA AND MONO LAKE When Sam Clemens arrived in Nevada in 1861, he wanted to get rich quick. He tried silver mining at Aurora, Nevada near Mono Lake not far from Yosemite National Park. Clemens didn't strike it rich but his hard luck mining days led to his literary career. 32 rare photos, mining deeds and maps to places where Clemens lived, wrote and camped. 100 pages. AUTOGRAPHED. $6.95 quality paperback; hard cover, $12.95.

NEW! MARK TWAIN: HIS LIFE IN VIRGINIA CITY, NEVADA While reporting for the *Territorial Enterprise* in Virginia City, 1862-64, Sam Clemens adopted his well known pen name, Mark Twain. Here is the lively account of Mark Twain's early writing days in the most exciting town in the West. Over 60 rare photos and maps to places Twain lived and wrote. 208 pages. AUTOGRAPHED. $10.95 paperback; hard cover, $24.95.

Mark Twain: Jackass Hill and the Jumping Frog by George Williams III. The true story of Twain's discovery of "The Celebrated Jumping Frog of Calaveras County," the publication of which launched his international career.   After getting run out of Virginia City, Twain settled in San Francisco in May, 1864. He went to work as a common reporter for the San Francisco *Call.*   After five frustrating months, Twain quit the *Call* and began hanging around with Bret Harte, then editor of the popular *Golden Era*, a West Coast magazine. When Twain posted bail for a friend and the friend skipped town, Twain followed and headed for Jackass Hill in the foothills of the Sierra Nevada near Sonora.There Twain lived with his prospector friend Jim Gillis in a one room log cabin on Jackass Hill. After a discouraging prospecting trip, in a saloon at Angel's Camp, Twain was told the Jumping Frog story by a bartender. Twain's version, published eleven months later, became an international hit. "The Celebrated Jumping Frog of Calaveras County," is included in this book.
72 pages, index, bibliography, 35 historic photographs, guide maps for travelers. AUTOGRAPHED. Quality paper $6.95; hard cover $12.95

New for Spring 1992! On the Road with Mark Twain in California and Nevada Here is a handy, easy to read guide to Mark Twain's haunts in California and Nevada 1861-68. Has road directions to historic sites, guide maps and lots of photographs of Twain, the historic sites and Twain's friends. Gives brief run-downs of each place and tells what Twain was doing while there. A must-have book for any Twain fan who would like to follow his trail in the far West. 150 pages, many photos, road maps, index. $12.95 quality paper; $24.95 hard cover.

Order Form

To order books Toll Free with *VISA* or MasterCard call **1-800-487-6610**, 9AM to 5PM West Coast time. **Phone orders are shipped the same day received.**

Name _____

Address_____City_____

State_____Zip_____

Yes, George send me the following books, autographed and inscribed:
___Copy(ies) In the Last of the Wild West, 12.95 pap.; 24.95 hard cover
___Copy(ies) Rosa May: The Search For A Mining Camp Legend, 9.95 pap.; 16.95 hard
___Copy(ies) The Redlight Ladies of Virginia City, 5.95 pap.; 10.95 hard cover
___Copy(ies) Hot Springs of the Eastern Sierra, 6.95 pap.; $12.95 hard cover
___Copy(ies) The Guide to Bodie, 10.95 pap.; 16.95 hard cover
___Copy(ies) The Murders at Convict Lake, 4.95 pap.; 12.95 hard cover
___Copy(ies) Mark Twain: His Adventures at Aurora, 6.95 pap.; 12.95 hard cover
___Copy(ies) Mark Twain: His Life In Virginia City, Nevada, 10.95 pap.; 24.95 hard
___Copy(ies) Mark Twain: Jackass Hill and the Jumping Frog, $6.95 pap.; 12.95 hard cover
___Copy(ies) On the Road with Mark Twain In California and Nevada, 12.95 pap.; 24.95 hard cover
Shipping by postal service is 1.75 for the first book, .75 each additional book. Faster shipping via UPS is 3.00 for the first book. 1.00 each additional book.

Total for books_____
Shipping   _____
Total enclosed in check or money order _____
Mail your order to:

Tree By The River Publishing
PO Box 935-W
Dayton, Nevada 89403

Order Form

To order books **Toll Free** with *VISA* or MasterCard call **1-800-487-6610**, 9AM to 5PM West Coast time Monday through Friday. **Phone orders are shipped the same day received.**

Name _____

Address_____City_____

State_____Zip_____

Yes, George send me the following books, autographed and inscribed:

___Copy(ies) In the Last of the Wild West, 12.95 pap.; 24.95 hard cover

___Copy(ies) Rosa May: The Search For A Mining Camp Legend, 9.95 pap.; 16.95 hard

___Copy(ies) The Redlight Ladies of Virginia City, 5.95 pap.; 10.95 hard cover

___Copy(ies) Hot Springs of the Eastern Sierra, 6.95 pap.; $12.95 hard cover

___Copy(ies) The Guide to Bodie, 10.95 pap.; 16.95 hard cover

___Copy(ies) The Murders at Convict Lake, 4.95 pap.; 12.95 hard cover

___Copy(ies) Mark Twain: His Adventures at Aurora, 6.95 pap.; 12.95 hard cover

___Copy(ies) Mark Twain: His Life In Virginia City, Nevada, 10.95 pap.; 24.95 hard

___Copy(ies) Mark Twain: Jackass Hill and the Jumping Frog, $6.95 pap.; 12.95 hard cover

___Copy(ies) On the Road with Mark Twain In California and Nevada, 12.95 pap.; 24.95 hard cover

Shipping by postal service is 1.75 for the first book, .75 each additional book. Faster shipping via UPS is 3.00 for the first book. 1.00 each additional book.

Total for books_____
Shipping   _____
Total enclosed in check or money order _____
Mail your order to:

     Tree By The River Publishing
     PO Box 935-W
     Dayton, Nevada 89403